A WOMAN'S WORK

The Storied Life of Pioneer Esther Morris,
the World's First Female Justice of the Peace

MARIAN BETANCOURT

TWODOT®

GUILFORD, CONNECTICUT
HELENA, MONTANA

A · TWODOT® · BOOK
An imprint of Globe Pequot
A registered trademark of Rowman & Littlefield

Distributed by NATIONAL BOOK NETWORK

British Library Cataloguing in Publication Information available

Library of Congress Cataloging-in-Publication Data available

ISBN 978-1-4930-2729-3 (paperback)
ISBN 978-1-4930-2730-9 (e-book)

∞™ The paper used in this publication meets the minimum requirements of American National Standard for Information Sciences—Permanence of Paper for Printed Library Materials, ANSI/ NISO Z39.48-1992.

Printed in the United States of America

The beginning is always today.
—MARY WOLLSTONECRAFT

An Englishman is a person who does things because they have been done before. An American is a person who does things because they haven't been done before.
—MARK TWAIN

*To the memory of my maternal grandmother, the late
Maria Riinkinen Hyvarinen, who also made a long westward journey
to take a chance on a better life for her family. Traveling through the
Karelian Forest across Europe and the Atlantic Ocean in 1909, Maria left
her native Finland, where in 1906, women were the first in Europe to
vote, and arrived in New York, where women did not yet have that right.*

*And to the memory of my late paternal great-aunt,
Dagmar (Dollye) Petersen Dietrich, who proudly marched in
the Woman Suffrage Parade in New York City in 1916.*

Author's Note

Although she's been dead for more than one hundred years, Esther Morris has been my kindred spirit since I met her when feminism was revived in the 1970s. I was viewing a slide lecture about little-known women in history. (We called it "herstory" then.) There, in front of the Wyoming State Capitol was a statue of a woman striding across the Plains carrying a book and a sheaf of flowers. The single paragraph beneath Esther Morris's image told me she was six feet tall and had made it possible for women in Wyoming to be the first in America to vote—in 1869. She was also the first female justice of the peace in the world.

Is that all there is? I was astounded. I had to find out who she really was and why I was so drawn to her.

Curiosity soon became obsession, and over the years—before the Internet made research a bit easier—I tracked even the smallest lead. What little information I found was often contradictory. But the more I learned, the more I liked Esther. In a variety of history books on the American West and the few about women, Esther received a paragraph or two as possibly being involved in the suffrage struggle in Wyoming Territory. There was a legend that she hosted a tea party at which she extracted promises from the territorial legislators to create an amendment giving women the right to vote—and own property and receive equal pay. But this tea party was dismissed for lack of proof. Yet Esther throughout her lifetime gave "sociables" for any excuse, so it is quite likely that she would have had such a party not only to promote the cause, but to introduce her family to her new neighbors.

Early historians, such as T. A. Larson, author of the 1965 and 1978 official history of the state, assumed Esther was not literate and had left no diaries or correspondence. How lazy these historians! And how wrong! Had they looked further they would have learned that Esther and her sons, part of a very literate family scattered all around the country, left more than one hundred letters. Along with Bill Dubois, Esther's great-great-grandson and a historian himself, I ultimately discovered these letters in the possession of Rosalind Day in California, the great-granddaughter of Esther's favorite niece, Frances "Franky" McQuigg Stewart. Throughout the book I quote directly from these letters, but I take some liberties with creatively imagined scenes and dialogue.

I began to see the sweep of Esther's story, the formation of her character. I loved Esther's compassion, her courage, her integrity, and her quick wit. I laughed at her jokes and read the books and poems she liked. I was proud when Esther managed to hold her large family of sisters and brothers together after her parents died, when she refused to leave a church building in upstate New York until black people were permitted to worship there, when she took up the cause of women's rights.

I enjoyed meeting her family and friends. Esther and I both dreamed of better things, were always tempted by what might be over the next horizon. We loved books and ideas and a good fight. In a shadowy dream one night, I was on my knees in a vast prairie trying to open a cellar door while Esther stood by, encouraging me to keep trying.

Reconstructing Esther's life convinced me she was the kind of woman who had to get involved. She had always been present at political gatherings and some very important conventions. She could not simply support a cause "in her own quiet way," as suggested by Larson. Esther wasn't quiet. She was born under the sign of Leo, a natural leader who basked in attention. She was big-hearted, gutsy, idealistic, and pragmatic. She was smart and assertive and liked to influence people, a quality she passed on to her sons. And she loved politics. I have no doubt she was a force behind that landmark legislation on the frontier, where in her later years she was known as "the Old Politician."

While there is certainly enough research material available to make a nonfiction biography possible, I am not a trained historian. For me, historical fiction provided the form I wanted to bring Esther's spirit into the story in a way that would not be possible in nonfiction. And by reading and rereading all of those letters, I found that the book pretty much wrote itself.

Esther's life spanned the entire nineteenth century and with it, every major issue—abolition, women's rights, western expansion, the railroads, the Civil War. It also spanned the entire country, from New York to Illinois and then to Wyoming, which Esther pioneered at the age of fifty-five. All of Esther's energy and experience came together in Wyoming, as if her whole life had been preparing her for South Pass City, that rugged mining town that would be the core of something much more important than gold.

Esther did not arrive on the western frontier in a covered wagon. Nor was she wearing a calico dress with bonnet and apron. This fastidious, cultured, middle-class woman arrived in one of the first transcontinental trains bringing with her many years of practical pioneering experience, political savvy, and an unshakeable optimism. She was a reformer, a suffragist, a Republican, a businesswoman, and a humanitarian. In her baggage she carried recent copies of *The Revolution*, Susan B. Anthony's newspaper, along with legal documents to present to the territorial government to petition for suffrage. But she was not without apprehension about this risky new venture undertaken with borrowed cash. Hard work and struggle were nothing new to Esther. She had suffered economic uncertainty, family conflict, and personal tragedy.

During her lifetime Esther collected a circle of friends that included not only suffrage leaders Susan B. Anthony, Elizabeth Cady Stanton, Mary Livermore, and Anna Dickinson, but also governors and generals, many men and women who were the movers and shakers of their time. There were abolitionists, spiritualists—even a vegetarian! Her tolerance for differing ideologies was apparent in her immediate family. Esther and her husband disagreed on everything—except what was best for their three sons.

Esther and her friends and family cut a path through this country and made it more livable for all of us. And who knows where we would be today if Wyoming had not been the first state to give women the vote. Historians who hadn't bothered to fully look at her considered her an ordinary woman. But of course! Like so many ordinary women who struggle to earn a living, support their families, nurture their children, fight for their civil rights, and try to make the world a better place, Esther made a difference—a really big difference—although not without a price.

—MARIAN BETANCOURT, MARCH 2017

Contents

Contents

PREFACE

State Capitol, Nashville, Tennessee
August 18, 1920

SOMEONE JUST TOSSED A VERY LARGE AND VERY RIPE TOMATO INTO THE speaker's face and I am tempted to leave these vulgar proceedings with the endless chest thumping and table pounding. I fear I will become deaf in my remaining good ear. Half the delegates are drunk so it is no wonder they cannot restore order and get on with the business at hand. The liquor industry has been spending vast sums of money—and whiskey—to defeat suffrage. They fear once women can vote, we will also have prohibition. And I hope we do! I cannot help but think that without whiskey men would prove better citizens and with women having a say, perhaps every disagreement in the world would not need to be settled with fisticuffs or war. Families would certainly be safer with fewer drunken husbands and fathers to abuse them.

But outside it is just as bad. Arguments erupt in the streets as people wave placards and flags at each other in this so called "war of the roses." The suffragists carry yellow roses and their opponents carry red. As if the south is not unpleasant enough; what a swamp in August! They say this is the hottest August in recorded history. I keep extra handkerchiefs in the pockets of my suit, for the constant mopping up of perspiration on my brow and neck. How I miss the sharp, dry mountain air of Wyoming. Nevertheless, I will keep my composure until I find out if Tennessee will ratify the 19th amendment and women will once and for all be able to cast their ballots everywhere in the United States. We need 36 states and Tennessee would be that number. It is going to be close. I can tell by the desperation in the opposition.

I am sitting in the gallery of this beautiful new building with plush scarlet seats and long gold window drapes. The behavior of those on the floor below is an insult to this city's founders who, in 1779, wanted to create a city of culture and education. To honor that intent they built the world's only exact replica of the Parthenon. And just across from the capitol, is a hotel named for Andrew Jackson's Hermitage. This beaux arts beauty was built in 1909 by the financial leaders, who felt their city should have a million dollar hotel and hired the famous architect William Strickland.

I find it ironic that The Hermitage is a Russian word for place of rest. Hah! Since Mrs. Catt arrived by train six weeks in advance of the vote and checked into suite 309, the hotel has also become a battle ground, much like this one. Word of Mrs. Catt's arrival galvanized the opposition and they reserved the hotel's entire mezzanine for their campaigning. The magnificent hotel lobby, with its soaring carved ceiling, is festooned with vases of yellow roses and red and the antis brazenly give out free liquor in the lobby.

The Hermitage is this city's first modern hotel to have electricity as well as a bath and a phone in each room. (Yet those phones are now giving my suffrage friends apoplexy, because they claim there are spies on the open lines.)

"I know my telephone is not private," Mrs. Catt told me. "And I know the whisky men are paying the bellhops to spy on us." Mrs. Catt is like a force of nature and when she turns her gaze upon you, with her pronounced dark eyebrows and deep bright eyes that peer right into your soul, you feel you must stand at attention.

Suffrage leader Carrie Chapman Catt is a very composed and determined lady from Wisconsin, who now lives in New York. She knew my mother well and told me yesterday the struggle for ratification involved 56 referendums to get states to write suffrage into their constitutions just as we did in Wyoming 50 years ago. It is this persistence and tenacity of women breaking new ground that is so exciting to me. Mrs. Catt said, "When we win the vote—and we will—I will quit the suffrage association and organize the League for Women Voters, so that all women will learn how to vote with their own hearts and minds, and not those of their husbands."

While the liquor industry provides free alcohol to keep men on their side, women use their wit and their will to make things happen. All my life I have watched women doing exciting things. They have been going every day to work in textile mills, operating farms and ranches, writing novels, showing their might by demanding fair wages and property rights and custody of their children. And on the frontiers more was possible. My mother, Esther Hobart Morris, was the first woman in the world to become a justice of the peace.

It has been 75 years since the Seneca Falls suffrage convention, and 50 years since the women of Wyoming were granted the vote because of my mother. Our government tried to keep Wyoming out of the union because of it. I remember little Joe Carey, our territorial representative to Congress, standing on his chair and shouting in the House of Representatives during the statehood battle 30 years ago. "We may wait a hundred years to come into the union," he shouted, "but we will come in with our women." I was secretary to Mr. Carey then, and still feel the passion of his words that fateful day. How we cheered and thought soon all the states will do this. I would have scoffed then at anyone who told me it would take another third of a century. And here we are still waiting!

Those who believe the propaganda that women are weaker, smaller brained, surely never met my mother! Or Aunt Eliza Jane! Or Cousin Franky! We had some glorious women in our family and among our friends we counted Mary Livermore, Susan B. Anthony, Elizabeth Cady Stanton, Isabelle Wallace, and the wonderful Anna Dickenson. Only once did I come close to falling in love and it was with Anna. Her emotion and fervor came from the heart and as an orator Anna would send every hair of your body standing at attention. People called her the Joan of Arc of the Civil War. She came to visit our home in Wyoming when she was campaigning for suffrage, but I don't want to recall the pain of that time when I tried to reveal my heart. Now it matters not at all. I am 70 years old and content with my bachelor life. Like me, Anna is alone and she is now the subject of a bitter family feud in New York City. Her relatives apparently will not allow her to keep her eccentric ways as well as her money. Did not this same thing happen to Mrs. Lincoln, when her only surviving son, Robert, had her committed to an asylum because she tried to sew her bonds inside her petticoat? Women need the vote so they can change such restrictions.

Uncle Edmund, one of mother's brothers, who became the richest man in Flint, Michigan with his lumber business, told my mother she would never live to see women vote. I can still see Mother's smile as she sent a telegram to Flint that day in 1869 when the legislators and governor of Wyoming territory gave women the vote. I was excited to have thought up our official state motto. The Equality State!

Unlike the women around me I moved from job to job, unable to find my calling. I was also the weakling of the family, physically at least, catching every plague that came along from agues to neuralgia, to the typhus that nearly killed me. I was sometimes given to fainting. It was Cousin Libby Chatfield, who helped me find a career by encouraging me to learn stenography so I could be a clerk in the state or in Washington and be involved in politics, which turned out to be a very good idea.

Libby, a true sophisticate, lived in a brownstone house in Greenwich Village in New York City, and worked as secretary to Susan B. Anthony, a position she acquired through some connection of Mother's. She married Levi Chatfield, a wealthy older man, retired from the Union army. Uncle Chatfield's friend, an editor at New York *World*, helped finance *The Revolution*, the suffrage newspaper, after the original money from George Francis Train ran out. I helped set up the office on Park Row near the great arches rising over the East River for the bridge to Brooklyn. I remember Libby bustling around *The Revolution* office, her golden hair pulled back and tied with a velvet ribbon, impatiently pulling her long hoop skirts out of the way of the office furniture as she rushed by. Libby was busy with suffrage until she died three years ago at 74.

But enough of these reveries, a wild scene has erupted and I am on my feet with everybody else. A young legislator from the eastern part of the state, Henry Thomas Burn, who wore a red rose in his lapel and had opposed suffrage all along, has just changed his vote he says, "Because my mother, whom I hold in high esteem, asked me to be a good boy and help Mrs. Catt put the rat in ratification." Yellow roses are raining down from the suffrage supporters in the galleries but the violence on the floor is getting ugly. Burn's irate colleagues are chasing him around the room and the poor man is perched on a window ledge looking for an escape to the street. What irony! The youngest representative in the state cast the deciding vote so his mother could vote and makes it possible for all women in America, once and for all, to vote. I suspect one hundred years from now, women will flock to his grave with yellow roses. As I once more mop my brow, I sit down, lean back and laugh out loud at the irony. And somewhere in the chaos, I can hear my own mother saying quietly, "Well, the men have finally come to their senses."

—Robert Charles Morris (as imagined by the author)

PART I
OWEGO, NEW YORK

Chapter One

The Flower Garden

A SOFT JUNE BREEZE RUSTLED THE PAGES OF THE BOOK TEN-YEAR-OLD Esther Hobart McQuigg was trying to read as she lay on her stomach on a faded patchwork quilt spread on the grass in her mother's flower garden. Napping beside her was her two-year-old sister Charlotte, named for their mother and called Lotte.

Esther had been anxious to read Mr. James Fenimore Cooper's new novel, *The Pioneers, or the Sources of the Susquehanna*, about the early days in this part of New York State where she lived. She had borrowed the book from the new lending library of Mr. Nathan Camp, who did not like to lend his books to children because they did not always return them in good condition. However, he knew Esther to be a good and careful reader and she had begged to get this one! She loved stories of adventure and romance and had read many of Sir Walter Scott's Ivanhoe stories.

Today Esther was unable to concentrate, and she impatiently closed the book when another page caught the breeze. She was worried about her mother and once again glanced through the swaying pink hollyhocks to the front porch of the two-story farmhouse with the green painted shutters. Her mother and maternal grandmother were pacing back and forth; the younger woman in her shapeless gray muslin dress leaned heavily against the older one. Grandmother Mehitable Hobart, called Hetty, had told Esther that walking would help ease the birth pain that her mother had begun to feel. Esther did not understand why people had so many children, why they went to such great risk and wore themselves out. This was her mother's eleventh child. A few weeks ago their neighbor Mrs. Cooper had died giving birth to her eighth child.

Esther had been jittery all day, ever since the predawn hours when she had awakened from a bad dream. She could not recall the details, just that she had been running through the woods, frantically searching for her mother. The sound of her own voice woke her up as she called out, "Mama, Mama, where are you?" The darkness itself frightened her and she curled up closer to her older sister Jane in the soft feather bed. Across the room in another bed her sisters Mindwell, Eliza, and Lotte slept. The bad feelings of the dream would not go away and Esther stayed close to her mother all morning, following her about, wanting to fix her some tea or biscuits. She had noticed how little her mother had been eating these past weeks.

"Your mama will be fine," Hetty said impatiently, trying to get Esther out from underfoot. "She's borne ten healthy children before this one." Finally, her grandmother asked Esther to take the whining Lotte outside for a nap to allow Charlotte some rest. Perhaps it was the brusque tone, but Esther suspected that her grandmother, too, was worried about Charlotte, who at forty-three had had difficulty with this pregnancy from the beginning.

In recent weeks Esther had tried to urge her mother into the flower garden, hoping it might cheer her. Charlotte had always loved the flower garden with its sweet scent, bright color, and occasional butterfly. It was a place of softness, a respite from the hard work of caring for such a large family and farm. But she had not been able to bend over to do the garden work lately, so Esther had been caring for it on her own after school and her chores at home. The garden had begun as a small plot on the south side of the house. Then it became two facing plots along a winding path. Her brother Daniel built a trellis connecting them. Now, with climbing blue petunia, the trellis also provided a shaded pathway through the garden. Plants grew easily in this fertile region west of Albany near the Pennsylvania border along the Susquehanna River, which, at more than four hundred miles, was the longest river on the east coast of the United States. In early summer lavender and foxglove grew two to three feet tall. China asters, daffodils, and peonies created a meadow of color. Esther liked to imagine growing up to be a grand lady with a large flower garden where she would serve tea to her friends in the afternoon.

After the War of the Revolution, Massachusetts ceded Tioga County to New York and gave land grants to New England veterans, many of whom eagerly moved from their hardscrabble rocky soil to this lush county to prosper. Soldiers who had fought in the area during the war had described orchards with juicy apples the size of pumpkins and corn that grew more than two feet high. It was called "the garden place" by the Iroquois and Seneca Indians, before they were driven out by the Continental army. Esther's grandparents were among the first families to settle the area in 1795. Her paternal grandfather, Captain John McQuigg of New Hampshire, and maternal grandfather, Captain Edmund Hobart of Connecticut, received 130-acre grants.

"It took seventeen days for Daisy to pull our wagon over the Indian trail. And all of us, seven little ones, and our possessions packed into that wagon," Grandmother Hetty had told Esther. "That stubborn ox did not want to pull the cart, nor did she favor leaving Connecticut. We often got out and walked, hoping we could inspire her to move a little faster." Although Esther had heard this story many times, she asked her grandmother to tell her again what happened to Daisy when she arrived.

"After that trip anyone who came near Daisy with a wagon or harness got a smart kick," her grandmother told her. Esther always laughed at this part and said, "I remember, you told me she spent the rest of her life eating up your profits."

Creating a farm from the wilderness was a backbreaking task. The pioneers managed to clear about four acres a year, while building a house and barn, hunting and fishing for family food, and helping neighbors cut roads. After clearing acres to grow wheat, the best cash crop, they added corn, beans, squash, and other vegetables. Captain McQuigg's family settled at the confluence of the Susquehanna River and Owego Creek in what is now Owego, while the Hobarts settled in Spencer, a few miles northwest. Esther's father, Daniel, the second oldest in the McQuigg family, married Charlotte, the second of the Hobart children. When Charlotte's father died, Daniel came to the Hobart farm to carry on the work. Both grandfathers died before Esther was born, but her paternal grandmother, Sarah McQuigg, still lived in their fine home on the river's edge in Owego.

———

"Essa?" Lotte's sleepy voice drew Esther's attention back to the garden and she snapped a bright lavender China aster from the row of flowers in front of her.

"Should we give this to Mama to cheer her?" Esther asked, tickling Lotte's nose with the flower. Lotte giggled and tried to catch the flower in her chubby hands. Esther's mother had always liked to pin a flower on her apron or in her hair, but had not done so in many months. A large round bud beneath the blossom reminded Esther of her mother, growing so large, her pale features and thin frame straining under the weight of the new child. Much as she worried, Esther did hope, however, that the new baby was a girl. She had enough brothers, five of them, and only four sisters. Suddenly, the sound of the porch bell startled Esther and she dropped the flower. She saw her grandmother pulling the rope and ringing the bell as Esther's mother limped into the house.

"Four bells," Esther cried, sweeping Lotte into her arms. "That's the signal to bring Pa home. It's time," she said, her heart thumping as she dashed toward the porch where Grandmother Hetty was guiding Charlotte into the house and speaking slowly and calmly, her custom in a situation that could send emotions into chaos.

"Get Jane to mind Lotte, Esther, and you go for Dr. Tinkham." Esther looked anxiously at her mother, who was pressing a hand against her lower back and held Hetty's shoulder with her other arm. Beads of perspiration glistened on her forehead, and for some reason Esther noticed for the first time all the threads of gray in her mother's brown hair.

"Put a saddle on that horse." Hetty's dark brown eyes flashed a warning at Esther, who liked to ride bareback. "And mind the traffic," she added with a quick glance over her shoulder as she started up the stairs with Charlotte.

Pressing Lotte against her pounding heart, Esther ran to the vegetable garden down the hill from the back of the house where her sister Jane had taken the younger girls, Mindwell, age eight, and Eliza, age five, with her to gather some early peas. After leaving Lotte, Esther raced to the barn but tried to check her nervousness as she climbed up on the rungs of the stall where a sturdy tan and white Indian pony had begun to prance about, sensing that it was about to escape the confinement of the barn.

"You've got to run fast today, Waverley," Esther said, hauling a saddle from the top of the stall onto the horse. Esther had begged her father to name the horse for the heroic knight of the Walter Scott novels of old England. She patted him affectionately as she fastened the saddle, hoping the solid, warm flesh would calm the tremor in her hands. The horse nickered and raised his head up and down as if agreeing. Esther hiked up her brown homespun skirt and jumped on Waverley's back and clucked at the horse to get started. They galloped out of the barn and down the path between rows of apple trees. The rumble of the wagon wheels grew louder as they neared the heavily trafficked Ithaca-Owego Turnpike, which paralleled the Catatonk Creek until it met the Susquehanna River three miles away in Owego. Esther knew she would not have time today to trot alongside the huge wagons of flour and salt and potash, to talk with the teamsters about the canal construction farther upstate.

"Aye, lassie, we'll be taxed to the poorhouse before Mr. Clinton's ditch is done," a teamster had complained just last week. The teamsters were as proficient with their tongues as with the long whiplash they carried as they walked beside their ox-drawn vehicles. They enjoyed any chance to gossip with the local farmers along their thirty-mile trek from Ithaca. Esther had heard the latest death count on the canal workers who had succumbed to malaria, or what the locals liked to call the "Genesee Shakes," while digging through the swamps above Cayuga Lake.

The Erie Canal had been the topic of continuous debate and speculation among York Staters for several years. Esther's father believed the canal would open new and more profitable markets for their grain and lumber, but her grandmother suspected the progress would bypass Owego, which prospered from the shipping of goods down the Susquehanna to the Chesapeake Bay and into the Atlantic Ocean and from there to other parts of the world.

"Everybody will go to the west once the canal opens," Esther's fifteen-year-old brother Edmund had said. Edmund, who most closely resembled Esther with their high brows, firm jaws, and deep-set gray eyes, worked at a store in Ithaca and frequently bragged that he was going to be a rich man one day. He was already planning to invest in a lumber business upstate near the canal.

Today the turnpike was a slow-moving pageant of wagons and stagecoaches. A herd of cattle had slowed up traffic, prompting a peddler to pull his wagon to the side of the dusty road and spread out his pots and brooms and crocks to tempt the frustrated travelers. Esther, a skilled rider, stayed low in the saddle and held Waverley on a short rein, staying close to the shoulder of the heavily rutted road. Racing past the lumbering wagons, she talked aloud to keep the pony from distraction and a skittishness she herself felt. Although Waverley was a swift horse and often won the village races, he was accustomed to taking his time on the busy turnpike, as if he, too, wanted to hear the latest news. The road dust lodged in Esther's throat, making her cough.

Before they reached Owego village, Esther pulled Waverley off into the shunpike, a shortcut behind the buildings on River Row, to avoid the congestion at the toll gates. Some of the shopkeepers lived with their families in wooden lean-tos behind the shops, and Esther skillfully avoided running into children and lines of hanging laundry. Chickens and pigs, which roamed the town freely, scattered as Waverley galloped through. Esther sighed with relief to see the doctor's wagon and horse outside his office. Her cheeks were flushed and her straw-colored hair stuck in matted ringlets around her smudged face as she slid from Waverley's back even before the animal came to a full halt.

"Dr. Tinkham, Dr. Tinkham," she called, running through the back door of Samuel Standish Tinkham & Son, Physicians and Merchants. "It's Mama, Dr. Tinkham. The baby is coming."

"Okay, Miss Esther," he said, smiling at her. "I'll be right along after I sew up this gentleman's finger." The doctor had white hair but a still young face. His shirt sleeves were rolled up and his black waistcoat opened. His small examining room was in the back of the store. It contained a cabinet of medicines and tools, and a small table with a chair on either side—one for the doctor and the other for the patient. There was also a long, flat table covered with a cloth where the doctor examined people. A farmer was sitting on that table now while the doctor held the man's hand and made stitches in it. A basin sat nearby with bloody water. Midwives were usually hired to deliver babies, but Esther's pa said his wife felt better with a real doctor, one who had been taking care of the family for many years.

⁓

By the time Esther returned home with the doctor, nearly an hour after she left, some of her brothers and sisters had gathered in the front parlor. She left Waverley tied to the porch railing and rushed inside to follow the doctor up the stairs. She was stopped short by her oldest brother, Daniel, who had come in from the sawmill with their father.

"Esther, stay here with us. Mama has enough help for now." Tall and angular at twenty-one, Daniel so resembled his father that Esther responded automatically to his authority and reluctantly came down the stairs. She sat on the floor with Lotte, who had been playing with a rag doll. Suddenly, a scream shot like a bullet through the bedroom door upstairs. Esther heard the muffled voices of her father and the doctor and her grandmother, too, but she was most aware of her mother's screams and then a continuous keening.

"Shall I read you a story, baby Charlotte?" Esther asked, pulling the toddler into her lap and pressing her face against Lotte's downy head to keep from shaking.

"It wasn't like this with Lotte," Esther said petulantly to Daniel. "Lotte came fast." Her mother's screams had diminished now to a muffled groan. Esther suddenly looked over at Daniel. "How long did I take?" she asked, wanting to know if she had caused her mother much pain. Daniel grinned at his sister.

"Esther, you were in a hurry, even then. Mama hardly opened her eyes and there you were asking a hundred questions." Esther's eyes filled and she was sorry she had asked such a question, as if making light of her birth, any birth that is so painful and risky. When Grandmother Hetty called down the stairs for more hot water, Esther asked about her mother.

"It's going to take a while," her grandmother said without expression. "Esther, go and wash yourself. Your face is streaked with road dust," she added as a way to avoid the questions. "And see to the horse. He belongs back in the barn with some water." Esther watched her grandmother wait for seventeen-year-old John, who was carrying a bucket of water to her. Without letting John into the room, she took the heavy bucket herself, her back straight, her step firm. Esther took Waverley back to the barn, removed his saddle, and filled his water bucket. She patted his flank and said, "Thank you for being a good pony, Waverley." She went out back to the pump and splashed some water on her face, but quickly returned to the others.

"Let us get supper," Esther suggested, unable to sit still and wanting only to rush to her mother. She forced herself to stay downstairs and think of the dinner. The others responded to familiar tasks, eager to keep busy while they kept their vigil.

"See if there are some dried apples in the cellar, Jane," Esther ordered. "I will get some meat from the smokehouse."

"You don't have to be so bossy," Jane said sullenly. "We've been through this before, and we do know how to get a meal on the table." Although Esther was four years younger than Jane, she was already as tall, reaching an equality of stature that Jane seemed to resent. Jane was thin with sharp features and a grayish pallor, and her blue eyes seldom reflected joy. Eliza, on the other hand, was naturally outgoing, want-ing to participate in all the family activities. Even now, with her sister Mindwell's help, she was putting forks next to the plates on the table and asking John to bring the spoons.

"There, it is all set," she said and clapped her hands.

Later, as they sat on the hard wooden benches around the table, they heard a faint baby's cry. Esther jumped, knocking over a cup of cider. The baby continued to cry but they heard no other sound.

"Why doesn't Papa come out and tell us what the baby is?" Esther asked anxiously. In the past Pa would step out and smile at them all and announce a boy or girl. "And everybody is looking and feeling fine," he would say. All of them continued to look toward the stairs, waiting.

"They'll tell us soon," Daniel said finally. "Finish your supper." Esther, who usually needed no encouragement to eat, pushed the pieces of smoked ham and apple in circles on her plate. The room began to darken, and Jane brought candles to the table and put them in the silver Paul Revere candlesticks, one of the few beautiful things their mother treasured. They had been a wedding gift from an aunt and uncle who lived in Boston. Except for the muffled voices from upstairs, no other news was forthcoming. John and Charles sat at the table playing checkers, while the others tried to occupy themselves with small housekeeping tasks. More wood was gathered for the fire, the supper dishes were washed, the lamps lit. John went out to check on the animals and lock up the barn. Another hour passed and sometimes they heard the baby cry, but the bedroom door had not yet opened.

"That's Pa," Esther shrieked suddenly as she heard a sobbing upstairs. Unable to conceal her alarm, she bolted up the stairs and pressed her ear against the door. "Oh, why doesn't somebody come out?" No sooner had she uttered this when they heard the door latch lifted and Esther's father filled the doorway. Sawdust still clung to Daniel McQuigg's damp forehead, giving his ruddy face an ashen look. Beneath the thick, curly gray hair, his reddened eyes sent a cold shudder through Esther.

"Is Mama all right?" Esther asked, her voice barely a squeak. Her grandmother appeared then with the baby, a faceless bundle of white flannel against her dark blue dress. Esther frowned at the infant and tried to push her way into the room. Her father caught her in his arms, but not before Esther saw the doctor pull the quilt over her mother's still form on the bed. Then Esther started to scream.

"She is with God now," Daniel said. Esther tried desperately to struggle free, but her father picked her up and carried her down the stairs. Hetty followed with the baby. The others stared up from the bottom of the stairs, mouths agape. Jane began to wail. Lotte, who had been awakened by the commotion, began to crawl up the stairs.

"Mama," she babbled. "Mama?" Charles rushed over to keep Lotte from the stairs. Esther's face burned against her father's rough muslin shirt.

"Why did she have another baby?" Esther sobbed, pounding her fists on her father's powerful shoulders, trying to reach behind him and strike at the baby in her grandmother's arms. "I want Mama," she wailed. "We don't need another baby." Daniel put Esther down in a chair near the hearth and sank slowly into another chair himself. As his children huddled around him he tried to pray, asking God to keep his wife in comfort and peace, but the words stuck in his throat. He fell silent and stared at the floor. Esther's brothers Daniel and John tried to finish the prayer. Daniel buried his head in his hands and made not a sound. John held the sobbing Eliza on his lap and had his arm around Mindwell.

Grandmother Hetty sat in a rocking chair near the window, the baby held firmly against her. She looked straight ahead. Only her feet moved as she pushed them against the floor to rock the chair. Hetty's face had gone deathly pale, the only sign of her grief. Her thinning gray hair was pulled back tightly in a knot, offering no softness or compromise to the sharp features of her face. Esther looked into her grandmother's eyes. The old woman watched her granddaughter for a moment, then turned and called out, "John, hitch Waverley to the wagon and we will go to the Giles farm so Aunt Esther can nurse the baby." John was broad in the shoulder although not as tall as Daniel or their father. He had large and very round greenish gray eyes under eyebrows so shaped to make him always seem surprised.

Unable to control her crying, Esther fled to the garden, dark now and filled with sweet dampness. She stumbled over her book and kicked it roughly away. The tender, flesh-like petals of the aster she had picked earlier for her mother were wilted now, but the little bud was still intact. Esther stamped on the flower and threw herself on the ground. The crickets, busy with their night games, made a deafening racket around her. Esther didn't know how long she had been curled up and shivering on the ground when she sensed her brother Jesse's presence. A year older than Esther, Jesse was an inch shorter. He sat down next to her and pulled up his knees and buried his face in them. "Pa sent Charles to get Grandmother Sarah," he sniffed, "to help with the burial, and Daniel has gone for Reverend Wilkes. Pa said we must make a place for him to stay the night."

"Who will get Edmund?" Esther asked. She knew he was more than a half day ride by fast horse. Suddenly from the darkness came the sound of hammering. Both looked up toward the barn.

"It must be Pa," Jesse said, "building the coffin." At this both children lost control and began to cry. Esther did not know how long they had been there, but when she became aware that her brother had begun to walk toward the barn she stood up and straightened her shoulders and shook the earth from her skirts and followed. She swallowed hard. "Will we see Mama once more, Jesse?"

"Maybe it won't be tonight," he said, his voice barely audible.

When the family gathered the next afternoon in the small graveyard on a hill above the village, Esther carried a sheath of brilliant pink peonies. She had carefully chosen the most perfect specimens of her mother's favorite flower. Nearby were the graves of the grandfathers Esther had never known. There were also the graves of the four of Mehitable's seven children who died in childhood and two of Grandmother Sarah's eleven children. Grandmother Sarah, with her wide bonnet tied with a black ribbon, was comforting little Eliza and Mindwell. Edmund was there, too, after Charles had ridden all night to Ithaca to get him.

Reverend Wilkes, a portly man with thinning hair, opened his Bible and began softly, "I am the resurrection and the light, sayeth the Lord." Esther could barely hear the words above the rumble of wagons on the road below, and the continuous drone of the sawmills along the river. Occasionally, the shout of a river man or teamster drifted up and mingled with the minister's words.

Esther looked past the others, down the hill. Men the size of ants in the distance hurried about stacking bundles of shingles and raw lumber onto the flat arks and Durham boats, shouting at those less skillful to make way as they manipulated their clumsy craft with long poles. Lumber was brought in during the winter on sleighs and piled up on the creek banks, in front of what must have been two dozen sawmills, to wait for the spring thaw. Then the arks were made and the shingles cut and shipped, forty thousand of them on a single raft. Some lumber was kept in a yard in town, of course, to build houses—and coffins.

Tears slid off Esther's cheeks and dropped onto the flowers as she watched her father and Daniel cover the simple box with earth. She wondered if God would have a flower garden for her mother to enjoy.

"We forgot to put a ribbon in her hair," Esther whispered hoarsely, recalling her last look at her mother earlier at the house as she was laid out in her best blue wool dress in the coffin. Now, when the grave was completely covered, Esther placed the flowers over it. She looked up when she heard the new baby cry. Her mother's younger sister, Esther Giles, for whom she herself was named, was holding the infant. They were surrounded by the large gathering of McQuigg and Hobart relatives. Retrieving one flower from the grave, Esther walked over and peered into the baby's face, able now to look at him, to note the resemblance to her mother in the shape of his nose and cheekbones. The baby had been named George. Months ago that had been decided, and now Esther remembered the discussion at the supper table.

"We will name a son for George Clinton," her father said, looking pleased, "not only because he was our first governor, but because he was the heart and spirit behind universal suffrage that was granted us this year. He brought true democracy to New York State."

"Does that mean I can vote, too?" Esther asked. Her father's face showed surprise and her brothers laughed out loud. Even her mother fell to giggling.

"That's man's business, Esther," her father explained gently. "The polls are no fit places for the ladies."

"I suppose," Esther said, enthusiastically pouring more fresh cream over her apple cobbler. But she did not understand. In school she learned just as much as the boys, so why would they be any smarter about voting than she was? Despite the commonly accepted idea that women did not have the same rights as men, they certainly shared the same work. She knew her grandmother had helped build this house. When Grandpa Hobart built the sawmill, Grandmother Hetty helped build the rafts and the arks and loaded them, too, when the river was thawed. There weren't many other people around to help, other than a few frontiersmen and Indians.

"This is for you, George Clinton McQuigg," she said, placing the flower in her aunt's hand. "Perhaps it's best you are not a girl." Esther kissed the baby's forehead and he wrinkled his face in a yawn. Esther wiped her hand across her wet face. In the distance, very faintly, she heard the music of a calliope.

"It's the circus; it's come," one of her young cousins announced, a bit too loudly.

"I hope it's not like the menagerie that came last year with that elephant that smelled so bad," another added. A few childish giggles erupted before a woman's voice hushed them. Esther wondered if she should go to see the circus. As she left the graveyard with Hetty, she realized that she was the same height as her grandmother.

"I will be strong, Grandmother," Esther said, taking the old woman's hand.

"I believe you will, Esther," Hetty said, squeezing Esther's hand ever so slightly.

In the weeks following Charlotte's death, the household was subdued, but there was structure in the lives of this large family, which made their recovery inevitable. There was wheat to harvest, sheep and cows to tend, cider to press, the lumber to cut and mill before winter froze the river. The older boys went about the heavy tasks without being reminded and Esther's father nursed his grief in an unending work schedule, and with a jug of hard apple cider he kept in the barn. Nobody ever talked about his "tippling," but the children privately referred to the jug as "the spirits of '76," for it was in 1776 that their father was born.

Aunt Esther Giles nursed the new baby, keeping him with her own family most of the time, such that the others never really got to know him well. Hetty, with Jane and Esther to help, continued to supervise the household. Esther's eleventh birthday went without notice in August. Birthdays had always meant a special cake for supper, and some homemade gifts, but this year Esther was glad no mention was made of the date. She wondered what baby George would think of every year when his birthday came around.

Esther began to mother the younger children, feeling comfort in providing the physical care and affection she so badly missed. She took to carrying Lotte around with her while she fed the chickens or gathered stray apples from under the trees. She walked along the creek or through the woods with Eliza and Mindwell, nervously calling them if they left her sight. She even allowed them to accompany her to her private spot in the garden under the white trellis. Sometimes she read to them from the few books the family owned. When she finished and returned the mud-splattered copy of *The Pioneers* to Mr. Camp in his library, he said she could keep it and enjoy rereading it. He would get another copy for the lending library. He told her that reading would help comfort her at this time.

Whenever Esther looked toward the porch through the screen of flowers, she saw the image of her mother in great pain, but she rededicated herself to maintaining the garden her mother so loved.

CHAPTER TWO

The First Steamboat Comes to Owego

"LET'S GO SEE IF THE NEW SCHOOL IS DONE," ESTHER SUGGESTED AS she sat next to her brother Jesse on the wagon seat. Behind them were baskets of beans, tomatoes, squash, and corn. In late summer it was the responsibility of Esther and Jesse to deliver vegetables from their farm to Uncle Jesse McQuigg's store in Owego twice a week. This gave them a chance to see what was going on in town and to visit friends if they had time.

"Oh, look, they've brought in a great pile of bricks," Esther bellowed as they approached the public square where the new Owego Academy was being built. It would replace the old one-room log building they all attended.

"You don't have to shout, Esther," Jesse said, slapping a hand over his ear. "I'm sitting right next to you."

"Sorry," Esther said, lowering her voice and recalling her grand-mother's recent admonition: "You sound like a turnpike teamster, Esther. You must learn to speak in more ladylike tones." She tried but sometimes forgot. Now Jesse stopped the wagon and he and Esther walked over to the wooden framing of the building.

"Well, it doesn't smell all moldy like the log school," Jesse said in a matter-of-fact voice as he hitched up a suspender that kept slipping off his shoulder.

"Let's go inside," Esther suggested.

"What for?" Jesse asked. "It's only a school."

"But it will have many rooms," Esther responded. "How do you think they will separate the classes?"

Jesse ran his hands along a board of the lumber, for he loved the smell of fresh-cut wood. He liked to build toys with scraps from their father's lumber mill. Both looked up through the ceiling timbers to the second story. Children in Tioga County were given formal schooling until the age of fourteen, and then most worked all day with their parents on farms or businesses in town. Esther favored geography and history lessons. Arithmetic interested her only because she wanted to learn the calculations needed to figure the cost of seeds for the flower beds or the coach fare to Albany. Jesse liked to figure the measurements of building.

"This is the first building in Owego made of brick," Esther said. "Won't it be exciting to come here?" Jesse shrugged as he got back in the wagon. Esther patted his arm when she sat down next to him, aware of the lingering sadness they still felt for the loss of their mother. Jesse pretended to be strong, but at times he could not help weeping and neither could Esther. That sadness now brought to mind a story Grandmother Hobart had told her about the original log schoolhouse built in 1797 and how it had cost her and Grandfather Hobart the life of their eldest son, Prescott, who died from an accident while he was building the school.

"We had no doctors then, and when Prescott cut himself with the axe, he got sick and eventually died of what they called lockjaw," Grandmother Hobart had told her. "How he loved that school. He was anxious to get it built. He was my oldest, but hardly more than a babe himself. He cared about the little ones so during that harsh trip with Daisy and the wagon." Esther clearly recalled how her grandmother's voice trailed off when she continued with her recollection, almost as if she were not saying it aloud. "We're so used to losing our infants that when a child grows up, it is almost impossible to face that kind of loss. We felt so lucky to have them." Prescott Hobart, who would have been an uncle to Esther and Jesse, was the first person to die in the new town.

"I wonder how Mr. Quincy will like the new school," Esther said, trying to shake the memories of death but not expecting an answer. The schoolteacher, Ezra Quincy, had suffered an accident that paralyzed one side of his face, and she wondered if that was lockjaw. Esther's father had told her that Mr. Quincy had been stricken with the palsy, but it was rumored that a sweetheart in his Connecticut town had rejected him for another suitor and Mr. Quincy was so distraught that he shot his pistol into his mouth. Now he had a constant reminder that he had failed not only in romance, but in suicide as well.

"Jesse, do you think Mr. Quincy really tried to kill himself because his sweetheart rejected him?"

"Why would a man do that?" Jesse asked, clearly perplexed by the idea. "He could find another sweetheart."

"Mr. Quincy should have a wife," Esther said, "so he won't be so lonely." She knew the schoolmaster boarded with a family in the village but was rarely seen at the town meetings or in church. Esther had heard girls say they could not kiss a man with his mouth so twisted. "It droops on one side and it does not close properly," her friend Electa Miles had once told her.

"If you look at him only on the right side," Esther had insisted to her friend, "he is quite good looking. A wife could kiss him on the good side, or close her eyes when she did it." Now addressing her brother, she said, "Maybe Mr. Quincy could wear some kind of a patch that would hide part of his face, like Uncle Jesse's eye patch." Esther realized suddenly that her uncle, who was almost forty, had never married. She had always believed he had simply not found the right woman. Now she wondered if his glass eye and wooden leg resulting from 1812 war injuries had something to do with it.

"Well, maybe you'll marry Mr. Quincy," Jesse said, "since you don't mind his queer face." The idea of being married to anyone and risking death to have babies snapped Esther out of her reverie.

"I'm not going to get married. I want to travel on all the rivers and go through the canal to see the West."

"Who will support you, or pay for your ticket?"

"I'll work at Uncle Jesse's store," Esther said defensively. "He already lets me work there sometimes," she boasted, feeling more sure of herself now. "I can cut cloth and I can count out money."

"Come on, we'll be late," Jesse said, urging Waverley into a trot.

——⁓——

"Uncle Jesse, why have you never married?" Esther asked when she dashed into McQuigg and Duane, General Mercantile Establishment. A smaller sign hung beneath, advertising "Lodging, Food, Fine Spirits."

"Why, Esther, when would I have time for a wife?" he asked, winking at her. Esther wondered if her uncle could wink where his other eye used to be, but thought it too impertinent to ask. Except for a slight limp, Uncle Jesse's wooden leg was not noticeable, hidden as it was under his trouser and boot.

They were in a three-story frame building on Lake Street that her uncle operated with his partner, Henry Duane, who was in the 1812 war with him. There were unpainted wooden counters and shelves with nails and bags of flour and barrels of soaps, tin pots, brushes, and leather harness in front of the counters and near the doors. A small wooden table and four chairs were placed near the stove in the back where travelers sometimes sat and smoked or had a mug of ale and some bread and meat. The outside of the store was painted yellow and there was a lean-to on one side of the building where extra stores and supplies were kept. The second floor had rooms to let out to travelers, and Mr. Duane and his family lived on the third floor. Uncle Jesse still lived in Grandmother Sarah McQuigg's house on Front Street.

"But don't you want a family?" Esther continued, noticing how like a mysterious pirate the eye patch made her uncle look. She could not imagine him without it.

"I have a family," Jesse continued. "There are so many McQuigg nieces and nephews and cousins in Tioga County that I would be hard pressed to keep track of my own children if I had any," he said. "Furthermore," he continued, hoisting Esther up onto the counter, "there are so many fair women in this county that I have never been able to decide which one to pick for a wife."

Esther thought her uncle the most handsome man she knew, with his wavy blond hair and broad shoulders and the rakish eye patch. Because his "deformities" were not as visible as Mr. Quincy's, perhaps people did not mind them so much. He charmed her, as well as his customers and guests, with tales of his adventures at Niagara with General Van Rensselaer in the war. The stories of the war always interested Esther because she was born when that war began.

"No militia man would cross the border into Canada," he had told her, "no matter how much the general threatened, so we simply danced around with whatever Redcoats we found along the border. Now mind you, we would not let those Tories into York State, but we saw no good reason to cross into Canada ourselves." Esther recalled that he told her of being afraid that, once in Canada, they would not be allowed back into their own country. Esther suspected her uncle peppered his stories with extra melodrama, but she enjoyed them all the same. Uncle Jesse had come to Owego when he was five years old. He had told Esther that his father came to get away from the rest of his family, who could not agree about anything.

"My father, your grandfather, Captain John McQuigg, had seven brothers and four of them fought with the Redcoats," Uncle Jesse told her. "My father's own mother was a Tory sympathizer and her husband a patriot, so my father came here in 1788 to find peace."

<hr />

Young Jesse suddenly burst into the store, nearly dropping the basket of corn and squash he had in his arms.

"The steamboat's here! It was just towed in from Chenango Point." Through the door behind him, Esther could see people already hurrying toward the river.

"Uncle Jesse, come with us," she said, hopping down from the counter.

"I wouldn't miss it," he said as some of the guests began leaving the inn to see the new contraption. Esther had heard about Mr. Fulton's *Clermont*, which went up and down the Hudson River. But she had not seen that river. She and Jesse pushed their way to the front of the crowd. A gaily painted little steamer glistened in the afternoon sun, and several of the village merchants who had financed this local vessel gathered at the water's edge with fiddles and banjos and began some lively tunes. Red and blue streamers waved from the railing around the pilot house, which was shaded with a green and white striped awning.

"It'll go nine miles an hour and carry twice the load of the river arks," they heard one of the merchants boast. Mr. William Camp, one of the promoters of the steam venture and owner of the grain storage house along with other Owego merchants, had already calculated their additional profits with this new fast freight service.

"It'll sink before it gets out to the middle of the river," said one of the river men watching contemptuously as the steamboat prepared to leave. His companion, leaning against one of the few remaining trees along the river, said, "Never get to Baltimore, too many rocky shallows in this river." He said the boat looked like a floating chicken cage with two very tall smokestacks. "Where will they stack the lumber?" He poked his companion in the side and the men laughed.

Mr. Camp waved from the railing as the captain signaled to let loose the ropes. So strong was Camp's faith in the venture that he had taken his seven-year-old son, George Sidney, aboard for the maiden voyage fifty miles downriver to Wilkes Barre, Pennsylvania.

"Oh, look," Esther said, poking Jesse in the ribs, "George Sidney is going. Don't you wish we could go?" Black smoke belched from the tall stack in the middle of the steamer and cheers went up along the shore. River men sat with arms folded as the musicians pepped up their celebration. "Bye, bye, George Sidney," Esther yelled, running along the shore, splashing mud and water over her skirts and shoes.

"Esther, stand back, or you'll get pulled in with the current," her uncle called from back in the crowd. "This is not a baptism." As Esther stumbled back up to dryer ground with Jesse, the boat was nearly at the center of the river. It puffed out so much smoke that most of the spectators had begun walking back toward the village to get away from it.

Esther felt the explosion before she saw it. The blast knocked her backward into her brother and both children fell into the mud. She heard screams behind her and out in the river where passengers were thrown into the water. When she was able to see the boat through the smoke, pieces of timber were still flying into the water. The cabin had disappeared and the wooden railing around the deck was broken. It looked just like a flat ark, and she didn't see her friend or Mr. Camp on the boat. The air was so filled with black smoke it was like a heavy fog blinding them.

"George Sidney's out there," she said to Jesse. Then they saw the boy splashing several yards out, and they raced along the shore to find a point where they could head him off. Esther and Jesse ran into the water.

"Esther," Jesse said when he felt the force of the water current, "we won't be able to reach him." Then, as an afterthought, he said, "We are not allowed in the river." The Susquehanna itself had been wisely named by the Indians with a word meaning "swift and muddy current." The river widens at Owego and divides to flow around a small island in the center that is known as Hiawatha Island, and this causes some very swift currents, depending upon the tides.

"We can't let him drown," Esther said, pushing on against the weight of her skirts. Jesse planted his feet firmly in the mud and struggled out of his sodden waistcoat and shirt. He tried to pull off his shoes, but couldn't do it without losing his balance. Esther forged ahead and could hardly keep her head above water, but she was closer to George Sidney. She strained to keep her arms and legs moving. Esther reached the boy just as he was going under. She pulled his face up, out of the water, then panicked. She couldn't move now, with the added burden. Jesse caught up then, splashing and coughing, but able to move more freely than Esther. Together they held onto George Sidney, hoping to be carried downstream to a place they knew where the land jutted farther out into the water. Esther felt her water-logged skirts hopelessly tangled around her legs. Now she realized how frightened she was. The current was carrying them down the river faster than Esther had ever moved in her life. The boats never seemed to be moving this fast, she thought.

"Hold on, Esther. Jesse, hold on."

"It's Uncle Jesse," Esther said. "He's near." She coughed up water, trying to call out, but she didn't have enough breath. Her brother succeeded, however, in hacking out a weak shout between coughs.

"Keep shouting," their uncle directed, "so I'll find you in all this smoke." Shouts bounced off the water and ricocheted in all directions. Esther thought she would never see the shore again, when a canoe pulled alongside and strong arms reached out and grabbed her, holding her against the side of the canoe. She clung to George Sidney, keeping his chin up, and her own, too, while Jesse clung to the boat with one hand and young George's arm with the other.

Five people drowned that day, including Mr. Camp, and no one talked about the next steamboat venture for some time. Progress was temporarily delayed in Owego.

"You know, if I could wear leggings like the Seneca girls instead of skirts," Esther said to her brother later, as the two sat wrapped in blankets in front of the stove in Uncle Jesse's store, "I wouldn't have had such trouble in the water." Jesse nodded, shivering, his lips still blue, his hair matted to his skull.

"I thought we were going to see the end of the river as you always wanted," he said through his chattering teeth. No one in the family said much to Esther and Jesse about the incident. There had been some discussion between their father and grandmother on whether the children should be punished for disobeying rules and going into the river. But it was decided they had learned a sufficient lesson by the experience. A firm lecture would suffice. Esther sensed that Jane was embarrassed at Esther's bold behavior, but Esther stuck out her chin when Jane approached, and neither one said a word. Only Hetty spoke directly of the incident.

"You did what you had to do, Esther." The old woman handed Esther a mug of steaming tea. "You and Jesse must watch over George Sidney now and see that he cherishes the life you saved." She paused, then added, "The loss of his father on this day will be difficult for him to forget."

And so Esther grew up like the village, in long continuous strides, and in bursts and spurts, sometimes awkwardly, sometimes gracefully. She was always around when something new came to Owego: a firehouse, another tannery, two more hotels, even a hat manufactory, which she especially enjoyed because she loved the flowers and ribbons on the hats. The town was losing its crude frontier look. When the sidewalks were laid down, she was the first to walk over them, after impatiently waiting while the carpenters hammered in the final nail.

Owego citizens complained about a steep tax for a courthouse and jail but paid it anyway, wanting more than anything to live in a law-abiding town. It was a planned town, after all, and despite its rapid commercial growth managed to keep its New England charm, a credit to its Yankee settlers.

The Erie Canal opened and New York, now the richest state in the Union, was dubbed the Empire State. Owego farmers raised the price of wheat and lumber and James Fenimore Cooper wrote another story about the good old days in York State.

DeWitt Clinton went to Ohio to break ground for a canal that would connect Lake Erie to the Ohio River and thus create a continuous inland waterway from New York City to the Mississippi River. Esther's eighteen-year-old brother Charles went, too, and was paid the astounding sum of a dollar a day to help dig the ditch. In one month he would earn more cash than his father would see in six.

Chapter Three

The Cholera Epidemic

ALL THREE DIED WITHIN HOURS OF EACH OTHER ON THE SAME SUMMER day in 1832, Esther's father and both grandmothers. The cholera struck fast and furiously, having come down from Canada by way of New York's lakes and rivers. Death could strike soon after the first symptoms of this painful gastrointestinal disorder that turned the insides to liquid. Cities as well as rural areas fell victim, for cholera was a disease of the industrial revolution as well as the frontier. Few people understood sickness and many believed the epidemic was God's punishment for leading an immoral life. Some blamed the Irish immigrants working on the Erie Canal and the riverboats, people who lived in crowded and unsanitary conditions and appeared to drink to excess.

Esther took care of Grandmother Hetty while Daniel looked after their father. They had worked tirelessly, trying with wet towels to keep the fevers down and changing the bed linens that quickly became saturated with bodily fluids. Esther boiled water and washed the soiled linens, hanging them to dry on rope strung between doorframes in the house because they would not dry outside in the rain. When Dr. Tinkham arrived he brought the news that their grandmother Sarah McQuigg had just died despite the efforts of Uncle Jesse and Aunt Elizabeth to save her.

"The old and the very young are the most vulnerable," he said, gently taking Esther's hand away from the towel she was placing on Hetty's brow when he realized the woman was already dead. "Your grandmother Hobart was seventy-seven and no longer strong enough to fight it off.

And your grandmother McQuigg was eighty-five," he continued, "so they had long lives."

"But old Mr. Post survived last time the cholera came," Esther insisted as she wiped her own brow with the sleeve of her dress. Her father, on the other hand, was only fifty-seven. Dr. Tinkham's voice was hoarse with fatigue and his black broadcloth coat wrinkled and soiled. He had visited a dozen people this day alone, and now went to Daniel McQuigg's room. The doctor took his pulse and shook his head.

"I wish I could give you hope, but your father's respiration is so diminished, he won't last the hour, I'm afraid. He has been weakened by the drink," the doctor said to Esther and her brother, who did not argue the truth of this statement. "His distillery with its stagnant water could well have been the source of the disease for him."

Thirty-five people died in Owego, Spencer, and the surrounding area, and there was no time for a proper funeral because the caskets had to be closed and put into the ground immediately to prevent spreading the disease. After Esther's father and grandmothers were buried she went to the flower garden, still wearing the clothes she had worn for the past two days without sleeping or bathing. She sat on the wooden bench her brother Jesse had built for the garden last year and cried. Feeling entirely bereft, as if God had taken everything from her now, she mourned most for Grandmother Hobart, whom she would sorely miss. Despite her gruff and silent demeanor, there was a solid presence in the old woman that required no verbal communication. It was as if the connection from Mehitable to her daughter Charlotte to her granddaughter Esther were a continuous thread. Esther had not been as close to Grandmother McQuigg, who lived in town. In recent years she had been ill and her mind seemed to have lost its bearings so that she did not remember anyone. Esther's father, too, had become less communicative since his wife died ten years ago. He had turned more often to his "spirits" and while he did look after the farm and sawmill, more and more of the responsibility fell onto the shoulders of his oldest son, Daniel, now married to Eleanor Cummings. They already had three children to care for and he and Eleanor often had rows over the senior McQuigg's drunkenness. Esther was sensitive to this conflict, but had kept the household going with her grandmother and by looking after Lotte, now twelve, and Georgie, ten years old.

In the years since her mother died, most of Esther's siblings had moved away. Jesse lived in Owego, where he worked as a carpenter, building new homes for the growing population. At harvesttime he came to help Daniel take care of the wheat crop and the grist mill, which was a significant source of income. Jane had married Alvah Archibald and lived on a farm near Oneonta. John had married Esther's friend Electa Miles and they moved to Pennsylvania, where her brother worked in a tannery. Edmund had his own accommodations upstate near Ithaca, where he had invested in a lumber business. Mindwell had married a boy from a neighboring farm and lived there now. Eliza, not yet sixteen, had run off and married one of the Parker boys and left for Iowa Territory. Charles, who had gone to Cincinnati to work on the canals, now worked in a tannery making shoes.

In their letters both Charles and Eliza wrote of the good conditions on the Great Lakes frontier. "There is much business for everyone and new houses and stores going up every day," wrote Charles. Since Andrew Jackson had become president, the American population began in earnest to move past the Appalachians, to expand farther west and stake their claim to a better life.

—◆—

Esther had always known that once her father died, the homestead would be turned over to her brother Daniel. Under the English law they still followed about property, the oldest son received the entire family inheritance. Nevertheless, it was still a shock when Daniel said he was planning to sell the farm to move north to his wife's family's farm near Albany. Despite the law Esther found it unfair that one child could decide the fate of others. Her siblings had always accepted this, for they had all moved on to marriage or their own occupations away from the homestead. Although Esther had learned the seamstress trade, it was customary for unmarried females to remain under supervision of the man who succeeded the father as head of the family, even if these females earned enough to support themselves.

When Esther's formal schooling ended at fourteen, her father had arranged for her to apprentice with Mrs. Jameson, a seamstress in Owego. Other than domestic service, this was the only way women could respectably earn a living. Esther found the handwork involved in making dresses—tiny stitching in many layers of skirts, petticoats, bodices, and sleeves—tedious and tiring. If she had to sit still for so many hours, she would prefer reading a book! However, she did enjoy selecting fabrics and picking fashion patterns from *Godey's Lady's Book*, which came up from New York City periodically with the mail. After her apprenticeship Esther began making and repairing clothing for the local farm women.

———

"You and Lotte and Georgie will come to live with us in Weedsport," Daniel said. Esther had no interest in moving to Weedsport to become the "auntie" of Daniel's growing brood.

"Can you not keep the farm if it pays a profit?" she asked. "I can stay here with Lotte and George and we can operate the farm while I work at my trade." She insisted he explain why he needed to put the money into his wife's family farm, but her brother said only, "That is not your concern." What about your own family, she wanted to ask but held her tongue as Daniel continued. "I cannot allow you and Lotte, both unmarried women, to live on the homestead and manage it on your own."

"But there are women on farms. What about Mrs. Hedgeman? She operates a farm alone near Barton," Esther pointed out.

"She is a widow, Esther, and quite old. It is not suitable for unmarried women and young ones to live without male supervision and protection," Daniel said with impatience. "You should be married by now, Esther; you are nearly twenty."

"Oh, Daniel, have some feeling," his wife, Eleanor, said. "We need to have compassion for Esther. God has tested her with the burden of too much height to find a husband." Esther understood that Eleanor did not want her outspoken sister-in-law at her home any more than Esther wanted to live there, but still, Eleanor's remark stung and she felt her eyes fill.

By the time she was sixteen, Esther was nearly six feet tall, strong willed and outspoken, hardly the feminine ideal of the time. However, she was also optimistic and had a sense of humor, traits that helped her deal with the awkwardness she often felt in school and the village, of being different than the other girls. Except for Jesse and John, her brothers were as tall or taller, but she was the only one of the girls to reach such height. Her grandmothers had suggested she find missionary work with the Baptist Church, because she was unlikely to marry. "No man would want a wife who was taller than he; how could she look up to him?" Grandmother McQuigg had asked. But missionary work had no appeal for Esther, who did not wish to be confined in a church or infirmary taking care of sick people all day, people she did not even know. And from what she had seen of marriage, she was not so sure she wanted that life either. The image of her overworked and worn-out mother was always in the back of her mind.

Esther was determined to not let her sister-in-law know her remark had hurt. She had never felt warmly about Eleanor, who appeared to be the compliant wife, never challenging you directly, but finding a way to diminish you by disregarding your efforts. She would quietly change the placement of a table setting or a flower arrangement after you had set it out to let you know your efforts were not quite up to her standards. Once Esther made what she thought was a pretty yellow gingham dress for baby Adeline, and when she asked Eleanor why the child never wore it, her sister-in-law brushed it aside as not a suitable color for the baby. Eleanor was a medium-size woman already growing stout who wore her brown hair braided in circles over her ears. Esther was often tempted to lift them and shout into her ear when Eleanor ignored something she said.

Now Esther closed her eyes and took a deep breath to control her emotion. She would not let Eleanor or Daniel see her tears, or let them know they had hurt her.

"I need to see to the horses," she said and quietly got up and walked out of the house. Esther walked with long strides along the creek to release some of her anger and pain. She walked through the pasture past two grazing cows and into the barn. Her beloved Waverley had died several years ago from a colic attack, and now they kept only three horses to pull the wagon and plow and one for riding, something she still enjoyed. She filled their water troughs and scattered some dried corn to the hens, who followed her.

After she closed the barn, she walked up to the flower garden and sat mulling over the inequity of her situation. Because she was a female she must let others decide her fate. She and her friend Eliza Jane Hall often had conversations on this subject, and about how the native Seneca women had much more freedom to make family decisions.

"It is the women who make the rules," Eliza Jane reminded her. "The oldest woman is in charge of the longhouse, which might be home to five or even twenty families." Esther thought about how Grandmother Hobart kept the homestead together after Charlotte died. And while Esther's father was legally in charge of the homestead, it was her grandmother who ran the household, kept the children healthy and fed, and got the vegetables planted. Yet, she had died penniless, without legal ownership of anything.

"Corn Planter's granddaughter told me that long ago when white women were taken captive by the Indians, most of them did not want to return to their white families," Eliza Jane said. "They liked belonging to the tribe where women were respected for their wisdom and the importance of their work and they were never beaten by their husbands." Both girls were also impressed with the Indian style of dress, especially Eliza Jane, who had fashioned her long, black curly hair into a braid that hung down her back. Eliza Jane's family had moved from Orange County when her father opened a newspaper and printing office in Owego. Eliza Jane and Esther met in their final year at the Owego Academy and had become fast friends. Eliza Jane had been to New York City twice and Esther loved to hear her friend's descriptions of the fashionable townhouses along the wide road known as Broadway. Also an avid reader, Eliza Jane shared her books with Esther. "I fear that if I marry I will become a captive," Eliza Jane told her friend one day.

"Hah!" Esther said aloud, as if her friend were with her now. "I am not married, yet I am still a captive!" Her walk had calmed her a bit, and now as Esther sat among the flowers in the garden, she realized she could not fault Daniel and Eleanor. It was how things were done everywhere among her people. The oldest boy always got the inheritance. Girls were expected to marry and fall in with the husband's family. If she did not want to follow prevailing custom, she would have to find a way around it. Arguing with Daniel would only cause anguish for all of them. No, she would offer her brother an alternative he might find acceptable. And Eleanor would certainly be receptive to a plan that kept Esther out of her home. Much as she loved this farm, Esther knew she would have to leave it, but most certainly she would not go to Weedsport, where she knew not a soul and would have no occupation or entertainment.

Esther would prefer to be part of Owego, which was growing into a place of great opportunity and change. York State was home to idealism and progressive thought and Owego was in the center of it. Abolitionists, suffragists, and spiritualists coexisted with millers and farmers and shopkeepers. There was no reason she could not find a respectable place to live there. This would bring her closer to her customers and she would attract more business and make more profits. Her brother Edmund would understand that argument! And she had begun to focus her attention on making hats. Ladies' hats were elaborately decorated with flowers, feathers—sometimes entire birds—and ribbons, supported by wide brims. Mr. Camp's store, now operated by his sons, including her friend George Sidney, had a millinery department where craftsmen made felt and flowers and dyed bird feathers brought in by market hunters. Esther would learn the milliner's trade and open her own shop. She would train Lotte to be her apprentice. After all, she was from one of the founding families whose influence was spread across a wide area of business and community politics. She would earn enough to care for Lotte and Georgie, as well. She would probably not have such a large garden in town, but she would have something, she was sure.

There were other men—Edmund and Jesse and Uncle Jesse—who could "supervise" her if she were able to find a home in Owego. They would offer any guidance or protection she might need. She would make them promise to support her when she spoke with Daniel.

The more Esther thought out the details, the more she liked this plan. Now she gathered some marigolds and nasturtiums, making a gold and red bouquet, and carried it back to the house. Her brother and his wife, who was nursing Adeline, were still seated at the table but suddenly stopped talking when she walked in. Esther suspected they were talking about her, but she ignored it. Her brother George was racing through the house with his eight-year-old niece Cordelia, who was his age, while Lotte tried to quiet them. Esther found a vase for the flowers and put them on the table.

"Here is something to brighten the room," Esther said, smiling at her brother and sister-in-law. She sat down and pulled her four-year-old nephew Horace into her lap and tickled him. As the boy laughed, she said, "Daniel, I have a plan you and Eleanor might find agreeable."

CHAPTER FOUR

The Young Abolitionist at the Baptist Church

"You can burn the church around me," Esther said, standing up from her bench and turning to face the mob. "I will not leave." About seventy men and a few women from local farms and mills and shops carried torches. A few men had muskets and some carried a thick board of lumber over their shoulder. They had first gathered at the entrance to the Baptist church in the town square to shout obscenities at those entering and to block their way into the church. Most of the parishioners pushed past, determined not to let the mob deter them from hearing Mr. Douglass speak. The protestors followed and crowded inside the doorway to jeer from the back of the church.

"Nigger lovers! Burn them out!" Some began pounding their musket stocks and lumber on the floor, chanting, "Burn them out, burn them out."

"This church belongs to the Baptist people," Esther continued forcefully, "and no one has the right to destroy it. If you propose to burn it down, I will stay here and see who does it." About two hundred townsfolk, also farmers and millers and shopkeepers, including a dozen free Negroes, were seated on the church benches. Some stood around the edges of the room. Many of the men, members of the volunteer fire department, had carried buckets filled with water into the church in case they were needed. Frederick Douglass had come to speak to the people of Owego about abolition as he had in several other churches in the region.

Last month a similar meeting in Utica had ended in violence, with the church being burned to the ground and many people injured.

"I will stay, too," said a man seated across the aisle. He stood up and faced Esther. "I am from Vermont, where we never allowed slavery and Negroes can worship how and where they please." Esther took her eyes from the mob momentarily to look over at this stranger. He was tall and very handsome, with light hair and a high forehead. She thought he must be a general, the way he stood with such confidence.

"Go back to Vermont!" came a shout from the crowd at the door. "This is not your state or your church." Now people on both sides were shouting.

"Is this the way to talk in God's house?" The minister was pounding on his lectern and shouting for order. "Everyone is welcome in God's house, even those from Vermont," he said. This brought a bit of laughter to the meeting and the noise quieted, long enough for the minister to ask the man from Vermont to introduce himself. "Tell us your name." Some in the mob seemed curious, too.

"My name is Artemas Slack, and I am a civil engineer recently relocated from Albany to Owego to help build the Erie Railroad between Elmira and Binghamton." Esther wondered why she had not seen this man before. Where could he be living? A railroad bridge was under construction spanning the Susquehanna and rails were being laid along the north side of town, so he must have been here for some time. She quickly brought her attention back to the crowd, which again began banging rifle stocks and boards on the floor.

"Was our country not founded on equality?" Esther asked, raising her voice over the din but without shouting. "Did not my family and yours fight for that right? And now you want to deny some citizens their right to worship a God who loves all of us? Think of the hardships we have all suffered to make this town one of peace and prosperity." She stood looking at them, waiting for an answer she knew would not come.

Silence fell over the church, a plain wooden structure painted white with a steeple at the center. The windows were tall and narrow and added a bit of elegance to the modest interior with simple benches and a lectern on a raised platform. Off to the side was a small piano.

Artemas Slack had been watching Esther with obvious admiration as he would a goddess, so tall and straight and proud in a simple broadcloth dress of forest green with white lace at the collar and cuffs. Her golden hair had been pulled back and tied with a black velvet ribbon, but some curls from the sides had slipped loose around her face. Her voice carried across that noisy mob with such assurance and without fear, the mob could think of no response. He had never before come upon a woman like this.

"Now let us welcome Mr. Douglass," Esther said. She turned to sit down, but stopped suddenly and turned back to the retreating mob. "Perhaps you would like to stay and hear what he has to say so that you can educate your opinions on this subject?"

———

The church was not burned that night. There may have been too many people inside for the mob to take on. Maybe they were not angry enough to destroy the church they themselves helped to build and used for worship with their families. Or perhaps it was those two very determined people facing them. Esther was well liked in Owego. She was from a founding family and had a wide network of friends and relatives. They would have some explaining to do if they challenged her. The railroad man could be a problem, too, if it cost them jobs with the new lines. After grumbling about "niggers" and "breaking the law to hide people," they shuffled out of the church. Some just shook their heads on the way out, most likely to go to the tavern across the square and nurse their grievances in rum or hard cider. This would either fortify their cause or weaken it. Esther and the others hoped for the latter.

When they were gone Frederick Douglass quietly got up from a bench in the front of the church and took his place at the lectern. He was a proud-looking man with broad shoulders, a wide brow, and a firm chin. His clothing was perfectly tailored with the finest broadcloth and linen. His waistcoat appeared to be hand-embroidered like tapestry.

"Thank you all for the important work you do to help our people." Mr. Douglass told them of slow progress in their efforts to make slavery illegal in all the states and territories. He also told them that many of the suffrage and temperance organizations were building a network in York State and assisting with the cause. He brought with him many copies of Mrs. Lydia Child's new publication, the *National Anti-Slavery Standard*, for the parishioners to take home and read.

People in Owego not only supported abolition, many helped slaves escaping from the South. The town was perfectly positioned as a station on what had become known as the Underground Railroad. Slaves were hidden on flatboats or steamers coming up the Susquehanna from the south. From Owego they traveled north and west and across Lake Ontario into Canada. Sometimes they took a land route around Niagara, but the water route was usually safer. Escaping slaves were hidden in homes and sometimes moved in shipping crates and even caskets delivered to the church. Esther risked her life to provide clothing and food to help people to freedom. Because her dresses were longer than average, she sometimes gave them to escaping men to disguise themselves. With gloves on his hands and a bonnet pulled low over his face, a black man could travel without notice.

Baptists became heavily involved in the slavery controversy, but churches in the North and South were splitting into separate organizations. Southern Baptists declared it acceptable by God for Christians to own slaves. Northern Baptists, who evolved from the New England Puritans, disagreed. Slavery, which had been abolished for more than a decade in York State, must be abolished everywhere.

Despite the eloquence of Mr. Douglass, Esther was distracted by the civil engineer from Vermont. Occasionally glancing over at him, she once caught him looking at her. She turned away quickly but a smile had escaped her lips before she could prevent it. And she noticed that he smiled back. She had never met a man who caught her interest in such a way. Her entire being, her spirit and her mind, even her body, was drawn to him. She felt she was becoming overheated and put her hand to her face to see if this were true. Is this why her friends went into such flights of silliness when they talked about a man they swooned over?

The recent wedding of her brother Edmund to her best friend Eliza Jane reminded her it was her brother who did the swooning in that courtship. Eliza Jane sang in the church choir and played piano, and Edmund said that was what made him fall in love with her, although Esther thought Edmund may have been influenced by her friend's stunning beauty. Edmund had not been a serious churchgoer and had reservations about the Baptist Church, having preferred something less fundamental and more refined, such as Congregationalism or Church of England, but Eliza Jane was in this one.

When Eliza Jane finished her presentation one Sunday and bowed her head gently in acknowledgement, Edmund wanted to stand and clap his hands. But, alas, they were in church and the minister simply moved on to the reading, asking all to join in prayer with him. Edmund continued to watch Eliza Jane and realized he was smiling. He looked around him, at the family bench, noting that Esther also seemed to enjoy the music, but she was Eliza Jane's friend. He had been careful not to make too much of a fuss over Eliza Jane, lest Esther tell her friend how besotted he was. In this small town most courting was done quite casually, but they were New Englanders after all, and certain manners were required.

Edmund had made it a point to study Eliza Jane's father and mother and get a sense of how best to approach them. He had been reading the *Owego Free Press* each week so he would be able to comment on Mr. Hall's editorials. He did not completely agree with his recent historic series about how cruelly the Iroquois Nation, including the Senecas and Cayugas, were treated in our country's early history. They were driven out during the war and then many were sent to reservations when the land for the Erie Canal was acquired. Edmund himself, with his lumber business, was well aware of the destruction of their territory. However, he was acquainted with several Indians, traded with them for horses, and some worked in the mill. He would find positive things on which to comment. For example, the colonists had kept the Indian names for rivers and towns. Edmund would assure the Halls he could offer Eliza adequate comfort. While he had worked in Ithaca for so many years since his youth, he had raised his own income with his astuteness about how to make people spend more money in the store by offering special sales, such as buying one bar of soap and then getting the second for half the price.

Edmund did not want to devote all of his time to business with individual customers. No, he preferred business at a higher level. He had invested in a large lumber mill that was making a handsome profit. This provided the capital to buy a new dairy farm just outside of town. He liked the modern idea of raising cattle just for milk and butter and cheese. Until now, cows were cows, milked until they got old and then butchered for meat. He introduced new methods to achieve more production from the cows and to interest other businessmen to buy milk wholesale; they in turn would make butter or cheese and sell it to stores. This way, Edmund was on the top of the chain, and his investment would pay off on several levels.

Around him that Sunday Edmund noticed others getting up to leave the church. Eliza Jane, who had taken her seat in the front row after finishing with the music, was now coming forward and his heart was beating so hard as if to come right out of his chest. He unconsciously put a hand over his waistcoat, checking to see if it was buttoned securely. With his attention to his tailoring and general appearance, Edmund had become a bit of a macaroni. Now, at thirty-two, a tall, solidly built and prosperous citizen, he was grinning like a twelve-year-old. Unable to take his eyes off Eliza Jane, who was walking toward her parents and siblings, he hooked his arm through Esther's and said, "Let us go and offer our greetings to the Hall family." Esther gave him a sly smile. Her brother did not know that she and her friend had discussed Edmund as a marriage prospect for Eliza Jane at great length.

Eliza Jane, who was ten years younger than Edmund, enjoyed teasing him by making outrageous statements, such as, "I think in another ten years women will have the vote, don't you agree, Mr. McQuigg?" Edmund, who did not believe that for a moment, was smart enough not to argue with her, but said, "I will pray that one day, you do get to vote, Miss Hall." Eliza Jane knew he was just flattering her, but she did admire Edmund's ambition and his modern ideas about business. The physical attraction she felt was a strong one. "Sometimes I get this mad urge to press myself against him and pull his lips to mine," she told Esther. Now, with Artemas Slack nearby, Esther understood exactly what she meant.

When Mr. Douglass finished his talk, many of the congregants gathered around to thank him. Where will he speak next, they asked, and had he heard any more reports of bounty hunters in the area? Artemas Slack introduced himself to Mr. Douglass and the minister. He mentioned that he had once before attended such a meeting, when Mr. Douglass spoke farther upstate. Mr. Douglass thanked Artemas for taking a stand and supporting Esther McQuigg, and others joined in with their agreement. The minister addressed Artemas.

"Please, Mr. Slack, may I introduce you to Miss Esther McQuigg, who has done much good work with us?"

"I am honored, Miss McQuigg," Artemas said, taking her hand. "I admire your courage and forthright principle. If I can be of service here with your work, please don't hesitate to call on me." It took him a few more moments to release her hand. Esther was barely able to take a breath, never mind find her voice. She almost curtsied before she caught herself in such an infantile gesture. Finally, she said, "I will do that, Mr. Slack. We need everyone we can get to help with this vital work." Her smile got through to him quite directly.

Esther wanted Artemas, but she told herself not to become infatuated, for she had no idea whether he already had a wife. At her age, now twenty-eight, she had learned to appreciate her independence and the good life she had made for herself. Losing her head to a handsome stranger could put that at risk. She had succeeded with her plan to live in town and develop her business after the homestead was sold. That family meeting had indeed been arranged with her brothers and uncle, who assured Daniel they would be responsible for Esther and Lotte's care. Georgie chose to go live with his older brother, where he would have more companionship with Daniel's children, who were closer to his own age.

Esther rented a small house a few blocks from Uncle Jesse's store. She devoted the front room and its two prominent windows to her millinery business. There was a small side room she used as a private sitting room to read and write letters, and a modest kitchen on the first floor.

She and Lotte each had a small bedroom upstairs. Now, after eight years, Esther was a fixture in Owego. As she strode into shops for victuals or went to church or town meeting, she was greeted warmly. She invited friends in for tea on Sunday afternoons and if the weather was fine, she served it in the small garden in back of her house. It was not a grand lady's garden, but it sufficed, allowing her to grow flowers and a few vegetables. Nevertheless, standing here with Artemas Slack, she now realized she wanted much more.

Esther left the church anxious to ask George Sidney what he knew about this stranger. She had remained close to her friend since the steamboat accident. He was only three years younger than Esther, but with his plump face and light brown hair, he had a childlike countenance. His family had sent him to Yale College to study the law with plans to work in New York City, but he came home from Yale suddenly when he lost his voice. It was still a mystery what had caused this condition. When George Sidney could no longer speak, Esther insisted they converse on paper. She kept a small notebook for him to use. She would ask him how he was, or what he was doing, or something about the business and he would write a note back to her. The Camps were the wealthiest family in town and had been business and civic leaders since the early days, so they would know all about the railroad construction and what Mr. Slack was doing here. She must think how to phrase her questions so her friend would answer honestly. And she must get a larger notebook so he would tell her every detail of what he knew.

CHAPTER FIVE

The Civil Engineer

IT WAS A BRIEF COURTSHIP. BOTH ESTHER AND ARTEMAS DETERMINED to know each other better after that first meeting at the Baptist church. Esther had learned from George Sidney, as well as from Jesse's sweetheart, Mary Freemont, that the civil engineer had been boarding with the Peters family on River Row, but was gone for days at a time. He hired a horse from the livery and rode out with his carpetbag and a canvas pouch with rolled-up maps and instruments.

"What more can I tell you?" George Sidney wrote on his notepad while giving Esther an innocent smile.

"Well, has he ever talked of a wife? Or a family?" Esther asked impatiently. "And stop smiling like that. You know exactly what I want to know." George Sidney acknowledged he had plenty of information about the railroad, but not much more about Mr. Slack. At the same time Artemas sought out the McQuigg men to learn more of Esther's availability. He was discreet, but nevertheless rumors traveled the town quicker than Paul Revere's famous ride, and while Esther and Artemas had not had so much as a casual walk alone together, they were already being paired by local gossip.

Artemas stopped at Jesse McQuigg's store to introduce himself. Now nearing sixty, Uncle Jesse's wavy hair was white and he took to dressing in a more formal style, as befitted the professional status of a store owner. The original yellow frame building had burned down and was replaced with a solid brick building. His partner, Henry Duane, had moved west with his family and Jesse now owned the store by himself with help from various young people from his family who needed work. The old McQuigg residence on Front Street was also gone, having been replaced by industrial buildings on the waterfront. Jesse now lived in the quarters on the third floor of his store, while the second floor accommodated paying guests.

Artemas asked the storekeeper if he might be so kind as to introduce to his nephews the subject of his courting Miss McQuigg. "That is, of course, if she would allow me to see her," he added. Uncle Jesse could barely keep a serious face, as he already knew how willing Esther would be. His niece was always looking for a way to start a discussion of the new railroad and the work of a civil engineer. Thus, Artemas was invited to Edmund's new house on a Sunday afternoon for a more formal discussion of his intentions. When Edmund married Eliza Jane, he had built, with Jesse's help, a new house on a ridge overlooking the Susquehanna. It was a two-story frame and stone house with an attic and a kitchen. There were flower gardens and a stable for two horses and coaches, one for his wife, and one for him to travel to his new dairy farm on the outskirts of town.

Once seated in the parlor, each with a glass of Madeira, Artemas assured the McQuigg men he had only Esther's interest at heart and he would do nothing to injure her position or reputation, or that of her family. He told them that his own grandfather and great-uncles had served with distinction in the War of the Revolution. In fact, he himself was named for the famous major general Artemas Ward.

"I am the second son of a family of pioneers in Windsor, Vermont. My father's name is also Jesse," he said, smiling at the two Jesses in the room. "My mother is Betsy Burnham and my brother is Allen Slack." The names of his other six siblings all began with the letter *A*. He had studied at the university at Norwich, a well-respected Vermont scientific and military academy directed by a general from West Point. "My brother and I were teachers in the district schools, but I eventually went back to Norwich to finish my studies," Artemas said. "Then, several years ago, I began my career with the railroads in Albany."

"Are you acquainted with Erastus Corning?" Edmund asked, referring to the Albany businessman who had invested a great deal of capital in railroads in New York. Artemas told them he did indeed know Mr. Corning and had worked on his Schenectady Line.

"Mr. Corning has a good idea to combine the railroad corporations so that they are not all building separate lines with no connections to each other," Artemas said. Edmund liked this idea of consolidation and control of the larger part of the business. The men were pleased for the opportunity to talk about the new railroads. The country was awash with railroad fever, and the industrialists with money were building railroads everywhere, claiming they would soon replace the canals and river barges in carrying freight.

"Here, in the Northeast, coal is a cargo that needs railroads," said Edmund.

"And don't forget the postal service," Artemas added. "Imagine if a letter to your brother or a business customer could get from Chicago to Albany in only two days, rather than two weeks by stagecoach or through the canals. In fact, this idea is tempting our government to invest heavily in railroads."

Uncle Jesse, with his thumbs hooked in his waistcoat pocket, shook his head. "We have heard much talk along the pike and on the river about the dangers of engines blowing up or rail cars running right off the tracks," he said. "The river workers said they had seen men covered in black soot, men who could not breathe from the smoke of the fires in the engines."

"Yes, the engines are dirty, but we are now putting an iron shield behind the engine to block the spread of the dust," said Artemas.

"I will not set foot on a train," said Uncle Jesse. "I'll leave this modern invention to you youngsters. I'll travel on the water, thank you very much. I even prefer a nice peaceful ride in a stagecoach, no matter how bumpy the road or slow the horses." The younger Jesse smiled at his uncle, then asked Artemas, "But won't your work keep you away for long periods, Mr. Slack?"

"Yes," Artemas said. "And for that reason I have not pursued marriage. I felt it would be a burden for a wife to have a husband away for long periods, but Miss McQuigg is so special I must now change my thinking." They all laughed, liking this man who would most likely be part of their family soon.

"Will you be able to support our sister? She is not extravagant, but she has made a comfortable life," Edmund said. "Her millinery business is the most successful in this part of the state." They would not be so indiscreet as to ask Mr. Slack's salary, but Edmund knew some railroad workers made very little money. In fact, they were sometimes hired on speculation; if the line made a profit, they would get paid. Artemas, dressed in a well-tailored coat of black broadcloth with tan trousers and a gold-colored waistcoat, looked as if he received adequate compensation. His family was not wealthy and, as the second son, he would not inherit anything even if it were.

"She does need to have time for her garden and her books," Jesse said, "so a proper husband would not prohibit these pleasures."

"And she likes parties," Eliza Jane said, entering the room with baby Frances, now six months old and called Franky. "You gentlemen have had enough time to discuss my friend's future, so I suggest you take a few minutes to admire my daughter." Eliza Jane, who knew all about Esther's infatuation with the civil engineer, had decided to find an excuse to come into the room to see this special man. "May I offer you some refreshment?" Eliza Jane asked. Artemas was relieved at the interruption, although he sensed Edmund was not pleased at his wife's breach of protocol.

"I see you have yet another fair female for the McQuigg family," Artemas said, smiling at the baby and deciding it was time for him to leave. "Gentlemen, madam," he said, "it has been my pleasure." Artemas bowed and then donned his hat. "I await your decision." The brothers knew they would, of course, grant their permission, but decided it would not hurt to let Mr. Slack wait a bit. After he left, Edmund took them out onto the porch to admire the river view. "It is a sight in the evening," he said, "to watch the sun set over the Susquehanna."

"Is Esther hiding in the other room?" Uncle Jesse asked Eliza Jane.

"No, but I'm sure she is watching from her window to see if Mr. Slack arrives back in town in a sprightly manner or with dejection."

"He seems a good match for our sister," Edmund said. "She will not easily overpower him." They were pleased for a potential husband for their sister at last. Not that she failed to attract suitors. There had been several, but Esther refused to marry someone in whom she had no interest or feeling. A year ago, they tried to convince her to marry one man they felt was qualified.

"No," she said firmly. "I sense he likes his cider too much and would turn into someone like our father, who once he was under the influence said only hurtful things. I am content to remain unmarried forever if that is God's plan for me."

Artemas began calling on Esther, but only when Lotte was also home, so as not to seem improper. They sat in the side parlor to talk and drink tea. In addition to their obvious physical attraction, they discovered common passions for books and politics. They talked with wonder at how fast the country was spreading west, and how each day seemed to bring some news from their friends or relatives who were discovering new areas of wealth in building the new nation.

"It's the beginning of everything," Esther said as Artemas told her about the new railroads, and how they would change the way people traveled and how goods were shipped. Artemas was invited to supper on Sunday sometimes at Edmund's home or at Esther's, but always with other family members in attendance. Eventually they did manage some time alone, however.

Esther for so long had been tending to the care and comfort of her family and her customers, she rarely had time for frivolity, except perhaps her girlish conversations with Eliza Jane. But now she was overcome with a giddiness she had never experienced before. She could not resist leaning closer to Artemas when they were together in church or in town meeting or walking along the river. They both enjoyed riding and walking in the country, and Esther showed Artemas the old homestead in Spencer where she grew up. Her flower garden, she was happy to notice, had been maintained by the new owners, a poet from New York City and his family, who used the house in summer.

One day Artemas took Esther to walk along the tracks of the new Erie Railroad and explained how he and his crew surveyed and measured the land to find the best location for tracks, decide what the most efficient route would be, and look for potential problems. Esther had heard about railroad accidents, many of them fatal, but Artemas reassured her that he was cautious. Most of his work was done without being on the trains, he explained, but he did have to ride in the engines sometimes to evaluate response to the rails.

Their first kisses, when he walked her home from the church after an abolition meeting, had been modest and proper. While walking in the country one Sunday afternoon, Esther closed her eyes as Artemas's lips brushed hers gently. When nothing more occurred, she opened her eyes to see him watching her with a grin on his face, but seeming awkward about the next step. She could not help bursting out, "Oh, I wanted more, Mr. Slack."

"And I, too." Artemas laughed then and throwing propriety aside pulled her close, took her face between both his hands, and kissed her with such intensity that Esther thought her legs would give out. She slipped her arms around his waist to keep upright and keep him pressed tight against her. When finally they drew apart, she whispered, "Oh, my!" She could not wait to find out what was next. "We'd best not wait too long for the wedding, Mr. Slack." He laughed and pulled her close again. "Oh, Esther, you are right about that. How I do love you."

—◦—

They were married on August 10, 1841, at the Baptist church with Uncle Jesse escorting his niece to her groom. Jesse and Lotte were witnesses and Edmund and Eliza Jane gave a dinner reception in their new home. Artemas's family in Vermont was unable to make the trip. He had hoped his brother Allen, also an engineer, could find a way to travel by rail, but the connections between this part of New York and upper Vermont were not convenient. Artemas told his family that he and his new bride would come to visit next summer, when he could get enough time off from his work.

Esther decided to make herself a grand gown for her wedding. Most brides at the time simply wore their best dresses, which might be of any color, but the previous year Queen Victoria had been married in an elegant white satin gown, and women in Europe and America began to follow her lead. Esther could not afford satin, but she made herself a dress of the finest cream-colored wool, adding satin insets in the bodice and sleeves. Eliza Jane insisted that Esther wear the wedding tiara that Esther had designed for her wedding to Edmund. Eliza Jane had long been enamored of the beaded, tiara-like headpieces the Seneca women wore for ceremonial occasions, so Esther had designed something similar for Eliza Jane's wedding. It sat atop her head with a trail of Irish lace flowing down her back and onto the floor. Another creation by Esther was a beautiful braided red silk turban adorned with gold beads, which Eliza Jane wore on special occasions.

—— ——

By the time the Erie Railroad had been completed between Elmira and Binghamton, in June 1841, a few months before their planned August wedding, Artemas's services were already in great demand by several railroad companies. He had considered the Baltimore and Ohio, for it would allow him to get home more often, but the Illinois Central made him the best offer. Planned as the connecting railroad for the country, the Illinois Central would have several lines across the state, and a terminus in Chicago would connect with railroads from other states as well ports at the rivers, canals, and Lake Michigan. This was the first railroad in the country to receive government land grants to encourage expansion across the country. The railroad, in turn, gave some of those parcels of land to men they needed to help build the railroad.

After first refusing their offer of employment because of the distance from New York, Artemas agreed to further talks when the owners promised to give him 150 acres of land in Illinois, in addition to a modest salary, in return for an eighteen-month contract. After talking it over with Esther, Artemas traveled to Chicago to meet with the owners and take a look at the land they offered. He agreed it was an excellent opportunity, but he would not do it if it meant that he would never see his wife. The owners agreed that he would get two weeks leave after each ten weeks of work in order to travel home to visit his family.

In the warmth of their feather bed, Artemas and Esther had talked long into the night about the sacrifices they would have to make if

Artemas took that job. They had refurbished Esther's little rented house. Both saw the wisdom in keeping her home and business as it was rather than finding another home. Artemas would be away most of the time and they would plan for the future, when they would live in Illinois. Both knew the future of the country was in the West and how the railroad would expand opportunities in new cities and towns that would be developing. Charles had been in Cincinnati for ten years and was doing well. Electa and John were planning to leave Pennsylvania to join Charles soon. Esther's sister Eliza, who now had three children, wrote from Dubuque, all about the business on the river and how many people were coming and going. Eliza's husband, Joshua Parker, was the chief pilot on the Mississippi River boats.

Uncle Jesse's youngest sister, Diadema, had moved with her husband, Mr. William Watson, to Pittsfield, not far from the state capital of Springfield. They had quickly acquired land and property there. The Illinois Central was also supported by the young Mr. Abraham Lincoln, a member of the state legislature who thought it a most progressive venture to connect the entire country. Aunt Diadema wrote to Esther, "You will hear of a pleasant young lawyer, Mr. Lincoln, who is in our government here. And he is very tall, like the McQuiggs."

Esther realized that while they had the security of family and friends and her work in Owego, it, too, was changing. Except for lumber, the railroad had already wiped out most of the riverboat freight business. The town population of eight thousand was half of what it was ten years ago. While Owego was getting smaller, the outskirts were growing. The early farms were becoming summer retreats for wealthy families from New York and Albany. While there was more wealth in Owego now, it was not going into commercial enterprises. There were no longer new merchants opening stores. The Camps and Uncle Jesse and other leading merchants and local government officials began cutting back to adapt. Edmund, who had invested in lumber land in Michigan, which had recently become a state, was thinking he would soon sell the dairy and move there to expand his lumber interests, although Eliza Jane did not seem anxious to go to a new wilderness.

Esther determined to learn all she could about Illinois while Artemas was away for such long periods of time. She kept at her millinery work and remained active with the church and library. In addition, she had a new diversion in the form of a new invention. Artemas had given her a sewing machine on her birthday. This was something Esther had been overjoyed to receive, and she made new petticoats, curtains, and covers for the bed and pillows. She could not believe how simple it was now to sew by turning a wheel with one hand and feeding fabric under the needle with the other.

However, she lived for her husband's return. She never knew exactly when he would be home, but he wrote to her every day and tried to give firm dates in his letters. "I beg you please, my love, to print your next letter for I have a devil of a time reading your script," he wrote to Esther. "I am assuring myself you are sending me your love, but cannot always be sure." Esther had been told by others that her handwriting was terrible, but as she explained in her next letter to Artemas, "I am in such a rush to tell you everything that perhaps I go too fast with my pen."

CHAPTER SIX

The Holiday Party

Esther had been watching for her husband, and as soon as she saw him coming up the road from the Owego railroad station, she ran out of the house. As Artemas dropped his traveling bag on the ground, Esther flung herself into his arms, which clasped her like iron bands. As his lips pressed hers, first tenderly, then hungrily, she tasted the salt of her own tears of joy as they rolled down her face. Esther was overcome by her own desire as much as she was by his desire for her. How she loved being so loved! She felt it was an obsession, something that would have embarrassed her had she ever realized this would happen to her. She pulled her arms more tightly around his neck until Artemas finally broke away for air, laughing. His voice was hoarse as he spoke against the warm flesh of her neck.

"Oh, how I've missed you. The thought of you keeps me alive during these long trips and drives me mad at the same time." He tightened his arms around her, as if it were possible to draw her any closer to him. Esther could only whisper his name as she pressed against him. Such was her desire that she wondered how she could ever again endure one minute without him, or saying goodbye again when his work took him west.

"Let us go inside," Artemas said. He pulled Esther's hands down from around his neck and held them to his lips and looked into her deep gray eyes that reflected such clarity and mystery at the same time, eyes that had compelled him so since the first time he looked into them. Esther held his arm with both of hers as they walked back to the house before the neighbors became scandalized by such a public display of affection.

"Sometimes I want to shout for joy even when you are not with me," Artemas said, kissing her again once they were inside the house. "But my men already think I am possessed, because I carry your image close to my heart and take it out of my pocket and look at it many times a day. Of course, I am always smiling." Shortly after they were married, a traveling "daguerreotype artist" came to Owego and took images of all those who were willing to pay. The first daguerreotypes invented in France were crude and required people to be absolutely still for long periods. Once they became popular in America, the practice was improved quickly. Now images could be taken in a few minutes rather than nearly an hour.

"Each time I see you I love you more," he said. "And while I am away I think of things I would like to bring you." Artemas took a small box from his coat pocket and gave it to his wife when they sat down inside. Esther quickly opened it and found a cameo with a hand-painted yellow rose hanging on a velvet cord.

"Oh, my darling, it is beautiful." Esther got up and went to the mirror over the maple chest while Artemas stood behind her and fastened it around her neck. "Artemas, don't tell me when you will have to leave again, for I simply cannot bear it. I cannot," she said and stamped her foot. He laughed and kissed the side of her neck. "But that's what you said last time."

"And it was unbearable." She leaned against him and he held both arms around her as they looked at each other in the mirror. "Tell me every detail about the West. Did you pay a visit to Aunt Watson? What are the Indians like? Did you bring a Chicago newspaper?" Artemas told her Chicago was a wild frontier town with shacks alongside stately new brick buildings. He said Lake Michigan from the Chicago shore was like a vast sea. Esther had not yet seen an ocean, but Artemas had been to Boston and sailed out of the harbor on a clipper with some university friends when he was younger. He stopped, suddenly noting the mischievous look in her eyes.

"And what is so funny, Mrs. Slack? Is my news laughable?"

"No, Mr. Slack, but I have some news, too, that could make you smile. I have been to visit Dr. Tinkham."

"Oh?" Artemas pulled her around to face him. "And what was that visit about?" He assumed from her sunny countenance that she was not ill.

"He said I am in a family way." Her husband gasped and his mouth dropped open. Esther giggled. "Artemas, close your mouth. This is not such a surprise, is it?"

"Oh, my dearest girl! What wonderful news."

The next day Esther packed a picnic hamper and they rented a horse and buggy and rode upriver toward Spencer. "Is it safe for you to ride in a carriage over bumpy roads?" Artemas asked. He had already made up his mind that he did not want her to ride on the horse's back.

"Dear husband, be assured that you have a strong and healthy wife. I walk some miles every day not just because I enjoy the activity, but because it will keep me and the baby strong."

Sitting on the grass near the river with their picnic of ham sandwiches and apple pie, they talked about their dreams for the future and about their coming family. Artemas knew his wife had fears about childbirth; most women did. For that matter, so did he, and he knew nothing about how to stem those fears, but he promised his wife he would be with her when their child arrived. Esther dealt with her considerable fears of childbirth by focusing on the healthy nieces and nephews she had, as well as her friend Eliza Jane, who was fine after giving birth to Franky. But the image Esther had of her mother's last day was never far from mind. And four years ago her sister Mindwell had died from an infection in the early stage of her pregnancy.

"What will we name this new person?" Artemas asked her, running his hand over her stomach.

"Oh, Artemas, let us be progressive and choose a name we like and avoid some traditions such as naming girls after virtues like Patience and Prudence. My late sister Mindwell hated her name always for the literal translation it brought—to mind well—but it was a Scottish custom to use such names. And look at Aunt Diadema, named after a garden spider!"

"The literal translation of my own name from Greek mythology," Artemas said, "is 'follower of the goddess.'" He laughed and pulled her down on the grass next to him. "So we were indeed fated to meet, for the moment I saw you I knew you to be a goddess."

"We could choose an alphabet letter," Esther said, "the way your own family named all of you with the letter *A*."

Esther and Artemas decided that to be modern they would find names they truly liked, and to respect tradition each would choose a favorite name from their own first initial. So Esther would make a list of boys' and girls' names beginning with *E*, and Artemas would do the same with *A*.

Lying on their backs and looking at the puffy white clouds over the river, Artemas described where their land was along the Illinois River, about one hundred miles west of Chicago in a town called Peru. "We will have some land sloping down to the river, so we can have our picnics," he said, "and where I will soon have to worry about watching out for a youngster who should not fall into the water." He leaned on an elbow to look into Esther's face, then kissed her. She touched his face with her fingertips, as if memorizing each detail.

"We will have ponies for the children," Esther said.

"And you can have a very large flower garden where you can entertain your friends," Artemas added.

"I will fill every room in our large, comfortable home with flowers from the garden.

"But, dear husband," Esther continued with a teasing grin, "if we stay here, I could be elected mayor of Owego." She began to laugh at his questioning look and told him that she had gotten ten votes for mayor at the town election. "I was flattered by this gesture," she said, "but do not take it seriously. Political office is only for men, although with all the suffrage activities in York State alone, it could change someday."

"Well, you are a good politician, Mrs. Slack. I always knew that." Artemas admired the way his wife could always find a reasonable way for people to get along. She was not a diplomat, not by any means. She was too candid and outspoken. But she was farsighted and could convince people that their short-term actions could lead to long-term discomfort, not just for those they wanted to hurt, but for themselves. She had been a mediator in her own family all her life, perhaps the only one who could find an alternative view in an argument, willing to look outside the accepted custom.

"Is it really so unthinkable?" Artemas asked his wife. "Perhaps you will become the mayor of Peru, Illinois."

"Why not governor of Illinois?" Esther quipped.

———

Esther put the baby back into his bed and watched as he drifted off to sleep. She had been holding her son, Edward (Archie) Archibald, now fourteen months old, and reading to him, something she did frequently. It was a way for her to finish her book and entertain her son at the same time. He often tried to grab the pages or pull them from her hands, and she would teasingly close the book gently over his hand. When he could not get free he giggled and tried to pull it out, then tried to put it back again. It was a new game.

As she watched him breathing softly she hugged her arms around herself, still enjoying the phantom feeling of his warmth and weight against her heart. She had forced her fears away during her pregnancy and come to enjoy the feeling of another life growing inside of her. Artemas, whenever he was home, would hold his arm around her belly at night as they slept like two spoons. Sometimes he would wake her when he felt the baby moving. Artemas kept his word and was home for the birth of their son, who took his time entering the world and gave his mother considerable pain. The new father did not leave home until he was assured by others that his wife had the help she needed.

Her husband was away so often that Esther sometimes felt like a widow, but she was an independent person and she knew how to enjoy her solitude, especially now with the work of caring for their home and their son, who seemed to have more energy than a schoolroom full of children. He had large gray eyes that seemed to absorb everything around him. He was a sturdy baby and strong and needed to be fed almost constantly for all that strong growth. Lotte was still helping with the millinery business, and Esther had hoped her sister would take over when Esther moved to Illinois. However, Lotte's upcoming marriage to their cousin Fred Brown, Aunt Elizabeth McQuigg's son, would put an end to that, for her new husband did not approve of a wife working. Esther wished Lotte would have waited to find a better man than Fred, who had a controlling personality. He also liked his drink a bit too much, Esther thought, but Lotte seemed to be smitten. Esther had begun planning to sell the business, for once she and Artemas and Archie moved to Illinois, that would be the end of it. Artemas earned enough to support them, but she did enjoy having the work.

—————

Whenever Artemas was due home, Esther would work herself into a frenzy of activity making everything ready, so he could enjoy time with his son and they could have a special supper together or go on a picnic. She planned many things, for she knew he would be gone again all too soon. Now she was getting the last-minute details ready for a party to celebrate Christmas. Artemas would be home in a few hours, coming on the Erie Railroad after connecting in Pennsylvania. She had scoured the woods for pine branches, whose aroma now filled the house. Fresh logs snapped in the hearth and warmed the room. Her mother's Revere silver candlesticks had been polished and placed in the center of the table among a display of pine cones. When the homestead in Spencer was sold, the family had divided up the few furnishings and artifacts as keepsakes and Esther had always loved the candlesticks.

"I have made your pa's favorite cranberry apple pie and squash pudding," she said to Archie, who was playing with a toy wooden train Jesse had made for him. "There is enough to feed the entire town, but I know with your pa's ferocious appetite there will be little left for them." She picked up her son to hug him and said, "And you have inherited his appetite, my boy." She straightened out the little gray woolen jacket she had made for him to wear with a white blouse and short pants. Esther herself was wearing a new dress with a red and green plaid wool skirt and black velvet bodice. Her cameo with the yellow rose was tied around her neck.

This was Esther's first official holiday entertainment, the first time, as a married woman and a mother, that she was able to invite her family members who still lived nearby. Eliza and Edmund arrived with their daughters, Franky, now three, and one-year-old Mary Elizabeth, called Libby. The toddlers immediately ran off to see Archie with Edmund following after them to make sure they removed their coats. Her brother, to Esther's surprise, was an adoring father. She thought he might be aloof around his children, as many men were who did not want to appear to be interested in a woman's domain, but Edmund doted on his girls. Eliza Jane wore her red satin turban with a dark green wool cape to celebrate the festivities.

"I gave Archie a long nap," Esther said to her friend, "so he would be awake for his father's arrival. It has been nearly three months since he has seen him."

"And he is twice the size he was then," said Eliza Jane.

Lotte's baby, Elizabeth Hobart and also called Libby, was three months old, and Esther had put some soft blankets in Archie's outgrown cradle for her new niece to use. Lotte seemed unsure as a new mother and frequently sought advice from Esther. She and Fred lived in a small house near the tannery Fred operated, but Lotte would often walk over with the baby to visit Esther. Jesse was expected soon with his sweetheart, Mary Freeland. Theirs would be the next wedding in the family. They had planned to arrive early and leave early in order to spend part of the evening at the Freeland family's holiday party. Now Esther was wondering why they were more than an hour late. And where was her husband? She had heard the train whistle, why, it must have been a half hour ago.

"Let's go look for your pa," Esther said and picked up Archie, who began to cry when Libby grabbed his toy train. Looking through the front window, Esther saw Jesse and Mary coming slowly up the porch step, not at all in a festive mood. She hoped they had not had a spat. Jesse removed his hat and held it across his chest. He wore a long coat, for the night was cold, and Mary's hands were encased in a green velvet muff. She took one hand out to touch Jesse's shoulder and urge him forward.

"I thought you would never get here," Esther said, opening the door and drawing them inside. Noting the grim look on her brother's face, she said, "It's Christmas, a time for smiles."

"We were delayed at Mary's house," Jesse said. "There was a messenger came to see Mr. Freeland, who as you know works for the railroad, and . . ."

"Is the train late?" Esther interrupted. "Will Artemas be late for the party?" Esther's heart started pounding.

"Esther, let me take the baby away from the cold." Mary reached over and took Archie from Esther's arms. Jesse, looking as if he were about to weep, pulled Esther into his arms and held her tightly.

"Jesse, let me go. What is it?"

"Come, Esther, sit down. I'm afraid I have bad news for you." He led her to the settee and sat down with her. Esther's heart stopped and her face went pale. The others, who had been pouring cups of punch, became silent, except for the children, who continued with their games.

"Just tell me what happened, Jesse. Why isn't Artemas here? Did he miss the train?" Jesse took a deep breath and said it straight out.

"Esther, there was a railroad accident and Artemas was killed this morning in Pennsylvania. The train was apparently going too fast on a curve and came off the track. The cars overturned. First he was thrown clear, although seriously injured, but then he tried to help the others, by getting them out from under a car, when an explosion killed them."

"No," Esther said, her face rigid. "No, he told me that would never happen. He knew the dangers and he would not have let this happen to himself." She pulled away from her brother, lurched out the front door, and ran down the street in the direction of the railroad station. It was dark now and had begun to snow.

"Artemas," she called as she ran down the road. "Where are you? I know you are only hiding; you are playing with me. Please come home now, come in the house." Eliza Jane, Edmund, and Jesse followed her from the house but Esther kept running until suddenly she stopped and sank to her knees. Edmund caught up to her and wrapped a cloak around her. "Esther, come inside and lie down. We will stay with you." As they picked her from the ground, she raised her face and shouted at the sky.

"What have I done, God, for you to take my precious husband? Why have you torn away a part of me so cruelly?" Her brothers struggled to keep Esther walking but she sobbed so hard she could not walk, and finally Edmund picked her up to carry her back into the house. "He promised me this would not happen. He told me he was always careful of the dangers," she wailed, banging her fists on Edmund's chest. Eliza

Jane instructed them to take Esther to her bedroom on the second floor while she ran ahead to remove the coats and hats that had been put on the bed by the guests.

"Leave us," Eliza Jane said. "I'll care for her. See to the others." Eliza Jane closed the door and sat on the edge of the bed with her friend and rocked her in her arms and cried with her. She knew how deep this love was that her friend had for her husband, deeper than her own for Edmund, for Esther was so pure of heart. There was no artifice in her. While Esther poured out her rage and grief, Eliza Jane thought she had never heard such painfully wrenching sobs in her life, not even when her own mother lost a young son to sickness.

"Why did God give me such happiness only to take it away?" Esther wailed. "Why?" She had so feared losing children, and now she had lost her husband, a man she had found late in life, a love she had not believed would ever exist for her, a partner of her heart and soul. "I have lain with him in this bed not more than a dozen times," she sobbed, and reached under a bed pillow to pull out her husband's nightshirt. "See, I keep this with me each night, so I can feel that he is with me." She buried her face in the shirt and cried harder. "Is God punishing me for my pleasure at such love?" She pulled the shirt away for a moment and looked at her friend. "I cannot live without him, Eliza Jane. I cannot." Sitting there in her festive red turban, Eliza Jane's own tears spilled for Esther, who had lost so much in her lifetime.

"Yes, you can, my dear friend," Eliza Jane whispered. "It won't be easy, but you will for what remains of Artemas, his son."

PART II
PERU, ILLINOIS

CHAPTER SEVEN

The Prosperous Merchant

"WHAT DO YOU MEAN I CANNOT HAVE MY HUSBAND'S LAND?" ESTHER hadn't meant to sound so impatient, but after an arduous nine-hundred-mile stagecoach journey from New York with a restless toddler, she could not bear to think it had been for naught.

"Now, now, Esther, calm down," her uncle William Watson said as they sat in the parlor of the Mansion House Hotel, which was both a business and family home in Pittsfield, Illinois. "It doesn't mean that you cannot have it—we will find a way. But according to law, unmarried women are not allowed to own property in any state other than Mississippi. And there it happened only so that plantation owners with daughters would not have to leave their land to greedy sons-in-law."

"I'm sorry, Uncle," Esther said. "I am weary from my journey as well as the injustice to women who are perfectly able and smart as any man." She had given her uncle the deed to examine, he being not only an attorney, but judge of the probate court here in Pike County.

"The land, as you know, Esther, goes to your husband's male heir." Age forty-five, Watson had a long, lean face and hair that was already silver.

"Yes, Archie is his heir, and obviously too young to do much about it, but am I not the guardian of my son and thus the land, until he reaches maturity?"

Hearing his name, Archie, now close to three years old, got up from the carpet where he had been playing toy soldiers with Henry, his seven-year-old Watson cousin, and ran over to his mother, who pulled him into her lap and hugged him. He had endured much during their journey, cooped up for weeks in a crowded coach and jostled along. Although he had napped frequently in his mother's arms and sometimes across the legs of other passengers, the natural restlessness of a boy his age made him cranky for a good part of the time. He had seemed happy to meet his new Watson cousins. The girls, Sarah Jane, twelve, and Ellen, ten, fussed over him and enjoyed dressing him up in Henry's outgrown clothing. But Archie was still showing some insecurity from all the changes in his life. To add to Esther's worry, he had been diagnosed by Dr. Tinkham with having mild asthma. There was little to do about it but try to avoid too much excitement. The doctor also prescribed strong coffee for the boy when he had difficulty breathing. But, of course, that meant he sometimes became overstimulated and could not sleep.

A German girl of about fifteen in a gray and white checked muslin dress and white apron carried a tea tray into the room and set it on a low table in front of the sofa. "Thank you, Annie," said Esther's aunt, Diadema McQuigg Watson, Uncle Jesse's youngest sister. She poured tea for her niece and offered Archie a biscuit, which he eagerly consumed. Aunt Di was a tall, sturdy woman wearing a smart burgundy frock with a lace collar and a cameo brooch. Her brown hair was pulled back in a braided circle on the back of her head, and striking green eyes were her most distinctive facial feature.

"There may be other ways of holding onto the land," Uncle Watson said. "As you know, your aunt and I have accumulated quite a bit of land here. If something happened to me, I would want her to be able to retain our properties, too, lest they end up in the hands of young Henry here," he said, ruffling his son's blond hair. Henry had been leaning against his father's chair, waiting for Archie to come back to their game. "With our friend Mr. Lincoln now in our state government in Springfield, we may hope one day to create more progressive legislation."

Esther had heard a great deal about Mr. Lincoln from her husband, who told her that he represented the Illinois Central Railroad in the courts, helping it get the land and the right-of-way it needed to grow.

Esther sighed and kissed the top of Archie's head. "I am grateful for your help, I truly am," she said, sliding Archie off her lap and sending him back to his game with Henry. "It was kind of you to invite me to stay here, while I get myself settled in a new place." After nearly three weeks on the road, a bumpy road, she was overjoyed to be able to stretch out for comfortable sleep and to have plenty of water with which to bathe. Esther and her son had been given a large bedroom in the hotel, one overlooking the front lawn, with its elm trees and flowering shrubs, a respite from the miles of scrub prairie and plains they had passed through in Indiana and Illinois. The feel of the soft, clean sheets of fine muslin and feather pillows in a real bed that first night had Esther so overcome she was almost unable to fall asleep.

The Watsons' house maid had laundered her clothing and Archie's. Esther brought only two other black traveling suits—mourning suits— but as much linen and as many outfits for Archie as possible without exceeding the twenty-five-pound baggage limit set by the stagecoach line. Books had to be left behind, but she did carry one, keeping it in her hand so it would not be counted as baggage. She had tried to read Mr. Dickens's new story, *The Chimes*, but Archie kept grabbing at the pages, wanting her to read it aloud, and she felt this would not be fair to other passengers.

"I have spoken with colleagues here," said her uncle, "and have been in correspondence with Theophilus Lyle Dickey, a good friend of Mr. Lincoln who practices in LaSalle County with a young attorney, William Hervey Lamme Wallace, also a friend of Mr. Lincoln. In fact, young Wallace had been invited to go to work with Mr. Lincoln in Springfield, but Dickey somehow convinced him to come to Ottawa, the LaSalle County seat. We will go to meet with them about your property tomorrow." Her uncle had told her earlier that he would travel with her upriver to talk with the lawyers there, go to the courthouse, and look at the land and see what they could find out. Archie would remain with Aunt Di and his cousins.

"We will file your claim with the attorneys there. Even though you legally cannot own the land, a petition to the court will delay proceedings long enough to find another solution." Esther felt only somewhat comforted by her uncle's assurance, but she and her husband had saved some money to start building a home on their land, and she was determined to carry it out. She had also planned to continue her millinery business and hoped to attach herself to an existing shop. Before setting out on her journey, she had written to a tailor from Owego who had moved to Peru some years ago, to ask if he knew of any possibilities. She would make the hats at home so she would always be with Archie.

"Archie and I need some exercise," Esther said, standing up. Thinking about the happy plans she and Artemas had made brought her emotions close to the surface again, and the best remedy for her was physical action. It would feel good to take long strides again. Her body ached from lack of exercise while cooped up in the stagecoach. "Will your children walk with us? Perhaps we can explore more of Washington Street." Esther was curious about Pittsfield, which had grown up so quickly into an elegant town of wide boulevards and stately brick and frame houses reminiscent of New England, where most of the population had come from.

The Watsons sat back on their horsehair sofa covered, like the side chairs, in dark blue velvet. A wide mirror with a carved wooden frame hung over the sofa. Atop the mantel were small framed photographs of family members. William shook his head after Esther left with the children. "It will not be easy for Esther to get that land. It would be best if she marries again. A young widow with property is a good match for an ambitious businessman," he said as his wife poured some tea for both of them. "There is a shortage of proper women out here. Most unmarried men have nothing but saloons and dance halls when they want female companionship."

"Is that the 'other solution' you mentioned? Would you match her with some poor farmer from the plains or a habitué of the saloons?" Di asked this raising an eyebrow, while her husband laughed at her.

"Di, you know better than that. There are some fine men, some who are very smart and ambitious and have already achieved success. I know Esther was able to be independent in Owego and had a successful millinery business, but here, she is in a new place where she is not so well known. We are her only family in Illinois, and even then, we are a day's trip away by steamer." Illinois was the northwest frontier; most of it was still a wild and muddy prairie, except for settlements along the rivers, like Pittsfield.

"She is still so grief stricken, poor girl, she cries at the drop of her hat," said Diadema. "It will be hard for her to be on her own, and lonely, I agree, but she had such love for her husband. How can she think of marriage so soon?"

"That will ease eventually," William replied, "and she must think of Archie. Can he be left to his own devices while his mother toils at her milliner's trade? He will be more secure with a man around him and Esther knows that. She is a practical girl."

"But you know, my dear husband, that for a woman to be intimate with a man she must have some desire to share her bed with him. Esther turned down a few men before she fell in love with Mr. Slack."

"Not all good marriages need to be based on such intense feelings," William said. "She needs to be safe and secure," he added, as if ending the debate. "Warm feelings will develop in time with a good man." He put his arm around his wife's shoulder. "Were you not introduced to me against your will?" he asked. "And were you so anxious to be intimate with me?"

Di leaned against him and put his hand over her heart. "You see how my heart is still beating a bit too quickly when I am near you?" William laughed and kissed his wife, who then got up and said, "Mercy, I am forgetting we have other guests in this establishment to care for." She left through a door leading to the section of the house that was the hotel.

Diadema McQuigg had met William Watson in St. Louis, where she had gone to visit her sister Rachel, who was married to a federal militia officer stationed at the Jefferson Barracks, the largest army post on the frontier. After they married Diadema and William became the first settlers in Pittsfield at the start of the last decade, having come up the Mississippi to begin a life there. Prairie farms produced vast quantities of wheat and corn, and the area quickly prospered because the grains could be sent south via the Mississippi River or north along the Illinois River, which was a gateway to the Great Lakes and the Erie Canal and across the ocean to Europe. William opened a small store and slowly began buying up property with their profits. Diadema ran the hotel—this was the second one they owned, having sold the first at great profit—and William, also a lawyer, was the city's probate judge. He and his friends, including the young Mr. Lincoln, were a forward-thinking lot committed to making their state one of the most prosperous.

———

It was exceptionally hot and humid this August day, and Esther remained on the deck of the steamer for much of the eight-hour trip eastward along the Illinois River. The breeze helped keep her cool and she was glad she was able to walk around. A steamer from New York across Lake Erie and through the Ohio River to Illinois would have been more comfortable than the stagecoach, she thought. However, the black smoke billowing from the stack above her brought with it the image of that early steamboat explosion on the Susquehanna that had killed so many people, including George Sidney's father. Esther feared steamboats as much as she feared steam trains, which had killed her husband. Her uncle had assured her steamers were safe now, but Esther was not so sure. As long as she could see the shore, she might have a chance to swim to safety—even if it meant taking off her cumbersome skirt.

"People have compared the land along the Illinois River to the land-scaped parks of England," her uncle said with a hint of pride in his voice. He had come out of the salon to join her on deck and was carrying his gray cutaway jacket over his arm. He had put a linen handkerchief around his collar to keep it from becoming stained with perspiration.

Esther noticed a few stately homes along the bluffs and many more under construction. There were no forests here as in York State, and she noticed that trees grew independently or in small clusters. Often a lone tree would appear after what seemed likes miles of prairie. Some were particularly stately trees with thick, cork-like trunks that grew along the bluffs. The leaves sparkled and shimmered as the branches shook in the breeze. Her uncle told her these were cottonwood trees. Fluffy white seeds produced in early summer gave the tree its name, he told her. When the seeds blew into the wind, they spread a cotton-like substance around the air. The seeds eventually would settle in the river and congregate into blankets along the banks. Barges and Durham boats hauled grain and lumber just as they did on the Susquehanna in Owego. The lumber came down from the thickly forested northern regions of Wisconsin and

Michigan. There were many small boats with duck hunters and fishermen, and her uncle pointed out a raft full of mussels.

"As a seamstress and milliner," he said, "you should know that this river is the major source of buttons. The buttons are made from the shells of mussels that are caught in this river."

"Yes, we have them in the Susquehanna, too," Esther said, smiling at her uncle. "Do you think they are bigger here?"

As they approached the port at Peru and the rail bridge under construction spanning the river, Esther recalled Artemas's passion about the railroad. The government, he told her, had granted the Illinois Central Railroad two and a half million acres to build a railroad to connect Chicago, on the shore of Lake Michigan, to the northern and southern parts of the state. Artemas had been working all over Illinois, surveying the land, laying out the track beds.

"Chicago will become the transportation hub of the nation," Artemas had told his wife as they sat with their picnic and the baby's cradle on the bank of the Susquehanna during one of his rare trips home. How he had doted on Archie and loved picking him up and holding him high in the air. The new father had been unprepared for the strength of his infant son, who bounced in his arms and pulled at his nose, laughing all the time.

Tears suddenly stung Esther's eyes as she recalled their times together in a mental picture book she would always have with her and which she visited often. Each memory, each occasion, was stored in her memory like a painting. She saw so clearly his high brow and the lock of sandy-colored hair that constantly fell over his left eye, the way his mouth twitched as he tried to maintain a serious expression when he was teasing her. After more than six months she still could not get through a day without tears. Much as she disliked wearing her small bonnet with the black mourning veil that impaired her vision, she was grateful that it also hid her frequent tears. Her son, however, disliked the veil and was constantly pulling it up as if to see whether his mother was still there.

In the immediate aftermath of Artemas's death, Esther spent days without talking or working or eating. Archie, missing his mother's usual brightness and energy, grew fretful. The boy hardly knew his father, and

Esther did not know how to explain to him what had changed in their lives. Eliza Jane and Lotte had helped Esther by bringing meals to the house and taking on the chores, washing Archie's clothes and keeping wood supplied for the hearth. Occasionally one of them took Archie to her own home to play with other children.

Now, as a reminder of the cause that had brought Esther together with Artemas, a Negro man and woman appeared on deck with two white women. Passengers gathered near the gangplank, preparing to leave the boat. Just like Owego, another river port, Peru, Esther learned, was a busy station for the abolitionists on the Underground Railroad. Her uncle told her that he and her aunt sometimes kept people in their hotel after they came up the Mississippi from points in the South. Then, they helped arrange their passage up the Illinois River to Chicago or across Lake Michigan into Canada.

"This is a popular travel route between the South and New York," her uncle told her. "They can come up the Mississippi and pass through the Great Lakes and Erie Canal to New York." Peru was on the northern bank of the Illinois River at the junction of the canal and foot of the railroad bridge. Steamboats arrived daily from St. Louis, and the population had been increasing.

"Once the Illinois and Michigan Canal from Chicago, ninety-six miles away, is finished, they will go right through that city to the lakes. Boats could then sail directly from the Great Lakes to the Mississippi River and the Gulf of Mexico."

As they disembarked, Esther looked at the workers digging the canal and was reminded of the men on the Ithaca-Owego Turnpike who always had news of the Erie Canal progress. She remembered the day her brother Charles proudly left home, at eighteen, for a job on the canals in Ohio to earn one dollar a day. In one week he earned more than their father earned in a month. Charles had done well. After the canal work he hired on in a tannery in Cincinnati making shoes, but last year he had died of consumption. He was only forty-one. Esther wondered if his lungs had weakened from fighting off the diseases (like malaria) the canal work caused. She knew the fumes involved in tannery work were not good for the health either.

Barges tied up at the dock were being loaded with sacks of grain. There were crates of squawking white chickens being piled onto one barge, headed for the Chicago markets. Esther and her uncle were greeted by twenty-four-year-old Will Wallace, whom Esther liked immediately. He had a kindly face with very curly brown hair that stood out from the side of his face and just above his shoulders like a halo.

"*Peru* is the Inca word for wealth," Wallace told them, "so the founders thought it would bring that here. Fourth Street is the main street of downtown Peru," he said after he settled them in the carriage. As they drove along he pointed out various buildings. "The Maze Nail Company just opened here." Turning the corner onto Pulaski Street, he told them that James Barton began a lumber mill there. "And over here in this fine brick building is the J. Morris Mercantile establishment. John Morris has made a name for himself in the eight years he has been here," Wallace said. "He is one of many Polish immigrants in Illinois." Wallace explained to Esther that ten years ago, in 1835, Congress had given 235 Polish exiles twenty-two thousand acres of land in Illinois. They had been political prisoners in Austria after the Warsaw uprisings and endured a four-month journey to Washington, DC, where the congressional gift was made.

"Many German immigrants are here, too," Uncle Watson added, "but most of the settlers are from New England and the East like us. The farmers you just saw with grains and chickens, from one hundred miles away, will buy supplies from Mr. Morris before returning home." A degree of prosperity was visible with a large trade, more stores and people. Plank roads, long strips of lumber with wooden crossties, similar to railroad tracks, lined the streets. But there were more muddy paths with wagons, coaches, and horses with single riders. Most storefronts had hitching posts.

Uncle Watson gave young Wallace the coordinates of the parcel of land owned by Artemas, and they drove a half mile outside of the town to stop to look at the land on Bluff Street, on a hill over the river. Esther got out of the carriage to walk around. It was a lovely setting, just as her

husband had described it, with a copse of elm trees and a few cotton-
woods near the end of the property by the river. By now it was dusk, with
a lovely view over the river, but Esther could not envision her house or
her garden as she had done before she saw this place. She was finally here
on this piece of land that had been the focus of so many dreams and plans
with Artemas. She felt a bit deflated now because, after all, without Artemas it was simply a piece of land. She remained silent, as if in a trance.
Sensing Esther's mood, Uncle Watson said, "You have had a long journey up the river and you will feel better in Ottawa, where Mr. and Mrs.
Dickey will give you a hearty dinner and a chance to refresh yourself."

"Ottawa is called 'the town of two rivers,' from an Indian word," Wallace
said during the thirty-minute drive to the Dickey home. "The Illinois
River meets another tributary, the Fox River."

The Dickeys lived on LaSalle Street, in a pretty white frame home
named Valley View. Several young elm saplings lined a long drive set
back from the road. T. Lyle, as he was known, had curly, sand-colored
hair and beard and a stern look, as if he were evaluating you as he would
in the courtroom. His wife, Juliet, and daughter, Martha Ann, both had
auburn hair and blue eyes. Two sons were away at school. Mrs. Dickey
showed Esther to her room, where a young housemaid brought her a
basin of fresh water. Esther was grateful for a place to be alone for a little
while. She removed her hat and veil and her jacket and washed her face
and arms with the cool water. She removed her shoes and rubbed her feet.
The shoes, the only ones she had with her, had worn thin, and she had
felt the stones on the roads through the soles as she walked around the
property in Peru. She brushed the dust from her jacket and skirt and lay
down on the bed for a moment before re-dressing.

Esther tried to cheer herself up before she went downstairs where
the others were gathered. She had always loved seeing new places and
meeting new people, but now about to enter this room full of strangers
she was filled with homesickness and grave doubts about settling here.
She had left behind all that was familiar and safe, all that she had worked
hard to build up. She missed Lotte and Eliza Jane and Uncle Jesse and

her brothers. Edmund had urged her to stay in Owego, "where you are so well known and cared for." He said that as a widow, a woman traveling alone, she would be putting her physical self and that of Archie at risk, and also risking her reputation. But hadn't Daniel said the same thing years before when the homestead was sold and she wanted to live independently? She had proved him wrong. Esther argued that she had strong family ties in the West.

"Aunt Diadema has often asked me to visit," she told Edmund. "Our own sister Eliza Parker is not far from there in Iowa Territory, just up the Mississippi River. John is in Ohio, just beyond the border of Illinois. And it is our generation of easterners that are moving west, like a blanket of humanity covering the continent." Edmund's exhortations only challenged her to insist that she must go forward. "Are you not planning to move west yourself, dear brother? All I hear is your talk of all the money to be made in the West. I want that land for my son." But at this moment? she now asked herself. What was she thinking? How could she possibly acquire the land and build a house and live in it without Artemas?

Esther took a deep breath and tried to make her face more cheerful. She had another life to consider, the one she had created with her beloved husband and whom she must raise and educate. Their son was a reminder, with every inch he grew and every word he uttered and every look he gave her, of what must come first. Their love had given her something more important than either one of them. Yes! She must also carry on the dream they had created. She would have her land and her son, Artemas's son. She must try. If she failed, if the situation looked completely bleak, she knew she could leave it and go back to New York.

As she entered the parlor, the men stood up, including one man she had not met earlier. He was a solidly built young man of medium height with thick, wavy dark brown hair and large, soulful brown eyes. His full mustache grew in a curve toward his mutton chop sideburns. He wore a well-tailored gray suit and carried a top hat. He had arrived, she was to later learn, on a big sorrel stallion named Nelson, which she recalled was the name of George Washington's favorite horse.

"Mr. Morris is one of our first settlers of Peru and a trustee of the town as well as a leading merchant," T. Lyle said, introducing them and escorting them all to the dinner table. "He came here from Poland ten years ago and has built a fine business." The table was lit with candles and a serving girl was bringing bowls of steaming food to the sideboard.

"But Morris is not a Polish name," Esther said.

"No, Mrs. Slack, it is a name I selected from the signers of the Declaration of Independence so that I could feel truly American." He told her nobody would be able to pronounce his name anyway. In the ten years he had lived in Peru, Morris had built up a strong trade with the farmers and river men. He had a large store and warehouse where he kept building supplies, farm equipment, clothing, and household goods.

"Do you like these dishes?" he asked her, nodding toward the table and lifting the coffee cup. "They are Meissen I was able to import from Germany, and Mrs. Dickey found them agreeable enough to buy a set for her new home."

"Oh, yes," Esther said, "they are quite beautiful." Morris told her he lived in rooms above his store and Esther was reminded of Uncle Jesse.

"Is your mercantile establishment also a hotel?" she asked. "My uncle Jesse has a similar business, perhaps smaller, with a hotel on the upper floor, as well as his own apartment."

"No, there is no hotel in my own establishment, but like your uncle, I do live on the upper floor," he said. "However, there are plans to build two hotels in Peru. Many people come up from Chicago to do business," he explained and told her of the fast coaches that made the trip in just six hours. Esther recalled her longtime wish to go to New York City, but it was such a long ride to Albany and then down the Hudson, she had never had the time to do it. Morris seemed a bit shy, and after a lull in the conversation he said, "I travel to New York once or twice a year to visit suppliers, but I find the place so crowded I am happy to be on my way back home."

"Mrs. Slack had a very successful millinery shop in New York," Uncle Watson said. Esther felt shy and said, "Oh, it was a way to keep myself together and care for my younger sister." She told Morris of her siblings scattered over the states and territories.

Morris described the town as "a suitable place for a family, too, for in addition to many stores, we have a school and two churches, and several newspapers."

"But do you not have family here, Mr. Morris?"

"I have no family in the New World, Mrs. Slack," Morris said. "Nor the old one for that matter," he added with a pensive smile, before turning his attention to the stewed chicken with gravy, potatoes, and carrots on his plate. He then looked up at her again. "I would like to have a family here," he added. Esther realized then that Mr. Morris had been invited here to meet her, a young widow who might be a suitable marriage prospect for him. And for her, being a married woman would mean she could claim her land in her husband's name. Esther looked over at her uncle, whose face betrayed nothing. She smiled at the cleverness, at how smoothly this had been arranged.

Meanwhile, young Wallace was chatting happily with the Dickeys' twelve-year-old daughter, Martha Ann, who asked him when he was going to get married. Wallace winked at her and said, "But, Martha Ann, I am waiting for you to grow up."

Chapter Eight

Building a New Home

Esther held one of Archie's hands and John Morris the other as they walked into the center of Pittsfield. Archie occasionally swung his feet off the ground to see if these two grownups would keep walking that way.

"Shall I carry him on my shoulder?" John asked.

"Thank you." Esther smiled at John, who bent down and asked Archie if he would like to have a better view. Archie eagerly held up his arms to be lifted. "I believe Archie is getting a bit tired from all this walking."

Having become familiar with the town during her weeks of visiting the Watsons, Esther pointed out the mercantile establishments, the livery, the lawyers' offices, and the other hotel. As they crossed the main street, dodging a few stray pigs, she told him that according to her uncle and aunt, Pittsfield had grown even more quickly than Owego, where she and Aunt Diadema had come from. It was the stores and mercantile establishments that gave these new friends something to talk about, and Esther showed John one of the millinery shops. John appreciated Esther's understanding of how merchants operated their businesses. He was relieved not to have to think up conversational topics to interest her, for he was not educated in the arts or philosophy. Esther explained how she improved her millinery business by creating the latest styles and by inviting some of the townswomen to come for tea and a fashion show.

"If ten women came to my little shop in the front room of my home, then I knew that at least two of them would become customers," she said.

"I also made some sample hats and bonnets, which my sister Lotte wore when she went out and about in town, so that other women asked where they could buy such pretty hats."

"Here on the frontier, with so many new settlers coming every day from Europe and from the East, we cannot keep up with the demand," John said. "I try to carry everything the farmers want and need, other than farm machinery. I have cast iron kettles, oil lamps, furniture, and dry goods. And I buy in large enough lots to sell to the smaller merchants in the farm towns north and south of the river."

At thirty-one, John was two years younger than Esther. He had a stocky build and was a bit shorter, but he stood tall, obviously feeling a confidence in all that he had achieved since coming to America on his own. His top hat added a bit more stature as well. He had cultivated the look of a successful businessman with his well-tailored suit of brown wool and his striped gray and gold waistcoat. After asking Esther and her uncle if he might call on her, John had been taking the morning steamer to Pittsfield each Sunday to visit Esther and Archie at the Watson home and hotel since the two had met in Ottawa two months ago. He arrived at the Watsons' in time for afternoon tea. This gave him a few hours to spend with Esther and Archie, before they returned to the hotel for supper. Then, John would retire to the room he leased at the hotel before departing for Peru at dawn the next morning.

Esther understood their meeting had been arranged with marriage in mind, but she let John know she could not promise anything more than friendship. Esther appreciated that John was also courting Archie, and she was amused at the way he sat Archie on his knee and talked to him as though at three he were already old enough to understand everything told to him. John seriously explained to Archie where and how he got his supply of toys, for he always brought a toy for the boy, a rubber ball or toy train, as well as something for the Watson children. It reminded Esther of the way her brother Edmund doted on his daughters Franky and Libby. And during a cold damp spell in early October, when Archie was suffering from the asthma, John rubbed the boy's shoulders, to relax him, while Esther gave him some black coffee to drink. Then John borrowed the Watsons' carriage and drove both Esther and Archie to see the town doctor.

John was too shy to bring Esther personal gifts, such as flowers, even though she often talked about her love for her flower garden back in Owego. But he did bring her books and the latest *Godey's Lady's Book* magazine. One Sunday he brought an elegant box of Crane's stationary along with a beautiful onyx pen and a bottle of emerald green ink because she had told him how many letters she wrote to her large family scattered all over the country. Now, as they arrived back at the Mansion House Hotel from their walk, Uncle Watson greeted them on the porch along with a very tall man neither one had met before.

"Come in Esther, John, and meet Mr. Lincoln. He's spending the evening with us before heading back onto the circuit in the morning." It was a common practice of lawyers to ride through the town to deal with cases for weeks or even months at a time in the local courthouses. Lincoln had many friends in Pittsfield, including Milton Hay, John Nicolay, and Edward Baker, and he often stayed at the Mansion House Hotel. Esther looked up at the gaunt man with the melancholy face, which became animated as soon as he spoke.

"Now, Billy Watson, you never told me you had such a grown-up niece. And who is this lad?" Lincoln stooped down to greet Archie. "Another relative?"

"This is my son, Archie Slack," Esther said, smiling at the stranger she had heard so much about. "And this is my friend John Morris of Peru," she said as the two men shook hands. Esther realized as she said "friend" that she did like Mr. Morris.

"Abe is joining us for supper," Uncle Watson told them, "so fill your plates as soon as the food is on the table, for this gentleman has an appetite that will leave little for the rest of us if we don't act quickly." Watson slapped Lincoln on the back and held out his arm to urge everybody inside. He picked up Archie and said, "However, I forgot about your appetite, my boy. You may eat more than Mr. Lincoln here." Esther and John, as well as the Watsons and the other hotel guests, laughed a good deal during that dinner, for Mr. Lincoln seemed to have an endless supply of stories about any topic that came up, including his early adventures on a flatboat on the Mississippi River.

One Sunday, Esther and Archie along with the Watson family traveled to Peru on the steamer, and they stayed at one of the new hotels in Ottawa. As hotel owners themselves, the Watsons often visited other hoteliers and tavern keepers to see how things were run. In Peru, John was shyly proud to give them, especially Esther, a tour of his mercantile establishment on Fourth Street, showing her all that was there, from iron stoves to building supplies to dry goods. He showed her the latest fabrics he had gotten in, which were mostly muslins and cottons for the farm families to make clothing and bedding, but he pointed out several bolts of silk taffeta and other fine fabrics he procured for the town dressmaker, who made gowns for the more prosperous townswomen.

"And where are the toys?" Archie demanded, causing everybody to laugh, including the two clerks who worked there.

"Archie," Esther admonished, "it is not polite to ask such a question."

John introduced them all to his clerks, both young men named Charlie and both from New York. "Whenever I call out for Charlie, they both answer, so I have to call them by their last names, Vose and Hewlett." Vose, nineteen, had pale blond hair, large ears, and a quick smile. Hewlett, seventeen, was short and wiry with red hair and freckles. Esther asked them where in New York they came from. Vose came with his family from Germany and lived on the lower east side of Manhattan, a neighborhood already known as Little Germany. There were now many German immigrants in the West, and in Peru about a third of the population came from Germany. John, who spoke German fluently, liked to hire them.

"They are hard workers," he said, "and want very much to make a good life here." Hewlett came from a town in western New York, not far from Buffalo, where his Irish ancestors had worked on the Erie Canal.

"Archie clearly likes him," Aunt Di said as Esther and the Watsons drove to the hotel in Ottawa, "and looks for him on Sunday afternoons at our home."

"Yes, and our young Henry looks for him, too," said Uncle William, "in hopes that Mr. Morris will bring a toy for him as well, which he often does." Henry Watson had become fast friends with Archie, even though he was four years older. Esther decided her son was being spoiled with all the attention from Henry and the Watson girls, and now Mr. Morris.

"Mr. Morris is showing you he cares," Aunt Di said.

"You know, even though you are a bit taller, you are a prize for him," her uncle added with a chuckle. "He has worked hard to help build Peru into a thriving town. He is not only an important part of the community, and one of the founders, but he is a very smart businessman. He would think of you and Archie as enhancing all that he has earned. He will be a good provider."

Esther thought her uncle probably right, but was this only a marriage of convenience? If she decided against a marriage with John Morris, she must make plans to return to New York. Her situation was not the same as it was before she was married, when she did not have a child's welfare to consider.

The next day, before she and the Watsons returned to the steamer dock in Peru, they drove with John to see the land once again. It would be easier if she didn't like him. She did like him, and enjoyed his company. But she liked him the way she liked her brothers, with affection. She felt easy in his company and she enjoyed talking about business, about how fast the country was expanding. The town and region appealed to her, too, for it was something new, rather than a place whose time might have already passed, like Owego.

"I can build you and Archie a fine house," John said the following Sunday in Pittsfield. "I would like to make a family with you and Archie." He sounded so wistful when he said this that Esther wanted to touch his hand to cheer him, but she only smiled. She felt a bit sad herself. Christmas was near and she was reminded that it was a year ago when Artemas died. She did not let those feelings surface, however. Esther felt affection for John, who seemed to have a gentle spirit, but her feelings were not romantic. She did not expect to find that kind of love again. Archie tugged at John's jacket, wanting to be put up on his shoulder again. The land, Esther realized, was really for her son and this was a place where he could grow up in a secure home and with a good father. She knew by the way he treated her son that John would be a good father.

"Your late husband would want you to have this home on the land he worked hard for, for you and Archie," John said, as if reading her mind. "I will put no pressure on you," he added.

"I am very fond of you, John," Esther said, feeling a bit shy herself. "I don't know if I will fall in love with you, but I will try."

"That is all I ask," John said. He looked deeply into her eyes but refrained from a touch to her hand or a kiss. "We both want the same thing," he said, "a comfortable home and family in this great country."

While Esther felt she was making a sensible decision, she was nevertheless apprehensive, and she admitted she was also still mourning Artemas. She was entering into an arranged marriage, and she tried to think of it like a business. However, what would she feel a year from now, or five years from now? How would she feel about sharing her intimate life with this man? She really knew very little about him despite the assurances of people close to her whom she trusted. Yet she was now in the place that had excited her so much when she and Artemas had made their plans to come here with their son and begin a new life. She and Archie were where her late husband had wanted them to be, a place she also liked because of its newness and its potential for prosperity. She hoped Artemas would somehow know they were here, and that another man, a kind one, was helping her carry out those plans.

❧

On John's next visit to Pittsfield, he and Esther spent some time alone in the parlor discussing how to proceed with the practical aspects of marriage. John had sold much of the land granted to him by the government in order to finance and expand his business. He owned his and several other buildings and land along Fourth Street, including the one in which his business and office were located. He also had a parcel at the edge of town with warehouses; some he used and others he rented to other merchants. Esther's land would be for their home and would ultimately go to Archie, who would become John's legally adopted son. They would draw up an agreement, with Uncle Watson's help, one subject to future revision if they both deemed it necessary.

"You would not ask me to change my religion, would you?" Esther felt strongly that she could not leave her Protestant beliefs.

"Oh, no, I have no feeling about that," John said with a chuckle. He took her hand and smiled broadly. "I will take yours if you like. I come from Jewish ancestors, but I do not practice their religion." In fact, after so many years of persecution in his family, which had been exiled from Poland into Austria when the Russians swept through Poland and Lithuania, he was happy to get away from the issue entirely. So as far as he was concerned, he would remain neutral and follow Esther's practices in their family.

"I rather like your Christmas," he said. "And now I will have family to buy gifts for and celebrate with." Esther had such a large family and John had no one here. She believed her family would like John and feel happy that she would be settled and cared for.

"I hope my being a Jew will not hurt you and Archie in any way," John said, "for there is still some hatred against us in America."

"There is often hatred for anyone who is different in any way," she said, smiling at him. She told him about her abolition activities in the Baptist church in Owego, and she told him about how being a tall girl had brought her antagonism from many people while she was growing up.

Esther and John were married in the middle of a blizzard in February 1846 at the Episcopal church in Ottawa. Esther had already stopped wearing the mourning veil, not only because Archie hated it, but because she felt it was time to look out on the world with a clear vision. It was a first step toward putting the past behind her and determining her path for the rest of her life. For the wedding Esther made herself a fine woolen skirt the color of grass and restyled one of her mourning jackets with pearl buttons and a white lace color and cuffs. Then she made a bonnet with green ribbons and yellow flowers. John wore his best gray suit. His shirt collar was so well starched that it made it difficult for him to turn his head.

The Dickeys, along with the Watsons and Will Wallace, hosted a small dinner celebration in the Dickey home, seating Esther and John at the same places at the table as when they were introduced. Dinner included roast beef, sweet potatoes, cabbage in cream, and apple pie. The new couple had rented a small house a few streets away from John's business while their house was being built. The two Charlies had made a sign for the front door with a pair of wedding bells and printed "Congratulations to Mr. and Mrs. John Morris and Archie."

— ❦ —

"Come, Archie, we will take Nelson for a ride." Now that Esther had chosen her path, she put all of her energy into building a new life. She began on a bright spring day by exploring what was around her. They hitched Nelson to the carriage while John was working and rode along the river toward LaSalle and a few miles inland. The Illinois countryside was abloom with spring violets and pink and red phlox, along with the cottonwood trees Esther had come to admire. She had looked through all the seeds that John carried at the store and asked him to get some China asters and hollyhocks as well as some seeds for a vegetable garden where she would grow carrots, potatoes, onions, squash, peas, and eggplant. John happily complied, although he was more interested in importing the best home furnishings he could locate from his network of dealers.

On her brother Jesse's recommendation they hired an architect from Cincinnati, where Jesse was now living with Mary and their first child, also named Mary. Jesse had traveled to Peru to see the land and helped them engage a German carpenter who had built many of the homes in the area. Jesse reminded Esther and John of questions they should ask before paying a carpenter for anything.

"Watch those places where carpenters sometimes tend to skimp, such as the depth of stair treads." He was firm on this, as "too narrow treads cause people to slip and fall, especially those with large feet like the McQuiggs."

"Leave my feet out of this, brother," Esther said, poking Jesse on the arm, but she was pleased that Jesse had come to advise them, and also get to know her new husband.

"Another concern is having enough space in water closets so they do not feel like a closet for a midget."

The Morrises built a traditional wood frame colonial-style house with tall columns at the front entry. These, along with the window shutters, were painted white while the front door was painted red and bore brass hardware. There was a white picket fence along the front of the property at the road, with a gate to a path leading to the front door. A wide circular drive allowed carriages to arrive at the front door or continue around to the back, near the small barn and stable that housed Nelson. Esther wanted to get an Indian pony for Archie, one as friendly and gentle as her Waverley.

On the first level of the home were a parlor and dining room of equal size and with high ceilings on either side of the curved entry hall. In back, French doors led to a wide veranda with a view of the river. Esther had already sketched plans for the garden, which would form around a terrace and lead toward the water. On the second floor Esther and John had a large suite with French doors and a porch where they could sit and read in the evening and watch the river. Archie had his own room on the second floor, also overlooking the backyard. There were shelves on either side of the window where he could store his toys and books, and his slate and chalks, for Esther had already been teaching him to read and write. Two other small bedrooms were located in the front on the second floor. On the third floor in the attic under the eaves were two small rooms for the young women who had been hired to help with the housekeeping and cooking. Catherine Matroin, twenty-two, was a German immigrant, and Emily Curtis, twenty-three, had moved from New York.

Beneath the high ceiling in each room, there was narrow shelving to store oil lamps, lanterns, and matches. A brand-new Winchester rifle was also carefully stored high on the wall of the entryway. Esther knew how to shoot but would not need that here. John rolled out the floral woolen carpet of reds and blues in the parlor, hoping the correct one had been sent. He had written detailed instructions to a dealer in New York City, describing the patterns and colors.

Lotte had shipped Esther's books and clothing and her sewing machine, along with the treasured Paul Revere candleholders. Esther polished these and set them on the maple dining table with brand-new tall tapers of white. Between them she placed a ceramic vase with some fresh wildflowers.

"Look what I purchased from the image peddler," John said, showing Esther a plaster bust of George Washington. With a growing middle class, people were beginning to look for more than just furnishings for their homes, and this created a need for image peddlers, traveling salesmen of sorts who sold decorative objects such as mirrors, dishes, paintings, and sculptures from their wagons. John sat the bust on a small pedestal table near the entryway.

With renewed energy to provide for his family, John spent long days at the second-floor office of his store keeping accounts and inventory and planning for new shipments. He frequently traveled to Chicago and St. Louis, and occasionally to New Orleans and New York, to arrange for new shipments with his network of suppliers. He was no longer the only merchant in Peru, which was growing so fast that each week several new families and commercial establishments appeared. Shops and businesses were spreading east along the river into LaSalle and farther to Ottawa.

All three Peru newspapers, as well as those in nearby LaSalle and Ottawa, announced that Mr. and Mrs. John Morris and son Edward Archibald had set up housekeeping on Bluff Road. Esther bought several copies of each and clipped the stories to send to her relatives and friends. In the back of the first floor was a sunroom of sorts where she could look out on the garden. She sat at a maple writing desk John had given her where she stored her pens and ink and papers. She kept family letters and photographs here. The government had recently issued postage stamps that eliminated the need to have the letters weighed and paid for at the post office. Now she could just lick the stamp and put it on the letter. Of course, it still had to be taken to the post office, usually located inside a grocery store. But now she need only drop the letters into a slot for "stamped mail." She let Archie scribble a note at the end to his cousins Franky and Libby, seal the envelope, and lick the stamp. Esther had to watch over her stamps because Archie liked to stick them on everything in the house.

Eliza Jane had sent daguerreotypes of the girls, who were well, and she always asked, "When can we see Archie?" But trouble was brewing in the marriage of Esther's friend and sister-in-law.

CHAPTER NINE

A Trip to Owego

"OH, ESTHER, HE HAD ME THROWN IN JAIL," ELIZA JANE WAILED AS SHE related her story in the kitchen of her sister Rosalind's home in Owego. "The sheriff came with two deputies, as if I were a lunatic and could harm them. They tied my hands and marched me outside the house with a rifle at my back. One threatened to put a hangman's hood over my head if I did not stop protesting. The neighbors thought I must have murdered my children, to be carried out of my house like this. Even in the sheriff's wagon, they kept the loaded gun aimed at me for fear I would overpower three big men and leap from a moving wagon to escape detention.

"And the jail!" Eliza Jane continued with increasing fury as her friend and sister-in-law listened in disbelief. "A stone room with no light or warmth, just a slab to sit or lie on. And a chamber pot in the open so anyone passing could see me at my personal business. I am convinced your brother, with his network of business and political cronies, arranged my jail stay to be as terrible as possible. And he will not tell me where the girls are." Eliza Jane began to cry but quickly wiped her eyes. "They are so young, only five and six." Eliza Jane leaned toward Esther and took her hands in hers. "Imagine if you could not see Archie." Esther knew exactly how she would feel. She would murder anyone who threatened to take him from her.

"I will talk with Edmund," Esther said, but she knew her brother's stubbornness. It would be like trying to knock down a brick wall. She recalled how perfectly cheerful and pleasant he had been yesterday when he, along with some of their other siblings, greeted her at the train station when she arrived with John and Archie. Edmund acted as if nothing were out of the ordinary.

Esther's first journey back to Owego had been more pleasant than her rugged stagecoach journey from Owego two years before. John had booked passage on the elegant steamer *Hendrik Hudson* for a luxurious five-day voyage from Chicago to New York City, where they spent one day before boarding a train to Owego, where they were met by a small crowd of relatives. Lotte and Fred were there with their daughters, Libby and Julia. Edmund had come with their youngest brother Georgie, who had grown into a tall and handsome young man with curly blond hair and a playful countenance.

"Oh, how the girls love him," Edmund said, smiling and clapping George's shoulder as Esther exclaimed her pleasure in seeing her baby brother. Edmund had been the only one in the family able to control George, who refused to seriously apply himself to school or a trade. After the homestead was sold, George lived with Daniel but often skipped out of school to hunt squirrel or fish in the canals near Albany. Jesse had tried teaching him carpentry to no avail. He seemed more settled living near Edmund, who had him working first at his dairy and then at the lumber and mercantile business. Now George was gallantly helping his sisters into the carriage and stowing the baggage behind them.

At Lotte and Fred's home, Esther and John settled their baggage into the small guest room. Libby, a sweet-natured five-year-old with soft brown hair and a mind of her own, immediately took charge of Archie, who was happy to follow his cousin. Lotte, now twenty-seven, had gained some weight and Esther thought the plumpness added to her rosy-cheeked demeanor, although her younger sister did seem slightly frantic and was overprotective of the girls, especially two-year-old Julia Frances. Another daughter, Mary Jane, had died last year just before her first birthday and Esther knew her sister was still suffering from this loss. Fred did not seem to offer much consolation to his wife, being mostly silent when he was home.

"I'm furious with Edmund," Lotte said as she and Esther settled in the parlor after the men went off to show John Fred's new mercantile establishment in the old Anson Camp building. John's new brothers-in-law immediately took to him, wanting to know all about business in the West. They planned to take their new kinsman around to Edmund's dairy farm, as well as his mercantile establishment, then up to Ithaca to meet the Hyatts and Turners, who were Edmund's partners in some of these enterprises. John had been looking forward to the visit, for Esther had told him how successful her brother Edmund was in his businesses.

Now Esther seethed as Lotte told her how their brother had hidden his children away because Eliza Jane had asked for a divorce when he refused to allow her to practice a new kind of medicine, a type of water therapy becoming popular in Owego.

"It's been done in Europe for a long time and here, of course, the Indians knew all about it at Saratoga Springs," Lotte said. "Now that a fancy hotel and spa have been built there, taking the waters has become the rage. Eliza Jane, who always admired the traditions and customs of the Native Americans, believes it will help people get rid of their aches and pains and malaise caused by overwork." Lotte explained to Esther that when Eliza Jane refused to stop her work and also refused to leave the house they shared, Edmund had her thrown in jail, where she remained until she was able to get legal help and raise the bail money. While she was in jail Edmund enrolled the girls in a private boarding school, whose location he would not reveal to anyone. And, of course, he refused to allow Eliza Jane back into the house where she had lived all those years with him and their children.

"There was no reason to do that, to hurt not only Eliza Jane, but their daughters, who cried for their mother," Lotte said. "Eliza Jane's father died, as you know, and he left his money and properties to his children. But, of course, Edmund took Eliza Jane's share because we women are not allowed our inheritance if we have a husband, who is considered to be the boss of everything about us. Eliza Jane said in that case, she would ask for a divorce and no longer be married." As Esther listened she sensed that Lotte, too, might be happier without her husband.

When Esther visited Eliza Jane the next day, they talked of possible ways to resolve this crisis. Their friend George Sidney Camp had presented legal papers to the court and raised the money to pay the required fine to get Eliza Jane out of jail. He had also helped her retain an attorney from a large New York City firm, who had more experience with divorce cases, but it would cost her money and Edmund was keeping her inheritance from her.

"I am penniless except for the fees I am paid for my work," Eliza Jane said, "and the people I treat are not wealthy. Some can only pay with foodstuffs or other types of barter."

According to the law in New York as well as most other states, when a woman married she lost any right to control property that was hers prior to the marriage; she also had no right to acquire any property during marriage. Esther certainly knew all about that! However, woman suffrage groups had been petitioning for change, and the state legislature was in the process of reexamining this law. Eliza Jane was adamant that Edmund should not control her portion of the inheritance left to her and her sisters by their parents, something that he had nothing to do with creating.

"Why should he reap the profit of the hard labor of my father? I wanted to use the inheritance for my business, to have my own carriage and horse—or at least a good horse and saddle, medical instruments, and supplies of mineral waters I need for paying house calls."

"And you also need to eat and pay for a place to live," Esther said, feeling overwhelmed at the obstacles facing her friend.

"Elizabeth Cady Stanton, the suffragist from Seneca Falls, was here," Eliza Jane told Esther. "She is a smart woman with many children, yet her husband supports her efforts. Although he does nothing to make her life easier, it seems. She brought a woman reporter, Margaret Fuller, from Mr. Greeley's *Tribune* newspaper in New York City who wrote down all the details of my situation. Mrs. Stanton told me about other cases where a husband was allowed to take all of a wife's inheritance and run off with another woman, or gamble and lose it all and then demand that his wife work as a servant to get him out of debt. There are awful examples, she told me, but the worst, of course, is that the man controls the children."

Eliza Jane was livid and began pacing back and forth in the small room. "Can you imagine such an outrage? How can they say the father is in charge of something the mother produces with her own body and at great risk? I created those little girls and nurtured them and cared for them, and now because I want a divorce from their father, the law says he owns them? How unfair is this world toward women? And we claim to be more civilized than the Indians. Hah!" Eliza Jane began to cry but quickly wiped her tears. "Remember how we admired the Seneca women long ago because they were the bosses at home?" She tried to smile, but the tears still came and she sat down. "I would certainly share the girls with him, but to be denied! My God, they are just babies!"

Esther could not imagine life without her son. She certainly understood her friend's humiliation, for she had felt some version of that herself in the past. She was forced to leave the old homestead after her father and Grandmother Hetty died even though she was earning enough as a seamstress and milliner to maintain the place, and more recently when denied the land Artemas had been given by the railroad.

"He won't even let me get my clothing," Eliza Jane sniffed. "I have to borrow dresses from my sister." Esther suddenly smiled and patted her friend's hand.

"Well, I've brought you something of your own, a new hat, which should help in that department." She handed her friend a box and watched her eyes as she opened it. Inside was a royal blue satin turban woven with seeded pearls.

"Oh, Esther," Eliza Jane said with a stunned look on her face. "It is most beautiful." She put it on and went to the mirror. "I will wear this every time I confront your brother in our legal pursuits." Esther shook her head and smiled. It was so like Eliza Jane to take the direct way, to challenge rather than appease, as a path to claiming her identity. "My red turban is in the house." She paused. "Unless he has destroyed all of my things." This thought silenced them both. "Maybe you can get my clothes when you visit him," Eliza Jane said softly, even as they both realized Edmund had most likely gotten rid of them.

"He probably donated them to the poorhouse," Esther said. As she listened to Eliza Jane's story, she tried to keep her anger at her brother's injustice tamped down, for she did not want to confront Edmund until she had all the details. She would also go with her friend to talk with George Sidney. Heaven knew there were enough lawyers among the family's relatives and friends that there should be some good ideas about how to help Eliza Jane get her children back.

Esther identified strongly with her friend's case, but she also understood their temperamental differences, that Eliza Jane would not be able to negotiate with Edmund. Esther tried to find a way to work around or through the situation, always believing there was a way to satisfy both sides, even while the injustice remained—for now. If the law said she could not have her land, no matter how unfair, then she would find a way around the law. Of course, she had help from Uncle Watson and his friends in Illinois to keep the land in Peru, and she was fortunate that John Morris was a fair-minded and kind man who accepted an arrangement that would benefit them both. The land was legally in the hands of her new husband, but would become Archie's when he was twenty-one. Mr. Morris had promised her that if anything happened to her or to himself before that time, the proceeds of the land would go to care for Archie. Both had drawn up a will and a written contract, witnessed by Uncle Watson and Will Wallace. This was an unusual document in a marriage of the time, but John agreed that marriage should be run similar to a business, so that emotion would not overrule common sense and mutual responsibility. Esther had no idea if the contract would stand up in a court of law, but she believed it was an honorable arrangement.

Eliza Jane, on the other hand, had a fiery temperament and clashed head-on with any obstacle. Esther recalled the day her friend and sister-in-law refused to sit on her horse in a side saddle as befits a proper lady. Like Esther, Eliza Jane and most women of the time had ridden horses since childhood and they rode like men. Riding astride while wearing a skirt meant the lower portion of a woman's legs would be exposed. And while young girls might get away with it, for adult women it was a definite impropriety. One day, to counteract Edmund's criticism that her legs would show, Eliza Jane tore her skirt up the center front and back and clipped the hems around her ankles with ribbons from her bonnet, making pantaloons, and galloped away, leaving her husband fuming on his own horse.

Edmund, who was methodically building a fortune for himself, did not want to be made a mockery by a wife who flouted propriety and custom. He openly scoffed at the suffragists, although he humored his own wife and sisters about the issue. On the other hand, Edmund had fallen in love with Eliza Jane because of her beauty and fiery temper. She got his blood rising. How he had begged Esther to introduce him to her beautiful friend. The things he so loved were now causing him pain. Esther knew his stubbornness and feared he would never back down. It would be best to go visit him with Lotte. Perhaps two could reason with him better than one.

— ◦ —

The first thing Esther noticed when she and Lotte entered Edmund's house was the missing photographs on the mantle. All framed daguerreotypes of Eliza Jane with Edmund and their daughters were gone. What remained were two individual pictures of the girls and one of Edmund with the girls. Also missing from its place over the sideboard was the gold-framed oil painting Edmund had commissioned to be copied from his wedding photograph. Esther was also struck at the silence in the house. Last time she was here, there were little girls running and laughing and Eliza Jane always inserting some controversial question into the conversation to keep it lively. There were no fresh flowers on the table, as well as other telltale signs of neglect in the housekeeping even though a housekeeper had brought them some tea.

"I like your new husband, sister," Edmund announced to Esther as she and Lotte arrived at his door. "He is a smart man and seems satisfied that he can care for you and Archie."

"You are prying, brother," Esther said stonily. "Obviously I am cared for very well, thank you." Edmund knew why his sisters were visiting and they did not want to make polite conversation, so he got to the point before they could accuse him.

"The woman is unstable," Edmund said when his sisters began to question him, "setting herself up to practice medicine. I am the laughingstock as she goes around town in her red turban like some kind of witch doctor," he said earnestly. Now thirty-six, Edmund looked vigorous, although his hairline had begun to recede. He was careful about his eating and he exercised regularly to remain fit, having become a steadfast believer in a proper diet of vegetables and grains as well as meat.

"She is not unstable," Esther replied with more heat than she intended, "except according to the male concept of any woman who has a mind of her own, or who thinks outside the rules set by men who, by the way, understand little about how women think or feel."

"You mean *if* they think," Edmund retorted. Esther felt her own blood rising and decided to calm down, or she would not accomplish anything with her brother. She had to use rational arguments because it was precisely this claim that men always used to keep women in their place, that women are not capable of rational thought, only emotional reaction.

"She is headstrong, yes," Lotte said, "but that is not a crime."

"I will let her get a divorce," Edmund said, "but she will have to find her way to Indiana to get it and she will get nothing else from me." Indiana was the only state that would grant a woman a divorce. The territories that wanted statehood quickly created some incentives, such as a place where divorce laws were lenient or where gambling was legal.

"Think of the girls," Lotte said. "They need their mother as well as their cousins and aunts and uncles. They are used to visiting with us and having us nearby, and Eliza Jane's family, also."

"Can you not both be parents to the girls?" Esther asked, trying to suggest a compromise. "Even if you live apart, why can you not both care for them?"

"I don't trust Eliza Jane to educate them properly. Her values are not in tune with society," he said, crossing one leg over the other as he sat regally in his green wingback chair near the hearth. Edmund told them he was also concerned about the girls' health, "how well they eat and exercise and how well they are doing with their music lessons. They both sing and play piano, you know," he said. "I want them to be the best educated and most cultured girls in the country," he added.

"Yet, you still want them to darn your socks," Esther mocked. "Edmund, be reasonable. Lotte and I have always loved those girls and we worry they are suddenly cut off from their entire family. We want to visit them."

"I cannot risk it yet," he said, "for fear you will allow Eliza Jane to visit with you. But I give you my word they are in good hands and have the best care. They have all of their own belongings with them, their books and music, their clothes, and I visit every week. They know I love them and have their best interests at heart."

"And what about Eliza Jane's belongings?" Esther wanted to know. She was about to specifically mention the red turban but held back, for she thought it would only inflame him.

"She has no belongings here," Edmund snapped.

Esther shook her head at her brother. "We will find the girls, Edmund, and we will visit and write to them to see for ourselves that they are well. Or have you given orders to stop their correspondence?" Later, Esther and Lotte talked with Eliza Jane, who had already begun searching the locations of all the girls' schools and private academies within the state and in nearby Pennsylvania.

"I have already hired a detective to find them," Eliza Jane said, "with George Sidney's help."

⚊ ⚊

While John and Edmund took the train to Ithaca, Esther and Lotte and their children paid a visit to their brother Daniel and his family at Port Byron on the Erie Canal. He and Eleanor had lost two of their grown daughters recently, one to typhoid and another to scarlet fever. Little Horace had died very young, only a year after Daniel and his family had moved out of Spencer and their son Charles had died at eighteen. Of their five children, only one, twelve-year-old Mary Jane, survived. Although Daniel had grown prosperous with the farm shipping goods downriver to New York, or west through the canal, Eleanor was ghostlike, going through the motions of serving tea and conversing with her sisters-in-law. Daniel seemed overly solicitous toward his wife and kept glancing over, as if fearing some kind of a breakdown or breech of etiquette. Esther wondered how Eleanor managed to carry on at all after such devastating loss, and she felt sorry for her early hostility toward her sister-in-law.

A visit to their older sister Jane was equally disheartening, for she had suffered from consumption for more than five years and was growing more frail by the day. Even as a child Jane seemed to know she would have an unhappy life. Her only child, Fred, now sixteen, had left home

97

two years before to work on a whaling ship. Her husband, Alvah, worked hard to keep their farm productive but seemed to find solace only in apple brandy.

When their visit to Owego was near an end, Esther took John for a walk through the town to show him familiar landmarks.

"He's gone off to the Wisconsin Territory," she told him as they passed the former store and hotel of Uncle Jesse. The little house where she had lived with Lotte and later with Artemas and Archie was now a photographer's studio, and her narrow garden on the side of the building had been replaced with a carriage shed. Esther noted how much change had occurred since she left this town only two years ago. She had visited the few friends who had not moved west. There were some vacant stores and others in need of repair. Unlike Peru, there was no new building in town.

That evening Esther sat quietly on the edge of the bed in their room at Lotte's and realized she was homesick. It was the first time she thought of it that way, but for days her mind had been wandering back to her house in Peru, to her new friends and to her garden. She was anxious to see if the pink foxglove she had planted was in bloom yet. She had been only half listening as John talked about his meeting with some of Edmund's associates through whom he found a new supplier for tableware and fine linens.

"Husband," Esther said as John was folding his trousers over the back of a chair, "it is time to go home." She thought John would like to hear of another reason to go home. "Shall I tell you what I learned at my visit to Dr. Tinkham yesterday?" As John stood in his underdrawers, he turned toward her, expectantly raising his eyebrows as a smile crept across his face and hers.

CHAPTER TEN

The Flood of 1849

"LET US PRAY THE ROOF DOESN'T LEAK," ESTHER SAID AS SHE AND Catherine struggled to haul the rolled-up carpet up the stairs with six-year-old Archie bravely holding up the end of the roll. Although the house was on higher ground than the business district of Peru, Esther took no chances. While baby Johnny was napping, she, along with Catherine and Emily, carried the stores of flour and corn and other perishable foods along with linens and books up to the second floor and the attic. They had moved the parlor furniture so they could save the precious wool carpet from possible water damage.

The newspapers were calling it the greatest flood of the Illinois River since the settlement of the country. Heavy rain began on the first day of 1849 and continued for weeks, causing the river to overflow. As the temperature dropped and the water froze, ice covered miles of the riverbanks. Great ice floes crushed Theron Brewster's warehouse along with trees, and some docks along the water's edge. More than a foot of snow covered the ice, and then in March the weather warmed and brought more rain along with the melting snow and ice. Now the river was twenty-five feet over its banks. The streets on either side of the river were like rivers themselves, with water rising over the door sills of the buildings nearest the shore.

John and both Charlies, along with two hired longshoremen, had been moving the inventory up to the second story of Morris Mercantile. They moved some merchandise to an inland barn John had rented and some smaller items to the house and stable. The men had worked without sleep for two days and were covered with sweat and mud, unable to change clothes or bathe. The air inside was thick with the smell of mold and rancid sweat.

At home Esther and Catherine put the carpet and some books in the new nursery on the second floor. The women had been painting and fixing up the room for Johnny, who would soon move in to this room of his own. Taking a short rest, Esther wiped the sweat from her brow with her apron and looked out the window in despair at the gardens she had developed into what she had once imagined as a young girl in Spencer. She had planted China asters, hollyhocks, and a mix of annuals and perennials in beds that were connected by winding pathways lined with low boxwood shrubs. A trellis of roses formed an archway along the garden path. Bricks and stones were laid down in a small terrace in one of the gardens where a round iron table and chairs were set up so she could serve tea to her friends, or simply sit and read.

Esther had been delighted to find so many like-minded women in the West, most of whom like her were from the East. Prudence Crandall, a slight woman with fair hair and a firm chin, was nine years older than Esther. They met at an abolition meeting in Ottawa. Prudence, too, had been put in jail for the "crime" of admitting Negro girls into her private academy in Connecticut.

"I refused to expel my Negro girls as the white parents demanded," Prudence told Esther. "Instead I opened the school to more Negro students." Esther laughed at this, sensing that Prudence and Eliza Jane would be staunch allies. Crandall had withstood months of angry protests and threats until the school's water was contaminated and a mob set fire to the school. "I feared for the lives of my students and closed the school," she lamented.

Esther recalled hearing of Crandall's exploits from abolition leaders in her own state, for she was still in Owego when this incident took place. She told Prudence about her experience defying the mob that threatened to burn down her Baptist church if Negroes were allowed to attend abolition meetings. In Crandall's case the town changed the law, making it illegal to teach Negro students, and so she was arrested and jailed. Although she was finally released on a technicality after two trials, Prudence and her husband went to Mendotta and she found a new teaching job. She continued her involvement with abolition and women's rights and was pleased to meet Esther.

Another woman who came into Esther's circle was Susan Hoxie Richardson, a cousin of suffrage leader Susan B. Anthony. She, too, lived nearby in LaSalle County and told Esther she was inspired to organize women after reading an editorial in the *Earlville Transcript* by A. J. Grover about the importance of woman suffrage. Richardson promptly sought out the Grovers, and they began efforts to organize the first Illinois Suffrage Association. Suffrage was becoming a central issue among her friends, and Esther herself had become more impassioned about it since her visit with Eliza Jane.

"You know," Esther said to these friends one afternoon, "years ago when the townspeople nominated me for mayor, I politely declined, thinking it unseemly for a woman to be mayor, but now I would accept gladly, for I more clearly realize the importance of having women leaders."

"We need the vote first," Richardson said.

Esther now missed these friends, for while the roads were flooded, it was difficult to travel and most were forced to stay home. It would be many more weeks, she thought, before the water receded sufficiently to restore travel. Now, when new spring buds should be coming up in her garden, she saw only a vast plain of mud.

***

The Morris family survived the flood but not the cholera that came on its heels. The disease had first devastated the more densely populated East, and this was the first time it had come west with such force, possibly because the flood had compromised the groundwater and the wells in the area. Several people died in April and May, and by the end of June it had become epidemic, killing hundreds in LaSalle County within three or four weeks. It took baby John Morris before he could celebrate his first birthday. Everyone in the house had been so careful not to expose him to anyone who had been in a house where there was cholera. But the disease could spread in so many ways they had yet to understand, and the young were most vulnerable. Esther clutched her baby in her arms long after the doctor said he was gone. She rocked him and cried in such anguish that John had to pull her arms away, so he could take their son from her.

"Let go, Esther, please, you must let him go." John himself was shattered that his first son, who looked so much like him with his dark eyes and brown curly hair, was gone. After working long days John liked to sit on the edge of the bed and watch his sleeping son in the nearby cradle. One night Esther came into the room as he was peering into the cradle, stroking his son's hand. "You can grow up to be president in this great country," John told him. When Esther asked him what he said, John grew flustered. "Just thinking out loud," he mumbled, and got up to change into his nightclothes.

Johnny had brought considerable joy to the household. Archie had recently begun school and liked to say his new vocabulary words to the baby, who would laugh and pat Archie's face and say "Chee," his name for his big brother, who was now inconsolable. Esther railed at God. If he had to be so cruel, why not take her baby sooner, she sobbed, before she came to know him as a child who liked to watch the butterflies when she brought him into the garden in his cradle. How her heart had swelled at the look of surprise and joy on Johnny's face when he had taken his first steps and realized he could toddle into his mother's waiting arms.

Burying her son in the small cemetery in Peru, Esther thought of Lotte, who had gone through this only a few years before when her baby Mary Jane died at the same age. She understood that babies were more vulnerable to disease, that it had to be endured by families, but it was more heartbreaking than she could bear. John kept Esther's hand pulled close to his chest and held it tight with both of his hands as they walked away from the grave. He later sought out the image peddler to commission a likeness of their son from the daguerreotype that had been taken; perhaps he could make an angel. John did not know if God would care for his son in heaven, or if there was such a place, but he hoped so.

⁓

Before the end of the year, cholera would claim another in their family.

"It's Georgie," Esther said to John as they sat in the parlor, he reading the newspapers and she her mail.

"What happened to him?" John asked, sensing from his wife's expression that it was bad news.

"It is the cholera again," she said, dropping her hand with the letter into her lap and lowering her head as tears welled over. "He was on his way home from the California gold fields. Edmund had a letter from a friend who was with him on the ship, the *Mosconoma*. They buried him at sea off the coast of Chile, near Valparaíso." John took the letter from his wife's hand and read it. They would have to tell Archie, who had taken a particular liking to his Uncle George, who had taught him magic card tricks during their visit to Owego.

For George, a boy who loved adventure, the gold rush had been too tempting to ignore. Edmund had staked him enough money to pay his passage, and with nine friends he sailed from New York around South America to San Francisco. He wrote elegant descriptions of his journey, and some of his letters to Edmund had been printed in the Owego newspaper so the whole town could share news of the gold rush. Esther had read the newspaper clippings, sent by Edmund and Lotte, who sometimes forwarded George's letters to her to pass along to the other siblings.

"We all had a turn of seasickness. Jud was very sick but has come out fine. We are all in fine spirits. Give my respects to all of my friends. You will kiss Helen and Lucinda for me." Esther's heart quickened at the mention of girls, for George seemed to have young women pining for him all over York State. However, five of George's friends who had set out with him turned back at Panama. Unused to the jungle heat and humidity along with the bugs, they remained on the isthmus, where the American consul promised to find them passage on a whaler headed for home.

"I shall not think of coming back until I see the elephant," George wrote, using a common expression for the moment of enlightenment when you finally understand you will not receive what you were hoping to get. He booked passage on a British steamer bound for Callao in Peru and wrote, "We went in the steerage and God deliver me from another English steamer. Stinky beef and wormy bread and mule soup was the fare which made me five or six days very sick." In the seaport town of Lima he described the bullfights and wrote, "The principal products of the country are Negroes, fleas, pol parrots, monkeys and jackanapes." George said he had not shaved and was tanned as black as the natives. "The fleas bite so that I am obliged to scratch with one hand and write with the other."

After months working in California, George wrote, "I began to see the gold diggers' fate. A great many work and only a few make money, and hundreds do not get anything. The Sacramento River is literally covered with men and more going there every day. Hotels charge $1 for sleeping on the floor. Hundreds are rolled in blankets lying on boxes and some be in the street. Hundreds leaving the mines and come here looking for work to pay their passage home." It was then he wrote to Edmund, "I have seen the elephant."

"I, too, have seen the elephant," Esther whispered. She buried her face in her hands and sobbed. "There is so much death," she thought, recalling the day her brother was born, the day that her mother died giving birth to him. And now, of her ten brothers and sisters, only seven remained. Joining Mindwell, Charles, and George among the lost were nearly all of Daniel's children, and daughters of Lotte and Jane, and baby John.

John put down his newspaper and came to sit next to his wife. He put his arms around her, pulling her head onto his shoulder, but she was inconsolable.

CHAPTER ELEVEN

Twins Arrive

"How can there be two of them at once?" Archie asked as he and John stared at the babies wrapped snugly in white flannel cloth. One, slightly larger than the other, had fallen asleep, but the smaller one pumped his tiny fists into the air and kicked his feet, demanding notice of his arrival. They were in two cradles, one borrowed at the last minute from a neighbor when the doctor realized there were twins. Unsure how to explain twins to Archie, John put his arm around the shoulder of the nine-year-old and changed the subject.

"This one is Edward John," he said of the sleeping baby. "And this energetic one is Robert Charles."

"But, Pa, if my first name is Edward, how can we have another one?" While Archie was never called Edward, he was certainly aware it was his first name. "Will he be Edward the Second, like the English kings?" John laughed. "Well, yes, he will be the second Edward, but it is because we liked your name so much we decided to use it again." Archie gave John a skeptical glance.

"Your ma and me, we each made a choice of names we liked. Your ma likes Edward, and John is for me. And Robert here is the name that goes with Morris, the last name I picked from the signers of the Declaration of Independence." He laughed because Archie had heard this story so many times it was now family legend. "Charles is for your uncle who died in Cincinnati a few years ago."

"Do you think they will get sick?" Archie asked. He remembered the sadness when baby John died two years ago, how Ma had held him against her heart, rocking back and forth, and how she cried after Pa took the baby from her and gave it to Catherine, who was also crying, so she could get him ready to put inside the coffin for the funeral. Then Pa went out, and when he came home he was walking funny. Ma said he had gone to the tavern and had a lot of rum because he was so sad.

"We will have much to give thanks for this Thanksgiving," John said. "We'll go hunting for a turkey. Would you like that?"

"Yes," Archie said, his eyes lighting up and losing interest in the babies temporarily. "And Ma has sweet potatoes in the root cellar to make the pie with the apples." John enjoyed this special American holiday, for he was truly thankful for all this country had given him: not only his new sons but his business and his home and a respected position in the community. Had he remained in occupied Poland, he would be part of a feudal system that nobody could change. You were either a lord or a peasant. There was no in between. Here, anyone who worked hard could begin a new life.

"Come on," he said to Archie. "Let's go buy some cigars from Mr. Jorgen."

—⁓—

"The mayor is here with the boy surveyor," John called out to Esther as he opened the big red front door on Thanksgiving afternoon. "Perhaps he is here to measure out your holiday dinner table." Archie ran to the door, and the young man with Mayor Gilson and his family stuck out his hand. A solid youth with reddish blond hair and a high brow, he wore a gray wool coat and a colorful red and green plaid scarf.

"And you must be Master Edward Archibald Slack." When Archie nodded, he said, "I am Master Thomas Edwin Greenfield Ransom, boy surveyor, civil engineer, and general slave to my uncle, the mayor." Ransom took off his plaid wool tam-o'-shanter and bowed. Archie laughed and ran off to play with the Gilsons' two children.

"Oh, Tommy," Esther said, coming into the foyer, "how good to see you." She hugged the seventeen-year-old, whom she had met years ago when she accompanied her late husband's body to Vermont for burial. Then, Ransom was Archie's current age. His father, General Truman

Ransom, had died in the Mexican-American War. His mother was Mayor Gilson's sister, Margaret, who now lived in New York City. Young Tom had been hired by the Illinois Central Railroad as soon as he graduated from Norwich University as a civil engineer. In Peru he was also the official surveyor and helped out in his uncle's real estate business.

"Ma sends her regards," Ransom said. "She wanted me to stay in New York with her, but Uncle George said all the money is to be made in the West."

With both hearths going in the parlor and dining room, the house was warm and fragrant with the scent of the roasting turkey and recently baked pies. Esther and John had invited those friends who had no extended families in Peru. They had always included the two Charlies as well as Catherine and Emily, who sat at the table with them for the holiday celebrations. In addition to Tom and the Gilsons, they welcomed the town's founder, Theron Brewster, who had been mayor before Gilson. His son Teddie was a good friend of Archie. Esther, who had lost considerable weight giving birth to the twins, wore the green skirt from her wedding and a velvet bodice with a lace collar. She had recently sewn a hoop into the skirt in keeping with the current fashion but found herself often impatiently pulling her skirt aside to pass through a narrow door or behind a chair. The hoopskirt, she felt, was one more impediment for women. Nevertheless, she was vain enough to want to be in fashion.

While Emily was laying the table and placing Esther's Revere candlesticks on either side of a spray of holly, John and Esther took everyone into the nursery to peek at the twins, now three weeks old. Gifts of calico cats and silver spoons with names engraved were given to Esther and John. Catherine and Emily had their hands full entertaining the Brewster and Gilson children, but Tom Ransom helped by telling them of his plans to organize expeditions into the mountains of the West.

"There's gold there," he said. "A man cannot help but get rich. Archie, one day you and I will go on such an expedition. Would you like that?"

"Yes," Archie said, giving his serious attention to this stranger from Vermont who had known his natural father's family, "but Ma says I must go to college, so it will be some time before I can go with you." Ransom laughed and patted Archie on the head. "We will plan on that, then."

While the women remained in the dining room for tea after dinner, the men moved to the parlor, where John gave each of them two Cuban cigars and a snifter of the best French brandy he was able to procure.

―❦―

This was the beginning of a happy and prosperous decade for the Morris family. Archie and the twins thrived, although Robert seemed to have a more delicate constitution, with frequent fevers and agues, causing his parents to worry. Archie's asthma attacks were less frequent and not as severe as they had been when he was younger.

The Morrises had frequent sociables at home. Esther had always enjoyed entertaining, and while John was a bit shy, he felt that as a town founder and trustee and now an alderman, it was good business for him to invite his friends and their families to dinner. Their home was a center of lively debates, with their network of friends including politicians, lawyers, and educators as well as suffragists and abolitionists. John was not as passionate about politics or suffrage as his wife, although he reluctantly agreed that women should be able to vote. However, he and Esther had an enormous rift the first time she insisted on going to the polls with him on Election Day, as an act of protest. She also brought along her doctor so he could publicly pronounce that going to the polls in no way made Esther sick or weak. This was a popular anti-suffrage argument, and many women vowed to include it as an unusual act of protest. Voting places tended to be filled with raucous and drunken men. Politicians seeking office offered free drinks to men who would cast a vote for them. It was considered an ugly atmosphere into which to bring ladies. When John made this argument to Esther, she said she had been exposed to worse conditions.

He knew he would not win the argument, so he finally said, "Esther, I believe that you will eventually be able to vote, but I don't like to be a public spectacle in your cause." Esther understood that John felt humiliated by this act, and while she sympathized with that, she managed to convince her husband that by accompanying her to the polls, he was showing himself to be a forward-thinking man, and perhaps her presence there would inspire some of the men to refrain from their usual crudeness. John never did get used to it, but he could not find an argument to counteract hers. He fortified himself with some brandy.

In addition to a comfortable home and a profitable business, the Morris family had the means to travel and made regular visits to Esther's extended family in New York, Ohio, and Iowa. Esther enjoyed traveling and wanted to take a pleasure cruise on the Mississippi River. To most Americans the mighty Mississippi was a mythological waterway. It was not only the biggest river, but the territorial dividing line between civilization and the vast wilderness leading to the Pacific Ocean. There was great mystery and romance about the river, and Esther wanted to see as much of it as possible.

One summer she and the boys took a trip up to Dubuque to visit her younger sister Eliza and her family. Eliza's husband, Captain Joshua Parker, was in charge of the riverboats and pilot of the *Davenport*, the biggest steamboat on the river. This job paid Captain Parker $500 a month, more money than the vice president of the United States was paid. The Parkers had built a beautiful white house on top of a hill overlooking the river, where they lived with their four children, ages three to fifteen. Captain Parker, a lanky man with prematurely gray hair and long sideburns, arranged for Esther and the boys to take a cruise downriver to St. Louis, with a new young river subpilot, Samuel Clemens of Hannibal, Missouri. He was working to get his pilot's license, and during the cruise Clemens spent some time teaching the boys the nautical terms for measuring the river's depth, emphasizing that a pilot had to know where in the river it was safe to travel.

"You see this line?" he explained to the Morris boys on the deck of a Mississippi River steamboat. "This tells us when we are in safe water of two fathoms or more. Now, what do you holler out?"

"Mark twain," the boys shouted in unison.

"Ah, how fine that sounds," Clemens said with a smile. "I do like those words." He told the boys that a thousand boats with names like *Crescent City* and *White Cloud* went up and down the river every day and it was very important that none of them ended up on the rocks.

Although railroads were booming, the rivers of America were still the focus of most shipping and community activity. This was true in Peru, where the Illinois riverfront was always the scene of some new excitement.

"Pa, come to the dock," seven-year-old Robert hollered one day in 1858 as he burst into the store. "Archie is reporting on the man rowing all the way down the river." Archie, who had ingratiated himself with the publisher of the *Peru Democrat*, was sent to check on a rumor that a young man named John Wesley Powell was rowing down all the rivers in the West. Today Powell was rowing the Illinois River out to the Mississippi. Newspaper stories said Powell was studying Greek and Latin at Illinois College, but seemed most interested in exploring the natural wonders of the West. Archie went to gather reaction from the crowd around the riverfront.

"I say, why not take the steamer?" said one longshoreman. "He'll get there a lot faster."

"Well, I think that man had the right idea," said one miller. "It's like riding your own horse instead of a coach and seeing the river close up."

By midcentury, a large middle class was developing in the United States. These families were having fewer children, not only because there was more awareness about birth control methods, but because there was a new conviction that children should be allowed to play and grow freely. With fewer children families could afford to educate them rather than simply keep them healthy until they were old enough to work, as earlier generations had done. Esther and John gave the boys every advantage; they were in good schools and also had lessons in music (Robert liked violin), dancing (Ed liked the girls), and German as well as sports. The game of baseball was becoming quite popular and Ed, a strong runner and batter, organized his friends into a team. The twins were enrolled in Peru Academy while Archie was just beginning the new high school, which students had already dubbed "Big Brick."

Robert was shorter than his twin and slight, with the brown hair and eyes of his father. Edward was heavier and somewhat taller, with light brown hair and gray eyes like Esther. Robert liked to sit with his mother at her writing table and compose his own letter to put in the same envelope. In fact, once he mastered printing and longhand, he was charged with fixing his mother's letters to make sure the recipients could read them. Esther had never been able to slow down her fast scrawl, and her family and friends begged her to "please print so we can read your letters." Her brother Jesse teased, "We have a contest in the household, that whoever can make sense of your entire letter will get an extra dessert for supper." Ed, who had less interest in sitting still, preferred to hunt with Archie and his father. Strongly influenced by his meeting with Sam Clemens, he had begged to be allowed to work on the riverboats, but did not get his way.

Archie was a budding newspaper man at a revolutionary time for the press, when for the first time the public was able to read the news within twenty-four hours in the many penny newspapers published in every town and city. As methods of reproduction with photography and type were becoming more sophisticated, advertisements were larger and often illustrated and boxed into their own space on the page. Archie liked to help John create his advertisements for the local newspapers each time he had new merchandise available. John's own attempts were simple and straightforward, stating that a new shipment of particular merchandise was available at Morris Mercantile.

Archie had a flair for the dramatic and created ads such as "First Time Ever Available in the United States" for the newly invented can opener. "Hurry into Morris Mercantile! These will go fast." Archie was allowed to attend printing school after his regular classes, although Esther insisted he was going to get a college education at the University of Chicago, which had just been established by Baptists.

Peru itself was incorporated as a city with a population of nearly four thousand. Most were born in the States, but more than one thousand came from Germany, five hundred from Ireland, and some from France, Poland, and Sweden. A city hall and a new market house were under construction in the city, which already had more than seven hundred buildings, including seven public schools, six churches, and two banks. Five tailors and four milliners were thriving; so were blacksmiths, coopers, a saddler, five lawyers, seven doctors, and a photographer. In addition to a match factory and a plow factory and several grain mills, three breweries produced beer for forty saloons and seven taverns, one of which was in the hotel.

"The church people are demanding a crackdown on drinking on the Sabbath," Mayor Gilson said at a town meeting. "They want the taverns closed." John, who always attended and sometimes led weekly meetings held at one of the stores or taverns, shook his head in frustration. With the other officials, it was his responsibility to help settle complaints and disputes over a variety of issues like zoning and fire safety. "We should have at least one day without men falling down in the street after a day in the saloon," said one protestor. Since Sunday was the only day off for most of the workers in the area, it was quite natural for them to relax at the tavern. They did not have the time to drink any other day. As the recently appointed coroner of LaSalle County, John also was responsible for solving crimes, which were often committed by drunks.

"But why punish the tavern owner?" John asked. "He is not responsible for any man's behavior. Should it be up to him to decide when somebody has had enough?" An immigrant himself, John did not want anyone telling him if or when he could have a drink. Besides, he knew and liked most of the tavern owners and visited these taverns himself at the end of the business day. These old New Englanders seemed to forget they all grew up on hard cider from the abundant apple orchards in the Northeast. His wife told him of the problems in her own family, especially of her father, who drank on any day he pleased, which was every day, from the "spirits of '76," as his family dubbed his cider jug.

<hr>

While John and Esther and the boys were living a comfortable life, it was Esther's brother Edmund whose wealth had increased most dramatically. After years of planning, he sold all of his holdings in New York and moved to Flint, Michigan, with his partners E. C. Turner, Judge Hyatt, and Henry Crapo, a man with political aspirations who would later become the state's first governor, to invest in what would be the largest lumber business in that state. Edmund had also convinced Jesse and Mary and their three children to move to Flint to build houses. This

Jesse did, and as a first-rate carpenter, he was hardly able to keep up with the demand.

Edmund had left his daughters in their private academy for girls in Elmira until they completed their course of education, when they would join him in Flint. He was still resisting Eliza Jane's claims to the girls or to any of his money (including the part that was her inheritance), and their divorce case stalled for years in the civil court in Indianapolis. Eliza Jane, with help from Esther and Lotte as well as her own sisters, had discovered the location of the girls, years before. Lotte was first to visit and ascertain that Franky and Libby were healthy and doing well in their studies. After that Edmund could not prevent visits, and over the years, Esther and Lotte and their families all visited and corresponded with the girls. Eliza Jane wrote regularly and visited as often as possible, but she was forced now to work to support herself and pay her lawyers. She took a teaching job in Cincinnati in order to be closer to the court in Indianapolis.

With enough money to hire the best lawyers, Edmund vowed to take the divorce case all the way to the Supreme Court if necessary. The case had been dragging on for years, while the girls were growing up without their mother.

Now Esther traveled by train to Indianapolis to testify on Eliza Jane's behalf, about her character and stability. She also testified to her brother's stubborn refusal to cede his wife her rights, not only to gain custody of her daughters, but to obtain the inheritance he had taken from her.

"She can have her divorce," Edmund said, "but she will get no money from me. Nor will she get custody of my daughters." He argued that Eliza Jane got her inheritance before the law changed in 1848 in New York State, allowing married women to retain any property they acquired during marriage. However, when Eliza Jane's attorney called fourteen-year-old Libby to the witness stand to testify for her mother, that her father had deprived her of maternal care, Edmund was visibly shocked. Libby told the court she wanted to live with her mother, that she had missed her all these years. Lotte and Esther had helped Eliza Jane see her daughters over the years, and helped arrange for Lotte to bring Libby to court to testify.

"It is not fair that my father prevented that," Libby told the judge, breaking down in tears. Edmund finally acquiesced, but Esther suspected it was not his daughter's tears that moved him as much as the need to be free to remarry. She had learned that Elizabeth Foreman, a relative of the Hyatts, was recently widowed. She was a sweet-natured and conventional woman, and Edmund wanted that kind of marriage now. The court decided in fairness to award custody of one daughter to each parent.

While Edmund remained bitter about Libby's defection, and Esther's "treason," he made a $3,000 cash settlement with Eliza Jane, stipulating that the money was only for the support of his daughter. It was not to be used to support her mother's unseemly lifestyle, for he had learned that Eliza Jane had had a lover for many years with whom she had borne a son, Charles Victor, now ten years old. Eliza Jane refused to marry the boy's father or change her name. Never again would Eliza Jane Hall give up her freedom.

"Libby chooses to go with her mother to a cold world. It feels like sending her to her grave," Edmund said. As he walked past the witness desk in the court, he stopped in front of Esther and said, "You are no longer welcome in my home, sister."

CHAPTER TWELVE

The Black Republicans

"FOR ONE, I AM OPPOSED TO NEGRO CITIZENSHIP IN ANY AND EVERY form. I believe this government was made on the white basis. I believe it was made by white men for the benefit of white men and their posterity forever, and I am in favor of confining citizenship to white men, men of European birth and descent, instead of conferring it upon Negroes, Indians, and other inferior races."

Congressman Stephen Douglas spoke from an outdoor stage in Washington Park in Ottawa on a muggy August evening before an enormous crowd. Some cheered the words of this short, bewhiskered senator from Illinois, but many did not. Known as Little Giant, Douglas, with a bold, jutting chin and deep-set eyes, was the chairman of the powerful committee on territories in the House of Representatives.

"Of course, he includes women with all those inferior races," Esther said with fury as she stood with her arms folded across her chest and her lips pressed together. She was in the crowd gathered in Washington Park along with Tom Ransom, the Gilsons, and many friends from Peru. The Watsons had come up from Pittsfield to stay with the Morrises. Their eldest daughter, Sarah Jane, had last year married Robert Scanland, the brother of the mayor of Pittsfield, who had recently held a sociable for Mr. Lincoln. Sarah and Robert named their first son Robert Morris Scanland, which so pleased young Robert Morris, now seven, that he wrote to all his relatives to report on his namesake.

Martha Ann and Will Wallace were there with their little daughter, Isabel. Martha Ann, T. Lyle Dickey's daughter, was now married to the man she had loved since girlhood. The strength of her love reminded Esther of what she had experienced all those years ago with Artemas. When Will returned from the Mexican-American War thirteen years ago, he was made the district attorney of LaSalle County and married Martha Ann. But the two families disagreed on the political candidates. T. Lyle, who had been a friend of Abraham Lincoln all of his adult life, had recently come out on the side of Douglas and had been campaigning for him—not because he believed in slavery, but because he felt there was no way to get rid of it without tearing apart the country. Dickey's defection hurt Lincoln to the core. Although the two managed a respectful acquaintance, their friendship had permanently cooled. Esther had noticed Lincoln's petulant glance at T. Lyle earlier as he had climbed up to the speakers' platform.

John was inclined to agree that Douglas was the better candidate because he would avoid war, but he felt that in America it would turn out right with either man. These were all ordinary people, just like him, speaking out and becoming leaders; look at Dickey and Wallace and Gilson, even his brother-in-law Edmund. He truly believed whichever way it went would be okay, although he did not like the way the United States had been expanding its territory into Texas and the Southwest, driving out Spanish and Mexican settlers.

"It reminds me of Europe," John had told Esther after the Mexican War. "The Russians overran Poland and Lithuania to claim it as their own." Yet he realized that the expanded nation would be a richer one.

Archie, now sixteen, seemed to be enjoying a flirtation with pretty Sarah Neely, the youngest sister of John Palmer's wife, Malinda. Sarah had recently moved from Kentucky to live with the Palmers. Like his friends Lincoln and Dickey, Palmer came from a hardscrabble life in Kentucky. Leaving a broken and poverty-stricken home at sixteen, he worked his way through college, read law, passed the bar examination, and had become a force in Illinois Democratic politics during the past decade. He was vehemently against slavery and very much for suffrage for women. He and his wife were involved in many suffrage activities and often in the same circles with Esther and her friends. Palmer broke with his party over the issue of slavery, however. He resigned from the state senate, where he had been elected as a Democrat, in order to join the newly formed Republican Party. He was working hard to get Lincoln elected to Congress.

Tonight was the first of many debates Douglas agreed to have with Lincoln in towns throughout Illinois. Two months earlier Lincoln had accepted the Republican nomination for the United States House of Representatives and made a speech in Springfield that people were constantly talking about.

"A house divided against itself cannot stand," he had said. "I believe this government cannot endure, permanently, half slave and half free. I do not expect the Union to be dissolved—I do not expect the house to fall—but I do expect it will cease to be divided. It will become all one thing or all the other."

Douglas always referred to Lincoln and other Republicans as "Black Republicans," implying that abolition was their only issue. Until then, the two main political parties were Democrats and Whigs, but the abolition groups at Ottawa preferred to be called Republicans. The name caught on and had recently become official. The name *Republicans* grew out of meetings at the home of John Hossack, a Scotland-born engineer who worked on the Illinois and Michigan Canal before settling in Ottawa in 1854. He built a large two-story Greek Revival house on the banks of the Illinois River that became the center of abolition activity in LaSalle County and the central station for the Underground Railroad. Hossack sheltered as many as a dozen fugitive slaves at a time.

Abolitionists had also gained momentum since the 1852 publication of Harriet Beecher Stowe's novel *Uncle Tom's Cabin*, which painted a picture of the horrors of slavery. It was to become the best-selling book of the century. Esther herself read it twice. Although she went to abolition meetings and showed her support, Esther refrained from hiding or transporting slaves, for since the advent of the 1850 Fugitive Slave Law, the risks for hiding slaves had increased dramatically. She would not put her family at risk. Now anyone aiding a runaway was subject to six months in jail and a $1,000 fine. The law also offered officers of the law bonuses for capturing a fugitive slave. At the same time, if those officers did not arrest a fugitive, they were fined $1,000. Esther showed

Hossack and the others a handbill Lotte had sent her, passed along from a friend in Boston.

"Caution! Colored People of Boston, one and all. You are hereby respectfully cautioned and advised to avoid conversing with the watchmen and police officers of Boston. For since the recent order of the mayor and aldermen, they are empowered to act as kidnappers and slave catchers. Keep a sharp look out for kidnappers and have top eye open."

Hossack had convinced Esther that it was not possible to compromise on the slavery issue, that it was the backbone of the entire Southern economy. "They will never give it up." Hossack himself was often arrested, but was surrounded by smart attorneys who got him released, usually on a technicality.

Lincoln's rebuttal to Douglas had taken all of Esther's attention, and as darkness enveloped the park, she realized that Robert had disappeared in the crowd. John didn't know where he was, either, as he had been off with some friends smoking cigars. Ed was with his father, so she searched the crowd and finally found Robert pestering T. Lyle.

"Mr. Dickey, please tell me the story again, the one about Mr. Lincoln in his nightshirt," Robert begged. They all loved this story Dickey had told them about his trips with Lincoln around the circuit courts in their early years as lawyers. They often shared lodging, and Dickey said it was impossible to get any sleep with Lincoln wanting to talk and argue cases the night long. One midnight, Dickey was roused from sleep by Lincoln sitting on the edge of his bed in his nightshirt, pleading his case against slavery. "Finally," Dickey related, "I had to tell him, 'Oh, Lincoln, just go to sleep.'"

As Esther and John reclaimed their son, Esther said, "I will vote for Lincoln when I go to the poll." They all laughed, except John, who rolled his eyes.

"You see why I must fortify myself every Election Day," John said.

"I hope you will change your mind," said T. Lyle, with a grin.

Chapter Thirteen

War Breaks Out

"Mr. Morris, are these not the best-looking boys?" Smiling at the two soldiers standing in her parlor, Esther rested her gaze on her nineteen-year-old son, now six-foot-three and grinning like a baby in his brand-new blue uniform with brass buttons. Archie was too tall for the Union army standard issue, so Esther had altered the jacket to fit properly at the waist and made the sleeves long enough to cover his wrists.

Standing beside her son and also grinning broadly was Colonel Tom Ransom, or T. E. G. Ransom as he was officially known, now twenty-seven years old and sporting thick, curly red sideburns, then known as "burnsides" after the general who began the style of hair growing down the side of the face to join the ends of the mustache, while leaving the chin bare. Ransom had been put in charge of recruiting and training the Nineteenth Illinois Volunteer Infantry, which had gotten a third of its members from LaSalle County.

"Welcome to Company E," Ransom said, putting a hand on Archie's shoulder. "General McClernand said we are one of the best drilled units in the western army." The Nineteenth was part of the second brigade in the first division, under Ulysses Grant, with whom Will Wallace and T. Lyle Dickey had fought during the war in Mexico. Now Colonel Wallace was organizing the Illinois infantry while Captain Dickey had been put in charge of organizing the cavalry for the state. John Palmer, also a colonel, was organizing the troops in Springfield.

"But where is your pistol?" Ed asked as he inspected his brother's canteen and holster. Archie swatted his ten-year-old brother's hand away from the holster and told him the pistols would be issued when they arrived at their camp near St. Louis.

"Here is a new pencil so you can write to us the details of all the battles every day." Robert also gave his brother several sheets of paper he had rolled around the pencil along with a packet of stamps. He waited to be sure Archie found a safe pocket where they would not get lost. Ed gave his brother a squirrel tail that he had dressed himself and attached to a loop that could fit around Archie's belt.

"You can put it on your rifle stock," Ed said. John had slipped some cash to Archie earlier in the day. Knowing the financial hardships the family suffered with the war, Archie protested at the amount—$100—but John insisted he keep it for emergencies or to buy whatever he needed that the army did not supply. Esther gave her son a slim volume of Ralph Waldo Emerson's essays, with his special favorite, "Self-Reliance." She hoped he would use Emerson's good advice to keep himself safe from harm.

Despite her smile and gracious hosting of the sociable to send the soldiers off, Esther was terrified she'd lose her son. She had nearly collapsed the day Archie told her he had signed up. She had already been upset about his plans to go with Tom on an expedition to the West. Archie had been excited each time he received a letter from Ransom outlining plans to meet in St. Louis and telling him what supplies to bring. "Fool's gold," Esther thought. Her baby brother had died on his expedition to the other side of the continent. The rush west, since the addition of new territories as far as the Pacific Ocean, had the country in a craze. Any number of expeditions had ended in tragedy, and those who made it suffered poverty and hardship. Esther humored Archie but she would put her foot down if he decided to go, because she was determined he would finish his education at the University of Chicago. But she was unable to stop him from interrupting his education to go to war.

"I refused to let him go to the army but he said he would die if he could not," Esther had written to Lotte weeks earlier, describing a kind of breakdown she had. Archie himself was shocked by his mother's behavior. The entire household was on tenterhooks, not knowing what she would do next. Catherine was still part of the household and she and the boys often had whispered hallway conferences on the best way to approach Esther, so as not to further upset her, or on how to induce her to come out of her doldrums. John, when he was not traveling, tended to avoid his wife, not quite knowing what to expect from her.

"She had such a tantrum, I feared for her life," Archie wrote to his cousin Franky, whom he saw more frequently now that she lived in Flint with her father. "She begged and pleaded with me not to go and resorted to the kind of hysterical behavior she abhors. 'If you are not shot your asthma will kill you sleeping in the damp and cold fields,' she told me. I had to remind her that my asthma had not bothered me in recent years. Then she tried another tack, saying I was needed at home, that Bob and Ed are too young to help out. I laughed out loud at that. I said, 'Ma that's an outright lie.' I also had to remind her she was the town's leading advocate for ending slavery and keeping the Union together. She cried and carried on for a week, and for a woman of such stamina and energy, this left her so depleted she looked pale and haggard and much older than her age and she is not yet 50.

"But the worst," he wrote his cousin, "was when she threatened to go to John Palmer and Will Wallace and our other friends in government to have me relieved of my duty. I told her I would never speak to her again if she did such a despicable thing." Archie's letter also included a plea to his cousin to come visit, for he believed his mother might be comforted with some female family companionship.

Now, as they left for the camp, Esther watched these two peacocks, these bold Lancelots, each pat the head of the marble bust of George Washington on their way out the door. It had become a custom, begun shortly after John had bought the bust for their new house fifteen years ago. John would take his hat from the table, tap George on the head, and say, "Wish me luck, General." The boys had picked up the tradition, and so had Esther after some reluctance because it seemed superstitious to her.

All the young men she knew had volunteered to fight. Whether adorned with chain mail or blue wool, men and boys were thrilled, even gleeful, to go to war. She could not understand this willingness to put one's self in front of bullets and swords. This was something only men felt. Women, who knew a great deal about keeping peace in families, would much rather get together around the tea table and talk it over.

Where could they compromise? How else could they look at the problem? Was there an alternative? Like a worm working its way toward the core of an apple, they liked to search for the solutions. Somehow the government, despite the recent laws of so-called compromise, which made it even more dangerous for the Negroes, failed to find a way, but then, there were no women in the government. "We need to vote," she often said to herself and her friends and family, "so we can change the way government does business."

Now these innocent boys were on their way to Hades. There would be terrible losses among her circle. Her own Uncle Jesse had returned from the War of 1812 missing a leg and an eye, not to mention many friends and cousins. In addition to Tommy Ransom, Will Wallace, and T. Lyle Dickey, there were her nephews William Parker and Fred Archibald (who had already been risking his life working on whaling ships), her young cousin Henry Watson, and Damon Stewart, Franky's newly betrothed, along with his two brothers, who had signed up in Michigan. Every day Esther closed her eyes and thanked God that Robert and Edward were too young to go. She kept the boys close to her, half fearing they would run away to join the war, especially Ed, who, like his older brother, thought this was a grand adventure. Unlike some who believed it would be a quick and easy war, Esther knew it would take a long, long time because neither side would give in. Men were stubborn. Just look at her brother Edmund, who made his family suffer for eight years because he would not compromise.

As Esther watched her son, she could not help seeing Artemas and wondering what he would feel now, had he lived to see his son go off to war. She was glad she had taken Archie when he was fifteen to meet his Slack relatives in Vermont, especially Artemas's older brother Allan. One day Tom Ransom had announced that he was going to visit his family in Vermont and invited Archie and Esther go with him. The only time Esther had met Artemas's family was when she escorted his body back to Vermont for burial near his parents. Esther was glad Archie had the chance to meet the Slack family, but on the trip home her son told her simply, "My real pa is in Peru." Esther knew this to be true. Archie and John had gotten along well, since the days when John was courting her at the Watsons' home in Pittsfield. John seemed genuinely pleased to show off Archie to his friends in town, and had spent time teaching him the way the business operated, for the boy seemed curious about everything. John sometimes took Archie with him on jaunts to neighboring towns on business, or to a meeting of the town trustees. "This is my boy, Archie," John would say when he introduced him, and he bragged that Archie, already tall for his age with a sturdy build, could chop firewood almost as quickly as he did.

<hr />

Esther tried to keep her anxiety about Archie at bay by keeping as busy as possible, leaving herself less time to imagine the perils her son faced. To add to her dressmaking duties, she made and sent shirts to Archie and Tom. The advent of the efficient sewing machine meant that clothing was now mass produced in loft buildings in New York City. Home sewing machines were still extremely expensive, but were available on the new installment plans, and John had bought one of the newer models for Esther a few years ago. Unlike the early machine Artemus bought her, Esther could now make the needle go as fast as she liked with the foot pedal that replaced the old hand crank. She and her friends sewed shirts for the soldiers and talked of the latest news, of friends and neighbors they knew who had been hurt or killed. They were always anxious to hear news from soldiers coming home. The Morris home became the scene for sociables the family hosted for returning soldiers, as well as a gathering place for Esther and her friends to collect clothing and food packages to send to the front.

The war provided women with new opportunities for public responsibility and leadership on a larger scale. When President Lincoln established the Sanitary Commission, Esther and her friends took the steamer to Chicago to help organize that city's branch of the commission, which became the most productive in the country. The force behind the Chicago commission was Mary Livermore, a Boston schoolteacher who had come to Chicago in 1857 with her husband, a Baptist pastor. With his support, a housekeeper was hired to care for the family so Mary could devote most of her energies to her job as director of the Chicago office of the Sanitary

Commission. Another woman, Jane Hoge, worked with her, and the pair ran one of the most efficient agencies in the nation. These women organized the Northwestern Sanitary Fair of October 1863 and raised more money than any other group. People came from all over to donate food, silver, and other valuables to be auctioned.

"President Lincoln donated his own copy of the Emancipation Proclamation," Mary told the others with great pride one day in 1863. "It brought $10,000 at auction, and we have now raised $100,000," Livermore proclaimed. It was an enormous sum at the time and inspired women all over the country to organize similar events.

"And, I might add, we had no help or even encouragement from the men in local government," Esther pointed out. The women gathered in the large room at the University of Chicago laughed and nodded. "Yes, much of the nation's work is badly done or not done at all, and that is why we need more women to show what can be done."

"We will put suffrage back on the table once the war is over," Livermore said gravely as the women organized their medical supplies and stacks of clothing, bags of coffee, and hardtack in the new Sanitary Commission office set up at the University of Chicago. "There is even greater interest now," she told Esther and the others. "A great number of women have become soldiers."

"I would prefer there was no need for anyone to be a soldier," Esther said, her heartbeat speeding up as she thought of her son, "but we need to be able to change things." She wished her son was here now, in this university set up by the Baptist Church and where he had studied before he went to war.

The Civil War was also the first time that women found such large responsibilities in the field of medicine. The Chicago Hospital for Women and Children opened in 1863 with Dr. Mary H. Thompson as director. Esther's brother Jesse wrote that Mary Bickerdyke, a Galesburg, Ohio, nurse related to his wife, served in hospitals with western armies in the field to such efficiency that General Sherman said, "She ranks me." Eliza Jane's cousin, Maria Hall, went off to set up her own hospital on another battlefield after Dorothy Dix told her she was too pretty to serve on her staff. For the past year, Dr. Mary Sutter, who had been working in hospitals in Washington and then Chicago, had been boarding at the Morris home. The family had taken in boarders during the war, to provide income, but Esther would gladly have given this doctor a place to live free of charge.

The war's disruption of the Illinois economy had a devastating effect on Morris Mercantile. John had substantial holdings in some of the Illinois banks holding Southern state bonds as backing for their note issues, and these bonds lost their value in the war's first months. Wartime speculation caused prices to soar. Coffee went from ten cents to one dollar a pound. John was a speculator in dry goods and other commodities. With the Southern markets closed, no cotton was going to the New England mills. It was impossible to get clothing and linens for the store. There was much profiteering going on during the war, and John was hesitant to trust anyone he had not dealt with in the past. However, his regular dealers in St. Louis and New Orleans were no longer available. Now he traveled to New York City more often to look for new suppliers, especially those who would grant him credit. His profits were down by nearly half. He had to cut back his staff to only one clerk.

At home they had to let one of their housekeepers go. Esther said she could manage without any, but John insisted they had to keep Catherine, who had been with them for so long. Emily, who had married and moved on years ago, had been followed by a series of young women who remained a year or two before marrying and settling with their own families.

John was a proud man, and for the first time in his life he feared he might not be able to provide for his family or maintain the level of business he had spent so much time cultivating. Other merchants in Peru were suffering, too, and John believed the city itself was on a downward spiral not only because of the war, but because gradually, while the rest of the nation seemed to be moving west, much of the commerce in this part of the state had been moving east into neighboring LaSalle, a city that was becoming the focal point of the county activity, especially at the expanded port facilities there.

"They made the port much bigger at LaSalle," he complained. "Along this outer edge of the county, it has become less attractive, perhaps because the buildings are older." John was not sure. He had helped build the town and now had to watch it die before his eyes. He did not want to relay his fears to his family, but keeping them inside meant he was relieving them with alcohol and drinking more heavily.

"Another mug, Krumm," he said to Charles Krumm at the German beer hall on New York City's Bowery in the Little Germany section. John felt at home with the Germans, knowing so many in Peru, but he did not like New York City. It was too crowded and dirty, and you had to keep your wits about you just to cross a road or find your way through a crowd. He had spent the day at the docks at South Street, finding out what kinds of goods were coming in, what merchandise was available, whether he could ship the goods—and how he would accomplish that—back to Peru. He was sharing an office on Liberty Street, working as a jobber and agent for stores in the West.

As he stared across the bar into the big mirrored wall lined with ceramic German beer mugs molded into faces, he felt as dark as the night outside. Just turning fifty, he had put on some weight. Indeed, his ill-fitting suit was also wearing thin, but he dared not go to a tailor for repair or replacement. He had some extra shirts and collars with him and underclothes in his carpetbag left at a boarding house in the area where he stayed.

The more John drank, the darker became his mood. He had learned in a letter from Esther that Edmund had just opened the First National Bank of Flint and had become the richest man in the state. Edmund had made a fortune in the lumber business that he began with his cronies in that city. John had to admit he was envious. Perhaps lumber, after all, was the real gold of this country, with houses and buildings going up as fast as men could cut down the trees. Esther suggested he ask Edmund for a loan from his bank, but John had too much pride to do that. He would feel inferior, that he had not been smart enough to invest his funds properly. Besides, Edmund was judgmental and he might say no, since he and Esther were not speaking to each other because of the business with Eliza Jane.

He wasn't sure what to think of Eliza Jane. She was very beautiful and spirited, but would probably keep a man off balance. Esther could be difficult and she was certainly opinionated, but he did not mind arguing with her because she could be reasonable except for this voting business. But he had done well to marry her. She provided a good home and was a wonderful mother to the boys, who loved her dearly. He loved her, too, he realized, although he had never told her that. "She knows I love her," he said aloud, and Krumm asked him what he was talking about now.

"Maybe the answer is in the Far West, Krumm." John had been thinking about the West; Archie had been encouraging it before he left for the war. "My oldest boy thinks we must go to the mountains."

"What will you find that you don't have where you are?"

"Maybe the same opportunity I found twenty-five years ago in Peru." He chatted with Krumm, who had come over from the Hesse region of Germany, the same territory that had sent soldiers to fight with the English against George Washington. He told John a story of an ancestor who came during the War for Independence and was shot in the backside by one of Washington's men while he was running from trouble.

"Now the Hessians come here to profit from what Washington helped create," Krumm quipped. "Where else can immigrants achieve so much?"

"Or lose so much," John mumbled. Krumm's young son, Charles Jr., was serving the bar with his father. He was thirteen, the same age as Robert and Ed, whom John missed with all the weeks he had been away from home. His boys had been a great help with the business, stocking the shelves and waiting on the few customers he had now, but he and Esther still insisted they must not work all the time, but devote their energy to school. Ed had spent some time with John in New York, but he had missed his mama and gone home.

"One more, Mr. Krumm," John said as he pushed the beer mug across the bar.

Chapter Fourteen

Archie Goes Missing

"Missing?" Esther said to the young officer who came to the house in early November of 1863, shortly after she had returned from the Chicago Sanitary Fair. "What does that mean? Why can't you find him? Has he been hurt?" Her voice began rising into high registers, and Bob and Ed came running at what sounded like panic coming from their mother. At the sight of the soldier, they, too, felt the panic, thinking he could only be bringing very bad news.

"He went missing at Chickamauga," the soldier said, "but we have no report of his body being found." Esther collapsed against her sons, who struggled to get her into a chair in the parlor. Bob fanned her face with a folded newspaper, while Ed went back to the soldier. He was angry that he had come with such news and had nothing else to tell them.

"Where is General Palmer?" thirteen-year-old Edward demanded, puffing up to his full height, still a few inches short of six feet. "He was at Chickamauga and Chattanooga, and he will know where our brother is."

"General Palmer is the one who sent me," the soldier explained. "Because he knows your family, he wanted you to know before you read it from the lists of those missing that the Department of War issues to the newspapers. He promises he will continue the search for your brother." The soldier paused and looked for a way to change his tone, so as to offer possible hope. "I am Colonel Jack Lutz," he said. "General Palmer expressed his regrets to me that he could not find your brother, that somehow he is at fault for letting him become separated from the unit, but he vows to keep searching." Ed did not know how to respond, so the soldier nodded and walked down the pathway to his horse hitched at the gate. Ed joined his brother and mother in the parlor, and now all three were crying.

When the war began, Archie's unit, led by Wallace and Ransom, had gone with General Grant to Fort Donelson and Fort Henry on the Tennessee River. These were the first important Union victories, but they had cost the lives of more than half the men in Archie's unit. Then it was on to Shiloh and Chattanooga and near starvation at Chickamauga. There were weeks without food until supplies could get through.

Esther dreaded each day's news reports, for several boys she knew had already been killed. Ed and Bob read as avidly as their parents and often fell back from homework to scan the newspapers. Most recently Archie had been transferred to a mounted cavalry unit under General George Crook as part of General Palmer's command. He loved riding, and now Esther cursed herself for getting him that Indian pony when he was a boy.

Esther rarely asked for help. She prided herself on being independent and self-reliant, but Bob and Ed begged her to ask Franky to come and visit. John was away so often, and the boys knew their mother needed more than they could provide. Although always affectionate, the boys began giving her more hugs than usual and asking if they could help her with the shopping or the gardening. She was so overcome by their concern, and the fact that they, too, suffered with worry for their brother, that it made her feel worse. Esther was haunted by the pain in her Grandmother Hetty's face long ago when she told about losing her oldest son.

"Come on, boys, we'll walk into town and see if Charlie needs any help at the store." Walking had always been a way to rid herself of bad feelings, but she knew it would not be enough to get her through this.

—✦—

Franky McQuigg did come for a hasty visit after getting a letter from Robert. Now twenty, Franky was a slim young woman with high cheekbones, dark blue eyes, and a broad smile. She was a bit taller than her sister Libby, but bore a close resemblance to her mother, except for having lighter hair. Esther had often wondered how her brother Edmund felt living with this constant reminder of the beautiful and spirited woman he had married.

"You will be proud to know, Auntie, that I am the first woman to enter the University of Michigan at Ann Arbor," she said as she hugged Esther.

"Oh, that's wonderful. I am indeed proud of you. But isn't your father afraid with so much education you will become one of those unbalanced suffragists he so despises?"

"I have already begun to organize a group." Franky told Esther she believed her father secretly did want women to vote. "Why else is he so proud to pay the tuition of the first woman to enter the university? He is a complicated man, but he has always loved us. I am working on convincing him to forgive Libby and you, too, Auntie." Esther had been to Flint several times in recent years, but while the boys visited Franky and her father, Esther's own visits were to the homes of the Hyatts and Turners, whom she had known in Owego. Edmund seemed quite pleased to welcome her sons, and Esther was grateful for that.

"Oh, I pray for Archie, Auntie, that he is safe somewhere. He will return, I am sure." Esther knew Franky was anxious, too, for she and Archie had always been close. They had many intellectual interests in common and often wrote back and forth about the books they were reading, and when together they would sit up all night talking about philosophy. Esther had once suspected a romantic attachment, until a young man in Flint named Damon Stewart began to court Franky. Esther asked her if she had heard from her mother and from her sister, and Franky said, "They are in constant touch. Libby already has a sweetheart in Los Angeles."

With the help of Seth Paine, a Chicago newspaperman who was also a friend in the suffrage cause, Archie's photograph was printed in the newspapers with a plea for information from anyone who might have seen him. Esther also wrote to Clara Barton, a woman in Washington who had been working in the midst of the Army of the Potomac and who had also been making a list to identify all the soldiers taken prisoner or missing. Young Bob was busy editing all of these letters with his mother's scribbles to be sure the recipients could read them.

Esther was unable to sleep through the night, and as each day broke she believed she could no longer endure the uncertainty. Her nightmares were filled with images of her son lying dead on the cold hard ground somewhere. She struggled to force these images away and replace them with others. Perhaps he was lost in the woods in the South and was walking home, something that could take months. Could he have amnesia? Could he be wounded and unable to talk, like her childhood friend Sidney Camp? Or worse, could he be in a Confederate prison? Perhaps he was in a hospital, wounded, and nobody knew who he was. This last image she felt was possible, and it gave her hope; she spent hours writing frantic letters to all the field hospitals for the Union army.

On a crystal clear morning in December 1863, a tall, emaciated young man in an ill-fitting and mismatched military uniform stepped off the steamer at the dock in Peru. He carried a bundle, a worn blanket tied around his few belongings. The sleeves of his coat were short, and his ungloved, reddened hands protruded. His trousers barely touched the tops of his boots. His blond hair fell to his shoulders, and much of his face was concealed behind an overgrown beard. Under a cap riddled with bullet holes, his bright blue eyes sunk deep into his skull. He walked a few blocks to the Morris Mercantile establishment and ducked his head into the doorway. Despite his ragged appearance and obvious need for food, he could not help but grin at the people standing there.

John Morris was not a demonstrative man, but he stopped breathing at the sight of the apparition in the doorway.

"Archie!" His eyes filled and he quickly pulled his hand across them to cover his emotion.

"I'm home, Pa," Archie said and went to put an arm around John and squeeze his shoulder, when suddenly Ed came into the shop with a carton of goods to be shelved. He dropped the box unceremoniously on the floor and ran to embrace his brother. "Oh, Mama's going to faint when she sees you, she has been so worried all these weeks since you went missing. Where were you? Were you shot?" In his excitement, Ed's voice went suddenly high. He had grown tall, but not as tall as Archie, and his voice was changing. He wore a leather vest over a wide-sleeved shirt that Esther had made for him.

"Well, I will tell you all about my adventures in the rivers and mountains and hollows of Tennessee, but I think I'd best go let Mama know I'm home."

"We will all go," John said, thinking the shock might be too much for his wife. "We will close up business for the day, since there is nobody in the store, and drive you home." As they rounded the driveway to the house, Ed jumped from the carriage and ran into the house, calling, "Mama, Mama, it's Archie, he's home, he's all right! And he is a colonel now, he's promoted. Maybe he will be a general." Robert, who had been doing homework at Esther's writing table near the back veranda, dropped his pen and ran outside to fling himself at his brother.

"Mama's in the garden," he said. Even in winter, Esther was trimming and snipping. She had in mind to trim some greens and give the house some cheer for the season, even though they had all been tense and frantic trying to locate Archie. It was her therapy when she was too restless to read or deal with her dressmaking, which was helping to add to the family income. Hearing the commotion in the drive, she walked toward the house, her cutting shears in one hand and the other carrying a basket of spruce branches. She dropped these and ran into her son's arms and hugged him fiercely and burst into tears. She wiped her eyes on her coat sleeve and stood back, her hands on his shoulders, feeling the bones beneath.

"Oh, you are thin as a rail; you have been starved. Are you sick? Are you injured? How did you go missing? Were you alone?" Esther was so relieved she felt weak, and the boys led her to the house; she could not stop crying.

"Ma," Archie said, laughing, "one question at a time. I am all right." They all went inside then, and while Bob refreshed the fires in the hearths, Ed went into the kitchen to find some cider for his brother, who he knew needed immediate nourishment. John put the horse and carriage away and returned quickly so as not to miss any bit of information.

The family sat around the dinner table for several hours that night. Esther brought more and more food for her starving son, who was delighted to have real food after months of moldy crackers and dried beef that was not fit for animals. John had gone to Munson's Bakery for the fresh pumpernickel bread Archie liked and whatever sweets were still available.

"At Missionary Ridge we got cut off from food supply lines, what they called the cracker line, and we had to go into hiding so as not to become prisoners. The Rebs got two of us, but the rest of us got away," Archie revealed. "We had to butcher one of our horses at Chickamauga so we would not starve," he said later as he told them about the fighting at Chattanooga. "I was with two others from my unit, and we got separated at the river. We kept heading north, hiding in ditches, behind barns, but mostly lying low on the ground. We crossed the Chickamauga so many times we became disoriented and did not know which direction we were going. There are sheer cliffs that rise up at the river's edge and offer little protection from sight," Archie explained.

"You are not going back, are you?" John asked.

"Not to the fighting," Archie said, "but I'm still on duty until next spring. General Palmer got me assigned to train cadets and guard prisoners at Camp Douglas in Chicago." Then Archie laughed. "Our friend Palmer got into a ruckus with General Sherman and resigned his commission. But President Lincoln said, 'Oh, no, you cannot resign,' and he made him the military governor of Kentucky and charged him with keeping that state in the Union." While popular sentiment in Kentucky was pro Union, state officials were pro South in attitude, the real reason a military governor was needed.

Esther and her family had read the accounts of Palmer's heroism there. After Lincoln's Emancipation Proclamation, slaves from all over Kentucky had run away from their masters, sensing the end of slavery. When Palmer heard that thousands of slaves had gathered at the racetrack in Louisville and asked to see him and petition for their freedom, he went immediately in full dress uniform, riding a white charger. He caused a sensation as he mounted the rostrum and announced that the national government could no longer enforce the Fugitive Slave Law, so they were for all intents and purposes free. They broke into celebration. Palmer, so moved by the joy of the people in the racetrack, raised his arms to gain their attention. "As military governor of Kentucky, I free you," he announced. Esther had read of this, and it brought tears of pride to her eyes as well as laughter at such a theatrical act by their friend, who was indeed a bit of a showman.

Archie laughed. "He had no such authority, but he knew that once the act was done it would not be undone. He returned to his quarters, cabled Washington to inform Lincoln and Secretary of War Stanton of his actions, submitted his resignation, and began to pack. Lincoln cabled back and told him to unpack, that the government would support his actions."

"And how did you become a colonel?" Robert wanted to know.

"I think General Palmer had something to do with that," Archie said. "I was no particular hero, but I did the best I could. It was terrible," he said in a hoarse whisper. "I don't want to relive it now," he added quietly, "so if it's all right, I'd rather hear about what you have been doing in my absence." He particularly wanted to know how John had been doing because he knew suppliers must have been cut off, and he felt that to make money now, they might have to go farther west.

After they filled him in on family news they busily prepared to give Archie a good grooming, which he so badly needed. Ed stoked the stove to get hot water for the bathtub. John got his shaving gear so he could get rid of the beard, which Archie had been scratching at all evening. Esther cut his hair, and then they let him enjoy his first night's sleep in nearly three years in his own bed in his own room. Bob and Ed kept peeking in to see if he was really asleep.

"He's snoring," Ed reported. The boys guarded their brother's door like sentries on picket duty, lest he be interrupted from his best sleep in years. They talked with each other outside the door, speculating on what horrors their brother had survived. Finally John told them to be quiet and go to bed.

"Archie will sleep without you guarding the door," John said. "Get into your own beds and tomorrow we will have a family holiday together." Later, as he lay next to his wife in bed, he held her hand while she cried tears of relief as well as sadness at all her son had been through. John didn't know what would have happened to her if Archie had been killed. But they both knew that whatever he had experienced and seen, it would change him forever. The horrors of the battles were vividly described by the newspaper reporters who were on the scene. And Esther and her family suffered greatly from what they read of the war.

The Morris family got another happy surprise a few days later when Tommy Ransom paid a visit. The general was on a short leave before heading back to Georgia to join General Sherman's troops. He had been seriously wounded at Fort Donelson, and Sabine Cross Roads, and again at Shiloh, and Esther worried that he had not had proper time to recover before heading back to battle.

"His wounds are grievous and we worry for him," she wrote to Franky. "He has been shot three times and still patches himself up and gets back on his horse. General Sherman has called him a great soldier. He had lost much weight, and his curly red hair had faded to the color of a corn stalk. However, he told me he was fine and ready after this short leave to go back." Libby McQuigg was also visiting on her way to Flint, and she and Archie and the general went riding into the country. They came home to a feast prepared by Esther.

Before moving on to his duties at Camp Douglas, Archie escorted Libby to Flint. He had been especially anxious to visit her sister Franky, with whom he had exchanged many letters during his two-plus years of war, although he suspected many of them had been lost along the way. He had looked forward to her letters and treasured them. She had been a friend of his heart all of his life, and during these lonely years he had convinced himself that Franky was his true love. He had learned about her engagement to Damon Stewart but was determined to reveal his true feelings, hoping she would change her mind. Franky, however, declined his advances.

"Oh, Archie, you are my dearest friend and I will always love you, but I must marry Damon, who loves and needs me more than anyone right now. He is the man I want to marry," she said. Dejected, Archie reported to Camp Douglas, wondering what he could do to apologize for his assumptions about his relationship with Franky, how he could avoid having her think him a fool. He understood, while listening to her talk of

Damon, how true her love for her intended was. Eventually he gathered up the courage and wrote to her.

"When I returned from the army my soul was contaminated with the approbations of camp life," Archie wrote to Franky. "In a word, I was demoralized. The standard of morals, which I then proposed to adopt are now as odious to myself as they then were to you. I flattered myself then that army life had made no inroads upon my morals however much it might have injured others, and that I was capable of resisting temptations in any form."

Feeling he had done his best, Archie changed the subject to his duties at Camp Douglas. "They are calling it the Andersonville of the North," he wrote. "The Secesh are left to starve and die of disease, they are treated just as inhumanely as Union soldiers had been at the infamous Andersonville in Georgia. Camp Douglas is but a few yards from the university and there have been fears among our officials that an attempt would be made by the Copperheads to liberate the prisoners." He told her that a large number of loaded arms had been found concealed in houses in the vicinity and this revealed a plot. A great many arrests were made the day before the election. "Then, in a ruse to draw out the terrorists, the officers at the garrison were allowed to go to their homes in order to vote the next day. While the military officers appeared to be away from the camp, the army had actually reorganized by arming postal clerks and students. The university was turned into a fort.

"The students of the university volunteered their services and were accepted. A company was organized and your humble cousin was chosen to command them. We drew arms, accoutrements, and ammunition and stood guard duty around the university during the two stormiest nights that we have had this season. It rained incessantly but the young men did their duty cheerfully." The planned escape was prevented.

"General Grant was here last week and we welcomed, processioned, receptioned, levied, and addressed until he was wearied out."

＊＊＊

"We lost many close to us," Esther wrote to Eliza Jane, who now owned and operated a citrus farm in southern California. Tommy, Brigadier

General T. E. G. Ransom, already wounded three times, refused to stop fighting until he eventually died from those wounds on the march through Georgia with General Sherman. Will Wallace, also a brigadier general, was mortally wounded at Shiloh. T. Lyle's son, Captain Cyrus Dickey, was with Wallace when he was shot through the temple and the eye. Cyrus tried to help him, but the rebels were right behind them and he could not stay. All he managed to do was move his friend to safety behind some ammunition boxes. When Wallace was finally carried off the field and taken to a tent to be treated, Martha Ann was summoned and stayed with him for four days until he died in her arms. Jane's son, Fred Archibald, was killed on Little Round Top at Gettysburg. His father, who had also signed up, was killed the year before. Esther was grateful her frail sister had not lived to know this. And Damon Stewart's two brothers were killed. Damon said they had been sent into an ambush because the officer leading their patrol had been drunk.

Six months after Archie's return Esther and her family traveled down the river to Pittsfield to comfort her family while they buried Henry Watson, who was killed at the Battle of the Wilderness. As Esther walked up the wide boulevard toward the Mansion House Hotel, she couldn't help remembering her first visit nearly twenty years before: the image of seven-year-old Henry, his father playfully tussling his hair as the boy stood by his chair, impatiently waiting for Archie to come back to their game of soldiers; the tiny metal figures spread out on the carpet, set up for their various battles and charges and formations. The game of soldiers does not always have a happy ending.

PART III

SOUTH PASS CITY,
WYOMING TERRITORY

CHAPTER FIFTEEN

Heading to the New Frontier

DESPITE HER DETERMINATION TO SEE EVERY INCH OF THIS NEW LAND-scape, Esther kept closing her eyes as the stagecoach rocked and bounced over the rutted mountain trail. She let her muscles go slack and tried to ride with the motion as she recalled another long stagecoach ride nearly twenty-five years ago when, as a young widow with a toddler on her lap, she had headed for what was then the northwest frontier to begin a new life.

Like that earlier time, she faced the unknown with fear as well as anticipation. However, unlike that earlier trip of nearly one thousand miles covered entirely by stagecoach from New York to Illinois, the greatest distance this time, from Chicago to Rawlins in Wyoming Terri-tory, was traveled on the Central Pacific Railroad. She and Ed, now sev-enteen, had periodically walked the entire length of four passenger cars to stretch and offset the monotony of sitting at a window covered with dust. In the vast emptiness of the West, when a town suddenly sprouted alongside the tracks like a mirage, it disturbed the vision, caused the eye to blink. The railroad towns, erected so quickly, looked as if they were simultaneously being built up and torn down, reminding Esther of the backdrop of a stage play she had recently attended at the Astor Place Theatre in New York City.

Now, as the stagecoach wound its way through the Rocky Moun-tains, here called the Green Mountains, the sweet smell of June grass drifted through the windows along with the flies. Esther and her son and the other three bone-weary, hot and dusty passengers rarely felt the cool breeze from the trickling mountain creeks they passed. The hundred-mile coach trip was a three- day journey—they covered thirty miles a day—unless the trail got too rocky and the team of six horses had to slow down. Ed, who had fallen asleep with his head on his mother's shoulder, suddenly jerked awake and slapped a fly from his face. The Frank Starr frontier adventure story he had been reading slipped from his lap to the floor. Ed, who had already explored Pikes Peak in Colorado with his father, was excited about going to Wyoming.

It had been nearly a year since John and Archie left for the territory, and Esther was anxious about their reunion. The move to the frontier was spurred on by her husband and oldest son, who believed there was great opportunity there for all the family. People were moving west in droves, for the war and Reconstruction had left the country's economy in shambles. John had bought into the Park Mining Company while working in a trading office he had set up on Liberty Street in New York City, looking for ways to support the family. However, Esther worried that her husband of twenty-three years, a man who loved trading in fine things, was not cut out to be a miner and she tried to talk him out of it.

"If you must go west, then why not establish a new mercantile business?" she implored.

"Have I not always provided well for our family?" John responded sharply. "We can use the profit from mining to establish a mercantile business later, once the territory is more populated."

"All are going west, Ma," Archie had told her. "It is the only place for growth and opportunity. Here all is stagnant." Esther knew her son, who had invested his own money with John in the mine, was anxious to start a newspaper and believed the new territory was the place to do it. Twenty-five years ago, Peru, Illinois, was considered the new territory, the Far West, and she and John had profited from the vast numbers of people moving there from the East.

John had experienced many fits and starts with business during the unsettled war years. At a low point they had rented out the house in Peru for $200 and paid $60 a month to live in a smaller one. During a hopeful period, John had made some profitable transactions in New York and come home to Peru ready to restore his business and their lives. They eagerly moved back into their home. John retiled the porch roof and repaired the barn while Esther repainted and papered the kitchen. John bought a new walnut and maple sideboard and some handsome dishes and chinaware. Both felt a sense of renewal, which reminded Esther of her husband's pride when they first set up housekeeping and he bought the beautiful woolen carpet for the parlor.

"My husband dresses up every day," Esther wrote to Lotte, describing John's new gray worsted suit and silk brocade vest. Her feelings of hope extended to her marriage, and she told her sister that she and her husband had even gone off alone in the buggy for a day in the country.

In the end, however, John had to auction his merchandise for a fraction of its worth, and the building and land brought less than they would have before the war. The town of Peru itself was fading, with most of the new business taking root in nearby LaSalle. She urged him to move the business there so they could keep their home in Peru. John had been so successful for so long that he could not adjust to what he felt was his diminished status in Peru. He seemed blind to any alternative to going west, where he believed he would be successful. Archie was encouraging the move, as well. Even before the war, it was a dream he had shared with Tommy Ransom, whom all the family had loved and who had stayed with them on his last leave before joining General Sherman in Georgia, where he died of his wounds.

"Don't you think my heart breaks, too?" Esther had argued before the business was finally sold and her husband seemed immersed only in his own distress. "This has been my home for nearly twenty-five years and I care deeply for it. I am too old to be a pioneer again." Her tears spilled out then and through great sobs she said, "I cannot leave my gardens." She had just restored what their tenants had failed to maintain. She nurtured seedlings in the greenhouse before putting them into the ground. She laid out the strawberry bed and a tulip bed that spring and separated currants and gooseberries, put manure on the asparagus bed, and ordered twenty-four new trees to set.

And the boys, who had grown up in Peru, had to leave their friends and their school. Esther felt such frustration with her husband—and with her situation. As a woman without adequate income, she had no choice but to go. Her boys came first and she would never put them at risk by breaking up the family. Archie could be independent and on his own but the twins were not yet old enough. Esther was saddened that unlike Archie, who had completed a three-year course of studies in literature, philosophy, and the sciences at the University of Chicago, there were no funds for the twins to go there. Nevertheless, Esther insisted Robert and Edward complete their education before moving to Wyoming. She found a school in New York City, a new Free Academy, where poor and rich were taught the classics as well as practical matters according to their aptitude rather than financial situation. There was also an Evening High School for Men. If she could educate the boys first, she would go to South Pass City, although reluctantly. John agreed, for his wife had worked out a sensible compromise, which, he admitted, she usually did. Ed wanted to go directly west with his father and big brother, but Esther put her foot down. For her, education was paramount. How she wished she had been able to go to college, but women were sent to school only until age fourteen, and then if they got any further training, it was to be apprenticed in the homemaking arts. Although Esther was better educated than most women of her day, she did it on her own with her great thirst for books. Most of her friends were also better educated than their spouses because of this.

In New York Esther and the boys boarded very inexpensively on the second floor of a brownstone near Park Row with Libby Brown, who had a salaried job at Humphreys Homeopathic Specifics, a company that made popular home remedies. Libby learned to operate a new machine called a typewriter on which she printed invoices and packing lists. Libby, who had often visited the Morris family in Peru, was a smart and spirited young woman. Esther thought her niece's talents were wasted at the homeopathic factory and through her friend Susan Richards she arranged an introduction to Susan B. Anthony, who was opening an office in New York to publish a suffrage newspaper. During her years in Illinois, Esther had made the acquaintance of the famous suffragist through her friends Mary Livermore, Martha Ann Wallace, and Anthony's niece, Susan Richardson.

"Libby has enough order to command a regiment," Esther said to her husband during one of her niece's visits to help them restore the house during the war. "What a pity that such talents should be lost in a woman just at a time when we need generals so bad." Libby was soon hired as private secretary to Miss Anthony. *The Revolution* was funded by George Francis Train, a wealthy eccentric who traveled the country promoting woman suffrage. When funds ran short, another donor came to the rescue. General Levi Chatfield from upstate New York was a major stockholder in the Atlantic and Pacific Railroad and former attorney general for the state. Chatfield's involvement with *The Revolution* proved fortunate for Libby, as well, for the two soon became engaged to marry. What pleased Esther most about the match was the general's acceptance of Libby's own work while also providing the comfortable living her niece deserved. Libby lived very frugally because she sent most of her salary home to Lotte, to help her mother make ends meet. Lotte's husband, Fred, had failed at his mercantile venture and, further impaired by alcoholism, was unable to provide for his family.

The Revolution operated from a small dark office on Front Street in Lower Manhattan, where Robert Morris could be found whenever he was not attending his classes. Esther knew her other sons would never think of working with women at this endeavor, even though they had grown up surrounded by women talking of suffrage and a female doctor had boarded with them in Peru for a year. Robert, however, had always wanted sisters and seemed to thrive in the company of these busy women, who worked so hard to get their newspaper printed. He soon became the official errand boy, taking messages all over the city, sweeping the floor, doing whatever needed doing. Libby convinced Robert to let her teach him shorthand and typing, because those skills were needed in government and politics and would enable him to get a job anywhere.

"Mother should learn typing, too," Robert said, "so everyone can read her letters." Meanwhile, Esther enjoyed the society of *The Revolution*, and during her stay accompanied Libby and some of the other women to the National Woman Suffrage Association Convention in Philadelphia.

—◦—

When it was time for Esther and the boys to leave New York, they made a few stops on the way to Wyoming. There were final arrangements to be made in Peru to ship household furnishings, and Esther wanted to pay a call on the Watsons in Pittsfield as well as the Palmer family in Springfield. Robert had gone from New York directly to Flint to work for two months at the store operated by his cousin Franky's new husband, Damon Stewart. Esther believed her niece had made a good match with this veteran of the Michigan volunteer infantry. Captain Stewart was a thoughtful young man who also loved books and history, and taught Sunday school. He had been wounded in the war, but two of his brothers had been killed following the orders of an officer who was drunk at the time. Damon vowed never to touch alcohol and became an outspoken advocate for reforming the laws regulating the production and sale of alcohol.

When Damon's family faced loss of their farm during the hard times after the war, Edmund bought it back from bankruptcy and gave it to his daughter and son-in-law for a wedding present. Damon loved to spend time puttering around the farm when he was not attending to the store he operated with a partner. Despite her lonely childhood in the boarding school in Elmira, Franky had grown into a warm and contented woman with a rich life. Esther had always loved Franky like a daughter, and was delighted when she gave birth to a healthy baby named Hobart after his maternal ancestors.

When Esther went to Flint to pick up Robert, she had a chance to meet with Uncle Jesse, now nearing eighty, who came over from Wisconsin, where he had relocated years ago to open a store and hotel. She had not seen her uncle in many years.

"Uncle Jesse," Esther teased, "you are as young and fine looking as ever." The black eye patch and the wooden leg seemed to offer no impediment to his enjoyment of life.

"And I could still pick you up, young lady, and sit you on the counter in my store." Esther laughed and stretched up to her full six feet. While she weighed nearly 160 pounds now, 30 pounds more than in her younger days, her weight was well distributed over her frame and she did not appear stout, even with multiple layers of petticoats and skirts. Esther's brother Jesse took his sister on a tour of all the fine houses he had built in Flint while his son Charlie, twenty-one, took Ed on a hunting trip.

Esther had made peace with her brother Edmund, who was now married to Elizabeth Foreman, a widow he met through Judge Hyatt. He never spoke of Eliza Jane, but he continued to make fun of the suffragists. "You will not live to see women vote," he scoffed when the subject of the suffragists came up. Nevertheless, he made it possible for his daughter Franky to be the first woman to enroll at the University of Michigan in Ann Arbor, where she organized a suffrage group and gave regular lectures on the subject.

"Mama is head of the suffrage association in Los Angeles," Franky told Esther, showing off a newspaper clipping. "And she has also written a book about suffrage." Franky gave Esther a supply of handouts from the local suffrage association.

"I'll give one to Mr. Morris and see what he has to say," Esther joked with her niece. "Your cousin Libby Brown has already stuffed my carpetbag with propaganda, but I will add these." Libby had given Esther copies of the sample woman suffrage amendment drawn up for the constitution as well as copies of *The Revolution*.

"In the West is where there is a chance," Libby had urged her aunt. "There is no establishment there with the power to put it down. They want women, decent women, in the West, so men there may be more inclined to give us rights." Esther recalled this was indeed the reason for her own marriage in what was then the Far West.

"She is right, Auntie, you can make a difference," Franky pleaded.

"We'll see what comes," Esther said.

━ ⁓

Now as Esther gazed out the window of the coach, her immediate worry was Robert, whom she had to leave behind in Flint. His health had always been fragile and when he had come down with typhoid fever, Esther insisted he remain where he could get proper medical care. She was not even sure there were doctors in the new territory. Robert would join them when he was stronger. If she and Ed did not go as planned, they would lose the money paid for their tickets.

"Heeyaa," called the driver as he let the whip fly over the team of horses when a sudden uphill climb caused the coach to lurch as they struggled through a hilly pass. Esther and Edward were facing forward, and the uphill climb flattened their backs against the rear wall of the stage. The three passengers opposite Esther and her son were pitched slightly forward, tensed for the next bump, lest they lose their balance. Careful arrangement of legs became customary each time the passengers got into the coach. All of this would seem amusing, Esther knew, when she wrote to her friends and relatives in the East, but right now her body ached, especially her long legs, always the first to feel fatigue, to rebel at physical restraint. She leaned against the side of the coach and looked out the window until the afternoon heat made it necessary to lower the curtain and shade the cab. The flies managed to slip in despite the barrier.

Eliza Houghton, a thin young woman from St. Louis, was going to South Pass to join her husband, the sheriff. The woman was pale and drawn, and although she did not complain, it was obvious the trip had been hard on her. The fourth passenger was a dapper little man who spoke little, jingled the coins in his pockets, and frequently looked at his time-piece. He kept his hat on inside the coach, and Esther had been unable to draw him out in conversation. A gambler, the man probably spent much of his life traveling between mining towns where money would flow. The fifth passenger, a tall, broad-shouldered man named John Kingman, sat stiffly with his knees pulled up close to the seat, his shoulders hunched forward as if his gray wool suit were too tight, his hands gripping the brim of his black hat, which perched almost primly on his knees.

"I recently reminded my son to avoid sleeping in a curled-up position, that being all bent up was not good for his body," Kingman said, trying in vain to find a more comfortable position. After they gazed out the window for a while, Esther said, "I wonder if there's as much gold in these hills as the miners seem to think."

"People are still coming in droves to find it," Kingman replied.

"My brother's friend Frank McGovern made $20,000 right away," Ed piped in. "He discovered Miner's Delight, one of the biggest strikes."

"Mr. Morris and my oldest son have an interest in three lodges," Esther explained, "thirty to fifty feet deep."

"Well, the government geologists are not so sure about the gold supply," Kingman said, "although they are certain there is a vast wealth of minerals here." Esther told Kingman about her youngest brother, George, who had gone to the California gold fields twenty years ago with such hope but soon became discouraged because there was not nearly enough gold to make the thousands who came looking for it rich.

"The desire for riches—and adventure—took his life," she said.

Esther was delighted to have John Kingman as a traveling companion, and they passed several hours talking about politics and books, discovering many common interests. He had lived in Keene, New Hampshire, the same town where Esther's paternal ancestors had lived before migrating to New York State after the War of the Revolution. Kingman had worked with Daniel Webster after graduating from Harvard. Esther told him that Webster's nephew owned quite a bit of land in Peru, where she had lived. Kingman had to leave his wife and five children behind when President Grant appointed him an associate justice of Wyoming Territory's supreme court.

"I miss my family already," Kingman told Esther. "I especially think about the evenings when we sat before a cozy fire popping corn and telling stories." Kingman had been away from his children years earlier when he served in the Civil War. "I didn't see my youngest until he was three years old." He talked with bitterness about the war, and it seemed to Esther as if it had been an affront to his fastidious nature, like poor posture, or improperly fitting clothes. He wore rimless eyeglasses while reading. He had a high brow and receding hairline with light, short curly hair and a very trim beard. A violent bump caused Kingman to groan in mock agony. Ed, who had been practicing tying lasso knots in a length of rope he pulled from his pocket, laughed as Kingman braced himself so as not to slip forward out of his seat.

"Would you like to change seats with me so you are pitched back rather than forward?" Ed offered.

"Thank you, young man, but I hate to think of hitting a bump in the road while we attempt such a maneuver while moving," Kingman replied with a laugh.

At the confluence of the Sweetwater River and Sulfur Creek, the stage stopped for the night. The crude accommodations of the stage station seemed luxurious to Esther after the cramped stagecoach, and she gratefully accepted Kingman's arm as they walked toward the low log building. He had offered his other arm to Mrs. Houghton, but she hurried on ahead. Once inside, it immediately became apparent that the food would be even less appetizing than the noon meal had been.

"More grub," Esther moaned, using the disparaging term for frontier food they had endured for the past week, "and ten dollars a day at that."

"I know there won't be any fresh vegetables," Kingman said. He had been telling Esther that the particular soil of Wyoming, with much alkali, produced very large, good-quality vegetables and he was anxious to try his hand at some farming. He had plans for a sheep ranch, too.

"Ma brought some seedlings from my cousin's farm so that we can have some greens before long," Edward said. "You'll have to dine with us when you crave a good meal. Ma is a wonderful cook."

"Well, she must be to have raised a strapping lad like you."

"My brother Archie is even bigger," Ed bragged. Taller than his twin brother, Ed had grown in spurts recently. He had a broader physique than Robert, more like his father, but his jacket sleeves were far too short at the moment. And Esther knew they would not be able to buy new clothing for some time. As they sat at a table with the other passengers, Ed eagerly watched the dinner being brought to table, hoping there was enough to quell his hunger.

The station keeper, a man with a tanned and wrinkled face, wearing leather leggings and with a damp red handkerchief around his neck, placed a large cast iron pot on the table. His wife removed the lid and gave the stew a stir with a tin ladle before telling them to "help yourself." She swatted at flies with her apron as she placed on the table a tray of biscuits so hard they too seemed to be made of cast iron, along with a crock of lard. Eliza Houghton ate only a biscuit, but Ed and the gambler ate heartily a second plate of the stew of meat and potatoes.

The passengers, keeping most of their traveling clothes on, went to sleep early that night on short, narrow cots in a crude bunkhouse, divided by a curtain to separate women and men. Esther said goodnight to her son and headed to the women's section. The joy of stretching out straight on her back sent Esther instantly into a sound sleep. She rose early enough to go outside and watch the sunrise and breathe deeply of the sharp mountain air. Beyond those high peaks, she thought, was the place she would soon call home, a very different landscape than the one she had left in Illinois. This was arid and rocky with few flowers, although there were some spectacular buttes and rocky outcrops. Some very tall pines were empty of foliage until near their tops, as if they had to first reach up to the sun.

The vastness of the space inspired her to speak aloud lines by an English poet, Joseph Addison, that the vista brought to mind: "Though in a bare and rugged way, / Through devious wilds I stray, / Thy bounty shall my wants beguile."

She turned suddenly, surprised to hear Kingman's voice behind her, completing the verse: "The barren wilderness shall smile, / With sudden greens and herbage crowned / And streams shall murmur all around."

Esther smiled at Kingman, obviously pleased that he knew the poem. "I hope we find those greens and herbage," she quipped. The driver called the passengers and Esther sighed, resigning herself to one more day in the cocoon-like coach. The Morrises and Kingman passed the day reading in turns from *The Celebrated Jumping Frog of Calaveras Country and Other Sketches*, which Mark Twain had recently published. Esther had several copies of the *Atlantic* that she shared with Kingman.

"My brothers and I met Mr. Clemens," Ed boasted to Kingman. "He was a pilot on one of Uncle Parker's riverboats." Mrs. Houghton declined to read, saying she had not the energy. The gambler, with his arms crossed over his chest and his hat pulled down over his eyes, dozed. Late in the afternoon, the stage driver shouted their arrival at the Continental Divide.

"It's from here that the rivers flow either east or west," Ed announced, and told them he had asked the driver to let them know when they reached this place. They would soon reach South Pass City. The passengers leaned toward the windows, waiting to see the town appear.

"General Sheridan is coming here to deal with the Indians," Ed said, referring to the famous Civil War cavalry general.

"My husband said there is no trouble here," the sheriff's wife blurted out nervously.

"The Indians are not as big a problem as the white prospectors," Kingman said, hoping to ease the woman's fears. "There are so many in jail we need extra court sessions." None of them spoke after that, not wanting to arouse the woman's fears. The stage made a steep descent into South Pass City, nestled between two hills. To Esther it looked like one more of those hurriedly constructed towns she had seen along the railroad route through the mountains and plains.

Chapter Sixteen

Setting Up Housekeeping Once Again

"STAGE IS IN!" THE COACH PASSENGERS HEARD THIS SHOUT FROM OUT-side as their drivers pulled the team to a halt. Ed jumped out first and helped his mother and Mrs. Houghton. They stepped out into a dusty, crowded kaleidoscope. Squealing pigs and clucking chickens dodged the horses and wagon wheels. The door of the Grecian Bend saloon opened, and piano music rolled out into the dusk. Archie, followed by John, came through the doorway and Esther wept as she embraced her son.

"Have you grown again?" she asked Archie, smiling up into his tanned face. His sandy hair looked lighter in contrast.

"No, Ma, I'm still only six-foot-three," he said, hugging her and smiling over her shoulder at Edward.

"But look at this fellow, will you," he said, breaking away to put an arm around his brother. "You are not nearly as skinny as when I left." Ed was still four or five inches shorter than Archie, and pummeled him with his fists, pretending to be insulted.

"How have you been, Mr. Morris?" Esther looked into her husband's face, not without some apprehension.

"I'm fine, Mrs. Morris. I hope your trip was not too uncomfort-able?" He looked at her, a little shyly for a moment, then smiled. "I know you hate being cooped up with little leg room." Her husband seemed to have aged, Esther thought. His hair had grown to his shoul-ders and he obviously had not been to a barber in some time. She also noticed stiffness in his gate and assumed his rheumatism was causing him pain. Esther quickly caught Kingman and Eliza Houghton before they left and introduced them to her family. The gambler had already disappeared. Archie told Mrs. Houghton that her husband had been called away to Mormon Gulch to settle a dispute.

"He asked me to take you inside to meet Janet Sherlock, the hotel mistress, who will look after you until your husband returns." Eliza looked crushed, but, anxious to get away from the stage, she followed Archie across the wooden walkway and into the Sherlock Hotel. Kingman chatted politely with John Morris, but sensing a reserve in Esther's husband, he said farewell and went into the hotel.

"As soon as I'm settled, I will invite you for supper, Judge Kingman, and to share our books." Esther waved at Kingman as John went off to fetch the wagon.

As her sons helped unload the stage, Esther looked around her at the crudeness of this town, which seemed to have more saloons than any other type of establishment. Already she missed the fine home she had left in Peru and the ease of taking a riverboat into Chicago to visit her friends. This would not be easy, but she determined that she would not feel sorry for herself. She would make a home here for her family. However, in her heart of hearts, she wanted to sit down and cry.

South Pass City, in 1869, was one of the major frontier cities, ranking with Denver and Salt Lake City, since the opening of the Carissa Lode two years before had brought the gold rush. Nine miles north of the historic Great South Pass of the Oregon Trail, this log and rough board community now had over two thousand permanent residents and served as the Sweetwater County seat. It was a busy, dynamic community where residents had their choice of doing business in at least six general stores, three butcher shops, several restaurants, sawmills, clothing stores, a sporting goods store, a jewelry store, and a furrier's shop. A horse could be left at one of five livery stables. One of the seven blacksmiths would also practice dentistry in a pinch. A gun could be purchased or repaired at the gun shop and used at the shooting gallery if no more serious business arose. A miner lucky enough to "strike it rich" could put his gold in the local bank or ship it home from the Wells Fargo office. Several doctors and lawyers had hung out shingles. In addition to the Sherlock, there were four other hotels and no fewer than seventeen saloons and "sporting houses" all supplied with liquid refreshment by two local breweries and a wholesale liquor establishment.

In the rented back room of the Grecian Bend saloon, where John sometimes worked as a barkeeper, Archie printed the *South Pass News*. The fatigue of her journey kept Esther from showing much enthusiasm for Archie's newspaper, but Edward looked through the latest editions while the family waited for John to return.

"Did you see Sally before you left, Ma?" Archie asked anxiously, offering his mother a seat at his desk. Before she could answer, Ed interrupted.

"Ho, ho, Archie has been pining for his sweetheart."

"Cut it out, Eddie," Archie said good naturedly.

"She's just fine, Archie," Esther said, "although I wonder if she will relish giving up living in the governor's mansion in Springfield to come here." Their friend General Palmer had just become the governor of Illinois. "I have a letter and package from her in my baggage."

"I wish I could send for her now," Archie said. Esther smiled at her son, who had inherited his father's good looks.

"I think you'll have to be married in Springfield," Esther said. "From what Sally says, her brother-in-law will not let her go off to some wild place without seeing that she is properly married at his home." Sally, whose name was Sarah Neely, was the youngest sister of Governor Palmer's wife. Esther knew the young woman had wanted to go to Iowa to teach school, but Palmer, despite his enthusiasm for women's suffrage, still felt women should not be allowed to venture into dangerous territory without a male escort for protection. Esther thought her future daughter-in-law a smart, sensible young lady, but with little education in politics. She was not a reformer by instinct.

Archie had been spurned by a young woman in Carlinville, where he had worked at a newspaper, and Esther knew Sally was not his first love. She had always thought that Franky would have been a true love for Archie but did not think it wise to encourage that relationship, which evolved over their lives with many letters, visits, and philosophical talks. Their friendship cooled down when Damon appeared in Franky's life. But Archie was twenty-seven years old now and very much wanted to start a family. Esther's own marriage to John was not a love match, but they had built a good life together and had grown close, at least until the upheavals of recent years. She hoped that would be the case with Archie and Sally. "We shall not urge her on too fast," Esther thought as she looked around at the crudeness of the town.

The log cabin that John and Archie were just completing was a half mile from the center of town, and Esther decided to walk there so she could see more of the town. She also wanted a chance to talk with Archie alone, while John drove the wagon home with Ed and their baggage.

"It feels so good to stretch my legs," Esther said, taking long strides. "It gets quite cool at night, doesn't it?" she said, pulling her shawl around her shoulders and taking Archie's arm.

"After the oppressive heat of the prairie, it feels good," Archie said, but Esther was sad about the loss of her prairie home and did not wish to argue. This had been a difficult move and she had not wanted to make it, but more than that she wanted her family to remain together.

"Has your pa been drinking?" Esther asked. Archie looked over at his mother's profile, the firm chin, set jaw, large sensitive eyes. He knew he would have to be truthful with her.

"I'm afraid he has," Archie answered quickly. "Working in a saloon is not the best thing for him to be doing, but when we have very meager results with the mines, he hangs around drinking with the miners."

"Well, he was doing that in Peru, too, as the business diminished," Esther said with a sigh.

After a pause Archie said, "I believe he missed you. He has only compliments whenever he speaks of you."

Once they passed the business area, the road was lined with simple wood homes, most built with logs topped with peaked roofs shaped with planks. Theirs was more a log cottage than a cabin, with five rooms and a wide front porch. Willow Creek, named for the stately willows lining its banks, flowed past the back door. Although the bedrooms were small, the main room was spacious with a peaked high ceiling. Esther thought about the gracious white frame house she had left behind with its tall windows, paneled walls, and rolling lawns. And her precious gardens! The small square windows in the log cabin had heavy shutters on the inside as well as the outside, to be bolted in case of Indian attack and to keep the cold winter winds out. Archie had a small cabin adjoining theirs that was not yet completed.

John and Archie had built a long wooden table and Esther counted at least twelve chairs around it. In Illinois the family often had sociables, and they tried to provide as many amenities as possible to make their new home in Wyoming seem less crude to Esther. John's meticulous skill was evident in the square corners and smooth finishing.

"Did you ever think of working as a carpenter, John?" Esther asked as she admired the woodwork. John had been helping the boys unload the trunks and did not answer. "Your work is as fine as Jesse's." She knew John did not enjoy carpentry, but he did like fine furniture.

The "cottage" challenged Esther's imagination. It would take some work, but she would create a home from this dark, rough structure, a civilized oasis in the wilderness. After all, hadn't her ancestors grown up in log cabins? She would begin with flowers. And she asked God to give her the strength to do what she had to do with grace.

Within a week Esther had the house arranged and her garden started. From curtains that had been shipped from Peru, she fashioned new ones wider and longer than the tiny windows, giving the illusion, at least, of larger windows. She arranged the books and picture albums and other small furnishings shipped from Illinois. One crate, she learned, had been stolen, although it was not clear if the deed was done by the local Indians or the miners. The crate had contained clothing along with dishes and linens. She was glad she had carried her mother's Revere candlesticks in her carpetbag with her. She placed them in the center of the table with some new yellow wax candles.

Archie and John had dug a well and an outhouse—for there was no indoor water closet here—and there was water in the stream to use for the garden. Ed helped his mother lay out the garden, digging rows for vegetables, herbs, and flowers. Esther was glad she had brought seeds with her, for the lack of variety in the stores discouraged her. She would write to Damon to order more. On her second day there, Esther, who always loved to take long walks, explored a few miles of the mountain woods and found some wildflowers and berry branches to decorate the house with. She was warned to carry a gun, as the area was not safe from Indians until the army sent more troops. She had never been afraid of Indians, as the Senecas in New York, and those in Illinois, had always been peaceful. It was her feeling that if she carried a gun, they would be more inclined to give her trouble.

"Ma, you need a gun for the wildlife, the snakes and wolves," Archie had insisted. Esther gave in, but the weight of the gun slowed her down. She decided to explore again, this time with Ed and the wagon, and dug up some bushes and two small pine trees to plant near the house.

Being naturally curious and creative by nature made it easier for Esther to adapt to change. She told herself she must make the best of the situation and went around to the shops and introduced herself to her neighbors. The Morris home quickly became a gathering place for neighbors who were hungry for news from the East and lively conversation. The population was largely single men, rough men, so the few families eagerly welcomed Esther. Congenial evenings were spent around the table until the lamps burned low. Talk centered around the politics of the new territory, the railroads, the vigilantes and the Indians. Esther had been telling them about her nieces, Franky in Michigan and Libby working at *The Revolution*. Her head was full of the suffrage propaganda when she arrived, and Esther, by now a savvy politician, was soon nicknamed "the Six-Foot Suffragette."

Less than two months after Esther had arrived, Archie came home with a dispatch from Cheyenne. "Look, Ma, the first territorial election is set." Governor John Campbell had announced that the first territorial election would be held on September 2. Archie gave the paper to Esther so she could read the details.

"I must go next door and tell Bill and Julia Bright about this. I think he is planning to try for a seat in the legislature." Bill Bright was a shy, unassuming man who looked older than his forty-six years. While he had no formal education, his wife did, and Bill freely acknowledged that she was his intellectual superior. Julia was from a wealthy Southern family and was twenty years younger than her husband. Bill, too, was from

Virginia but had served with the Union army because it was important to keep the Union together and he hated slavery. Bill came to South Pass City when gold was discovered in summer of 1867 and opened a saloon at the busiest intersection of town. The following year, Julia arrived with their baby to join him.

"What are the chances of getting suffrage legislation through?" Esther asked as soon as she announced news of the coming election date. "Oh, I haven't given it much thought, Mrs. Morris," Bill replied with a gentle drawl. The full brush of a gray mustache covered most of his mouth, muffling his speech and making it necessary to listen closely. "I'm concerned first with the lawlessness, getting rid of the vigilantes," he said. "There was a hanging recently when some miners accused another of being a claim jumper."

"But if you become our legislator," Esther insisted, "you would be in a position to see to all of these things, including suffrage."

"Do you guarantee I will be elected?" Bill asked, his eyes twinkling.

"Oh, Bill," Julia said, coming to her husband's side, "you know you would be elected. People here respect you. They feel confident in you."

"I think we can consider the deed done if you announce yourself before the voters of South Pass," Esther said. "And I know that you are sympathetic to women's suffrage. You told me yourself that if the emancipated Negro could vote, why not your wife and your mother."

"It won't be that easy," Bill said, fishing in his pocket for his pipe. "The legislature will probably be Democratic and our new governor, like President Grant, is a Republican. He may not approve the bill, and the work of the legislature would be in vain."

"Who would oppose you in South Pass?" Esther asked. "This is a chance to do what's right. My brother told me when I left his home in Michigan that I would never live to see women vote. I will see it," Esther said firmly. She and Julia walked over to the table and sat down. Bill brought some paper and pens to the table, sensing that Esther was about to draw up a logical battle plan, as a general would do before entering the field. She gave Bill a copy of the actual proposed amendment to the United States Constitution that she had gotten from Libby so he would have the wording to use for the Wyoming legislature.

"Why don't I have a sociable, perhaps an afternoon tea, before the election so we can make everyone understand how important it would be to put this into the legislature? In my own house Bob and I are the only outward proponents, but I think the other boys and Mr. Morris would go along with it if they see it will happen," Esther said. "They are all Democrats," she added, laughing.

Esther did not mention her "campaign" to her husband, knowing that he would oppose it, or worse, express no interest. He had never been sympathetic to woman's suffrage, although he admitted he could think of no reason why women should not vote. Even though he still resented her annual trip to the polling place with him, he had ceased to argue about it years ago, convinced that his opinion was of no concern to his wife. From the people Esther already knew, and that included most of the merchants, miners, and professional people in town, Esther concluded that most of the women and about half of the men favored suffrage. She had given out some of the brochures she'd gotten from Franky and Libby, but sparingly, for she did not have enough to be wasteful giving them to people who would toss them aside or make fun.

"Let us put this issue in everybody's minds so when the election is held, they will vote for the candidate who favors it," she said to Kingman when he stopped one evening for supper.

"Why not be sure that all candidates favor it?" Kingman said, leaning back in his chair. Esther's eyes widened with interest. She knew Kingman was very much in support of woman suffrage.

"But isn't it Captain Harry Nickerson who is planning to oppose Bill Bright?"

"I think so," Kingman said.

"He is always making jokes about suffrage," Esther said. "I don't think he considers it seriously."

"Have you talked with Mrs. Nickerson?" Kingman asked.

"I don't see her often," Esther said. "She is timid about company."

"Perhaps," Kingman said, "but her sister, Anna Kelsey, is studying medicine and planning to open a practice in South Pass. I think she might influence the Nickersons. Would they deny her the vote at the same time they say she is capable of being a doctor?" Esther found the

Nickersons amiable but noncommittal when she called on them. She decided that before the election she would indeed hold a tea party in her home and invite both candidates to declare themselves on the issue of women's suffrage.

——— ———

On an evening in late June, the Morris family gathered at the depot to meet Robert's stage. Esther was anxious to see him, hoping he had made a full recovery and that the journey had not weakened him again. But when he stepped out of the coach, she saw immediately that her son was feverish and pale. She quickly took him in her arms and felt his brow and noticed how weak he was. John helped him into the wagon so they could get him home where he could lie down. For the next four days Robert's fever raged and the family gathered all their funds, fifty dollars, to get the town's best doctor to care for him, hoping whatever medications and treatment he offered would work. Esther was frantic, berating herself for allowing him to come west so soon. She fed her son large quantities of soup and cornmeal and pots of tea, and gradually Robert began to get the color back in his cheeks. He seemed to respond well to the dry mountain air. One day, sitting up in bed, he began looking around.

"It is a fine building," he said to compliment his father and brother. "I promised Franky and Damon I would send them a sketch of our new home on the frontier," he added after filling them in with all the news from Flint. He regaled them with stories about the fancy chickens his new cousin Damon was raising. "He won't let anyone eat them until they are old and tough."

With Robert's health restored, the family settled in, and with their natural habit of industriousness, they soon had many jobs bringing money into the home. The chief justice for the territory, John Howe, also from Illinois, appointed Archie chief clerk of the territorial court because he was the best educated person in town. There were so many court sessions that soon Robert became his assistant, writing up documents for Archie and the lawyers.

"Criminals are sent to jail in Detroit and today a man got five years," Robert wrote to Franky. "Ed is keeping the books for the sawmill that

Archie is operating, and yesterday Archie's pony was stolen by Indians." The boys bought Esther a washing machine and promised her a new sewing machine so she could make them all some new shirts and carry on with the dressmaking business she had begun in Peru. The mining interests were paying some money, but not what they had expected.

The territory had attracted many newspaper men, and Archie had some competition for his *South Pass News* from Nathan Baker and James Stillman. Governor Campbell, as well as territorial secretary Edward Lee, published newspapers in Cheyenne, as did Jim Chisholm, who had worked at the *Chicago Tribune*. The Morrises' old journalist friend Seth Paine from Chicago was visiting with his wife and writing a series of articles for the *Tribune*, which the Morrises got regularly in the mail. Paine had been involved in many suffrage activities in Chicago, where Esther had first made his acquaintance. He was also a vegetarian and a proponent of spiritualism, two movements that were gaining wide popularity.

After filling in Franky with family news, Esther sent money for an order of seeds: beets, turnips, long radishes, onions, corn, peas, and rutabagas. "The cabbages are up and I have a hanging basket of wildflowers in my window," she wrote.

"I will keep you posted on the woman question."

Chapter Seventeen

The Tea Party

The tea party was set for the Sunday afternoon before the election. Esther had spent Saturday baking cornbread, molasses cakes, and a Sally Lunn. She prepared chicken pudding from the wild sage hens the twins had caught. The Sherlock store had just gotten a shipment of China tea, and Esther sniffed the fragrant leaves as she tied them into muslin bags for the pots. She had borrowed several teapots from her neighbors in order to provide a sufficient amount. Borrowed chairs were also collected. The whole family got into the flurry of activity on Sunday afternoon, and as Esther issued last-minute orders, the boys carried trays of cakes and fresh breads from the kitchen to the long table in the main room.

Esther retired to her bedroom for a few minutes to rest and tend to her appearance. Looking in the mirror above her dresser, Esther now combed the curls around her face and put on the silver and onyx earbobs that John had given her on their first anniversary. She still felt sad remembering the early years when she and John had been partners and good friends, pioneers together. "Are we too old to do this again?" she wondered. She recalled their romantic carriage ride into the countryside when they were fixing up the Peru house, hoping that they were on a profitable footing once again. Esther could be energized with new interests, especially the thought that suffrage might work here, but John seemed discouraged that mining was not more profitable. He spent too much time brooding, and drinking while he did this. Esther hooked a fresh wildflower from the riverbank in her collar ribbon, removed her apron, and fluffed the skirt of her blue and white striped lawn dress, shaking away her frustration with her husband.

Experience had taught Esther that it was not a good idea to get so involved in her preparations that she ignored John, so she went out to the porch where he was polishing his boots. She noticed his feet had swollen and he sometimes had trouble getting his boots on. Although he was willing to help with the heavy work, it was not of his own incentive, but more a duty to her and the boys. John had attempted to brush his hair down. Since it had turned gray, it was thicker and less manageable, giving him a wild look if he didn't keep after it. Esther patted the hair on the side of his head affectionately.

"That just doesn't want to stay down, does it?" she asked. She sometimes thought John resembled the infamous John Brown, but she never told him that.

"Is your party all set?" he asked, ignoring her hand. He bit the tip off a cigar quickly, concentrating on controlling the tremor in his hand. She wanted to ask John if he'd like to do something, but she thought, "No, let him be useful on his own. It must come from him." Esther was tired of thinking up ways to make John feel needed.

"How's this, Ma?" Robert called from inside. Esther smiled and turned into the house, expressing delight with the preparations. The table was a feast for the eyes as well as the palate, with flowers and fancy breads and cakes. Ed had caught some whitefish in the river, and Esther prepared it with a cream sauce and surrounded it with trays of dried fruits, and fresh vegetables that she bought from Jefferson Woffard, a young Georgia Negro who farmed outside of town. She added some early lettuce and parsley from her own garden. Archie carried in a bowl of fresh butter he had gotten from a neighbor on his way home from church services, which were held in the Magnolia Hall billiard parlor. John came in from the porch with Janet Sherlock, who had arrived with some pies she had baked.

"Can I help bring Peter over?" Robert asked Janet. Peter was Mrs. Sherlock's seventeen-year-old son who had been blinded in a mine explosion several months ago. Archie had spent time with him after the accident, hoping to help the boy overcome his handicap. He read to him and took him on walks so he could get his exercise. Edward and Robert, happy to find a companion their own age, befriended Peter as soon as they arrived and had even managed to make him laugh again. Janet, who had been a widow for two years, was grateful to the Morris family. With their help she was able to convince Peter to work with her in the store, and learn how to count out the goods and money for customers. The twins made a game of teaching Peter to enjoy using his other senses to get around. Riding out, they learned to identify the scent of the grass and trees, the sound of birds and animals. They especially learned to avoid rattlesnakes.

Young Franny Gallagher arrived with her husband, Patrick. She embraced Esther and then walked over to a side table where Esther had lined up some of her books. "I've brought back your *David Copperfield*," Franny said, replacing the volume neatly with the other Dickens books, Esther's leather-bound collection of Scott's Waverly novels and her beloved Scottish poets, as well as books by Gail Hamilton and Harriet Beecher Stowe. She had very much enjoyed *Uncle Tom's Cabin* but felt Mrs. Stowe's later books were less compelling.

"I loved his Mr. Micawber," Franny said, the Irish brogue still apparent in her lilting voice. "He reminds me so much of my Patrick, always somethin' appearin' to be just around the corner. How I wish I could speed things up a bit." Franny's husband put his arm around her shoulder and led her toward a chair.

"Don't be worrying yourself, Franny, and in your condition you should be sittin' down after that ride from the cabin." Patrick, a tall, dark-haired, thirty-two-year-old army major, had been "bob-tailed" from his command of Fort Bridger and was still trying to clear his name. He had been falsely accused of allowing men to leave their post during guard duty. Esther found him an intelligent and entertaining companion after the initial barrier of polite reserve was broken down. Franny had set out alone from Ireland at sixteen and found work as a maid in Boston. She taught herself to read and write and fell in love with Patrick as soon as she met him at a church social. No sooner did they meet than the war broke out and he enlisted. It was Franny's bright, loving, and sometimes misspelled letters that helped him endure the war.

After the Fort Bridger episode, they built a small log cabin near their stake and Franny worked the mine with Patrick. It was a lonely life but Franny loved having her own home, even so humble a cabin. She had carpeted the floor with buffalo skins and hung a protective canvas under the rafters. Now that she was expecting their first child, Patrick had joined Henry Black in his law office on Eddy Street and the Gallaghers had decided to look for a place in town.

Sheriff Houghton arrived with Eliza, who looked no less nervous than she did during the stagecoach trip three months ago. The Brights arrived and chatted amiably with the Nickersons. Major Noyes Baldwin and his wife, Josephine, came, followed by Jefferson Wofford and his wife. Nathan Baker, editor of the opposition newspaper, arrived and cuffed Archie on the arm, assuring him that his own report of Esther's tea party would be better than Archie's.

"Your report can hardly be objective," Baker said to Archie. "After all, your ma's a Republican and you're a Democrat, like Mr. Morris." Frank McGovern arrived with two other miners who lived outside the town. They had been frequent visitors at the Morris home and liked Esther's straight talk about politics, as well as her good humor.

John Kingman presented Esther with a tin of rock candy. Soon the house was filled with laughter and lively voices. Most of the men were standing in both front rooms, leaving the chairs for the ladies. Some were forced to stand in the doorways of the bedrooms and others on the porch, leaving the main door open so they could hear.

Esther and Robert passed around trays of food and Esther poured the tea, which she had brewed strong enough to satisfy those used to more rugged refreshment. She had a compliment and a concerned question for every guest. Most of the men and some of the women carried guns but left them on the porch. Several Springfield rifles leaned against the house, part of the supply the governor had delivered to South Pass residents to protect themselves against Indian raids. Three months before, three miners, including Mountain Bill Rhodes, had been killed by an Arapaho war party. Esther refused to carry a gun, but she did put a rifle in the wagon when she rode any distance from town. After all, this was wilderness and home to rattlesnakes, mountain lions, wolves, and bears.

Church Howe, a federal marshal from Massachusetts who had been smoking on the porch, walked inside with John for some food. Howe's heavy-lidded, deep-set eyes gave him a sad and sleepy look. His dark hair had receded, making his face seem longer than it was.

"Maybe we should put a guard on those guns, John. Never know what Ben Sheeks might do with them if he shows up," said Howe, one of the few friends John had in South Pass City. The two often spent hours playing billiards or auction pitch at the Grecian Bend. Sheeks, a young bachelor lawyer, had been outraged at the idea of Esther's tea party and had tried to organize a boycott.

"Will she have squaws and whores voting, too?" he asked during a heated conversation in the Miner's Delight saloon. Sheeks, who said he, too, was going to get elected to the legislature, had printed handbills urging all residents to boycott Esther's party. "Look at her husband," he told a storekeeper. "Would he spend all his days and nights in his saloon if his wife was womanly? He has been badgered by her insistence on equality. The Morrises are a good example of what will happen if women get involved in politics."

Esther was glad Sheeks did not show up, although she was not worried about his slander. Those who knew Esther were not influenced by Sheeks's lies. Her kindness and generosity had proven him wrong. Esther's friends felt that whatever was wrong between Esther and John Morris had begun years ago and would not be solved by Esther's acquiescence from her political beliefs. Her sons, too, were a testament to her womanliness.

Captain Nickerson, chatting with Franny Gallagher and Jim Stillman, who had opened a school in South Pass, said, "Well, I understand you women are not satisfied to be our superiors. Now you want to be our equals." He laughed as Franny squinted up at him.

"Aha," she said with a smirk, "and was it not you who said we should have a female schoolteacher so that we would not have to pay such a high salary?"

"Now why would you say that?" Stillman asked Nickerson, his voice rising. "You know we need more women in the territory. We should encourage them by giving them equal status."

"Besides," Franny said, "you wouldn't want the Utah or Colorado Territories to do it first, would you?"

Esther rapped a spoon against a cup, determined to get on with the day's business. "Boys, boys, behave yourselves. Let's not forget what we came here to do." Nickerson stopped talking and with a flourish bowed from the waist.

"Madam," he said, "we are at your service." Guests found a place to sit or stand and waited for Esther to continue.

"There are present two opposing candidates for the first legislature of our new territory," she said. "One of them is to be elected, and we desire here and now to receive from them a public pledge that whichever is elected will introduce and work for the passage of an act conferring upon the women of our territory the right of suffrage."

"Hear, hear," said John Kingman, raising his cup in the air. The people seated around the table rose and applauded Esther and then turned to Bill Bright. Appearing cautious, perhaps even hesitant, Bright spoke slowly. When he finally began, however, his convictions were firm. He looked at Julia before he spoke, seeking reassurance in her confident smile.

"I have never thought much about it until recently, nor have I been converted by a woman's lecture or newspaper, for I never heard a woman speak from the rostrum and never read *The Revolution*." Robert held up a copy. "Until young Robert here forced it on me," he added with a laugh.

"I know that this is a new issue and a live one, and I know there are many reasons for promoting it—some of them false. But I have a strong feeling that it is a just cause and for that reason alone I promise to use all influence in my power to have such a bill passed." Julia stood up suddenly during the burst of applause and kissed her husband on the cheek. He blushed as he sat down beside her.

"Well, Captain Nickerson?" Esther said. Nickerson sauntered over to the head of the table, his hands holding his coat lapels. With his shoulders thrown back, he addressed the party.

"Ladies and gentlemen, when I am elected—and I will be elected—I will introduce a bill for suffrage and see that the women in our territory are the first in the world to brandish the ballot for the betterment of mankind." As he started to smile at the applause, Nickerson added a thought. "For womankind, too."

"Hear, hear," Kingman said again. With his cup raised, he added, "and to Esther Morris, who can inspire the world." Robert Morris, who had always clapped the loudest, looked over at his father, who was standing near the door, examining the end of his boot. When Morris caught his son's glance, he turned slowly and walked outside, down the steps, and toward the road to town.

"Now, gentlemen," Esther said, "we must discuss how such a law will be worded. For not only must we vote, but we must be able to own property, and hold office, and be paid salaries equal with men.

"But first," she said, "let's have some more tea."

—◦—

The Democrats won by a landslide in this anti-establishment town, and although Esther was a Lincoln Republican, she was relieved that Bill Bright, a Democrat, had beaten Captain Nickerson, a Republican. She had more confidence in Bright's promise to introduce a woman suffrage bill in the territorial government. The victory of Ben Sheeks, another Democrat, might be a stumbling block, however. She knew he would oppose any such legislation. Then there was the final hurdle. Would a Republican governor approve legislation introduced by a Democratic legislature?

Six weeks later, when the new lawmakers met in Cheyenne, a town only slightly more populated than South Pass City, they proved surprisingly solicitous to women. A few ladies were permitted to sit in on the legislative sessions, a privilege usually reserved for men with political connections. Bill Bright was elected president of the Territorial Council, and when he introduced the woman suffrage bill, it passed with little opposition on the same day, as if they were talking about adding an hour to the post office schedule. In the Territorial House of Representatives, Ben Sheeks and some of the others fought it for a few days, dragging up the usual arguments. When Sheeks insisted such a bill include the words "colored women and squaws," instead of simply "women," he was overruled. He succeeded only in raising the voting age from eighteen to twenty-one.

Some would say later that the legislature passed the bill as a joke, thinking the young Republican governor would never sign it. Governor Campbell certainly let it be known that he did not want to sign it, although he had already signed bills giving women the right to own property, hold office, and receive equal pay. But bringing woman suffrage into the territory would only add to the grief he was already getting from Washington. They warned him Wyoming would never become a state if woman suffrage passed. He was under great pressure to straighten out the "Indian mess" and build schools, jails, and hospitals. But Campbell, an earnest young man, had grown up with suffrage talk in Ohio. He remembered being told to sit still on a church bench while his mother lectured on the subject.

The territorial secretary, Edward Lee, a charming and handsome bachelor, was committed to the suffrage cause. In fact, he had introduced such a bill himself, as a member of the Connecticut legislature two years before. The six-foot-two Lee, with two older sisters to spoil him in his comfortable Connecticut home, had figuratively and literally been the fair-haired boy. But Governor Campbell wasn't too happy with Lee, a man he thought drank and talked to excess—and was much too fond of women.

Esther was not able to go to Cheyenne. At the time, it cost forty dollars simply to get to the railroad in Rawlins, one hundred miles away, then another hundred miles to Cheyenne. But Amelia Post, a suffragist in Laramie, visited the governor, making a plea for him to sign the bill. The governor remained unmoved, even though he frequently played whist with Mrs. Post and her husband, who was a territorial delegate to the United States Congress and speculator in mines and cattle. It was John Kingman, finally, and Chief Justice John Howe of Illinois who succeeded. They went to the governor's drafty apartment at the Ford House on the evening of December 9 and talked to him for hours as the snow rattled the window glass. They would not leave until the governor had promised to sign the bill.

Esther knew that the two judges believed strongly in woman suffrage, but she wondered if they had actually succeeded in changing the governor's mind, or if it had finally come to a political deal. The governor, called "Little Johnny" by his detractors, had been making enemies in his own party. Perhaps Kingman and Howe offered him support in exchange for his signature on the landmark legislation.

Campbell promised Kingman and Howe he would sign the bill, but it was not until late the next day that he finally got around to doing it. He would take a lot of protest from Washington, although he expected President Grant was in favor of suffrage. Thus, on December 10, 1869, Wyoming women won the right to vote.

Kingman wired the good news to Esther before he left for his holiday visit in the East. What a joyous celebration at the Morris house, and as soon as Bill Bright returned from Cheyenne, Esther and Robert paid him a visit to thank him for his efforts. Esther could not stop beaming. She went home and wrote letters to all the family, while her son immediately wrote it up for *The Revolution*, spending his entire week's salary having the story telegraphed to New York City, so excited was he to let them know. It was like Christmas for the rest of the month.

The following weeks were hectic and exciting for the family and for South Pass City.

"Buildings going up and shafts going down," Esther wrote to Franky. The winter had been mild so far, and now the January "thaw" had Esther dreaming about her spring planting. She asked Franky to send seeds as soon as her supply was in.

"I'll need lettuce, radish, turnip, corn, rutabagas, peas, and onion sets," she wrote, "any seeds that come from a climate like yours, and can hold up under the frost should do well here . . . if they can later stand the grasshoppers!"

Franky had been lecturing on woman suffrage in Michigan and was eager to hear more about the cause in Wyoming so she could talk about it.

"This is no child's play," Esther wrote. "The Republican governor of Colorado has asked the Democratic legislature there to introduce such a bill. And it looks like Utah may get it, too. You say you expect suffrage organizations here, but I'll tell you, we don't need them. Here the men have a pioneering spirit. Many are liberal and well-educated. They are not afraid to let us share equally in the burdens and the rewards. Mr. Morris has been decidedly quiet about the issue of late, since it was his own Democratic party which brought it about. Now he assumes it must have some merit. But some from both parties are for it and against it."

Later, as Esther stepped into the busy new post office building on South Pass Avenue, she shook the dust from her skirts and looked around smiling.

"How do you like your new building, Mr. Dixon?" she asked, breathing deeply the spicy scent of fresh pine lumber. The young postmaster hailed her. He was called Alphabet Dixon because he had so many initials (G. W. B.) before his last name. Of course, the nickname could have come from his daily work of alphabetizing all of the mail and putting it into the proper cubbyholes of the post office.

"Hello, Mrs. Morris. Your new copy of *The Revolution* is in. Perhaps this one has Robert's story about our woman suffrage law?" He pulled a stack of letters and papers from one in a long line of cubbyholes behind him and gave them to Esther, waiting to see if she would open up the newspaper so he could have a look. Dixon knew that Esther's niece sent the suffrage newspaper from New York City, where she worked as secretary to Susan B. Anthony. It was the custom on the frontier to share newspapers from the East. *The Revolution* was as popular as the *Chicago Tribune* and *Harper's Weekly*, enjoyed both by those who shared its ideals and those who found it laughable.

Esther put her parcels down on the smoothly sanded counter and unwrapped the paper, attracting the attention of the calico cat sleeping in one of the cubbyholes. The January 13 *Revolution* did indeed carry Robert's story, crediting Bill Bright with bringing suffrage to Wyoming. They used all of Robert's exposition on "the glorious cause" and the "rights and freedoms of women in Wyoming" and concluded with his invitation. "I join Horace Greeley in urging the girls to come to this higher plain of Human Rights as well as to have a home in our high, clear, mountain atmosphere," Robert wrote.

"Sounds like you would like to see more women in the territory," Dixon said, winking at Robert, who lowered his eyes. Dixon folded the paper and returned it to Esther, who was holding the cat, which had come over to paw at the newspaper.

"We all would," Esther quipped. "It would give us women some rest from all the dancing we must do at the sociables." She put down the cat and picked up her things. "Please tell Mrs. Dixon to stop for tea one day soon."

Outside, Esther paused while a string of lumber-filled wagons rolled by, then continued on with her errands, frequently stopping to chat with neighbors and friends, enjoying the easy camaraderie of these busy pioneers. Walking home, Esther reflected on her new feelings of well-being. She felt confident that her family's fortunes were on the upswing again, after the years of struggle following the war. The fears and uncertainties she felt when she was about to embark on this new adventure had subsided somewhat. Pioneering had renewed the spirit of cooperation in her family, bringing them closer, with each of them helping the other to manage their many enterprises.

"All the family is helping each other," she wrote to Lotte. "Business has been good all winter. A church and school are planned and all dry goods we need are at the store where Robert is working. The family is getting along well, helping each other. We expect more mining in summer," she added. "There was an Indian raid in April and Archie went after them. There is [a] possibility of Indian war."

While they had been in town, some of the merchants had given Esther and Robert their advertising copy for the next issue of Archie's newspaper. Now, before going home to fix supper, Esther went into Archie's cabin, next door to her own. Archie had been away with Ed and twenty other men on a hunting trip, so Esther and Robert had been managing his affairs, while John looked after the sawmill Archie operated.

An old Washington handpress, made of heavy cast iron and shaped like a very tall spider, took up most of the front room in Archie's two-room cabin, which had become the newspaper office since a fire destroyed his rented office at the saloon. Stacks of books, mostly philosophy and the classics, were piled around the floor and window ledges. There were three tables in the cabin, each covered with papers and books, pans and dishes. Looking for a logical place to put down the papers in her hand, Esther shook her head at the disarray, recalling how often she had urged her son to create some system of order. She realized it was one cause she would never win.

"No wonder he says he wants a wife," she said aloud as she and Robert left by the back door. Picking up a shovel from the porch, she strode out to the garden to dig up some potatoes, while Robert went inside to create order by writing to Franky.

Chapter Eighteen

Madam Justice of the Peace

JOHN KINGMAN JOINED THE FAMILY FOR A SUPPER OF FRIED CHICKEN, mashed potatoes, and biscuits, with some tomatoes Esther had preserved from the summer crop. Kingman entertained them with news from the East, and Robert updated Kingman on the need for an extended court session because the calendar was so crowded. He had been handling his own job as deputy court clerk, as well as Archie's job while his brothers were away with the hunting party. While they talked John went to get some cigars.

When they were about to dig into blackberry pie and coffee, Kingman suddenly asked, "Esther, how would you like to be a judge?"

"I've always been involved in men's work," Esther said while pouring coffee, "so it would be nothing new."

"I'm serious," Kingman said. "Now that women have the right to hold office, it's time we put it to the test. Don't you agree? I've mentioned this in Cheyenne and there's no opposition. In fact, Eddie Lee and John Howe are all for it." As Esther looked at Kingman with real interest, he continued. "You would be filling the vacancy left by Jim Stillman, who resigned to spend more time on his other enterprises."

Esther was feeling the tug of interest, an invitation to adventure, but John suddenly snorted, "The wild bunch in this territory wouldn't stand for it."

"And why not?" Kingman asked, accepting a cigar from John. "Everyone here respects your wife. There are few people I'd trust more than Mrs. Morris to dispense fair and equitable justice."

"What does she know about the law?"

Esther looked sharply at John, struggling against her indignation. "And what does Mr. Stillman know?" she retorted. "He's a former newspaper man and a miner, whose intelligence has been considerably blunted by alcohol, I might add."

Kingman sipped his coffee before responding to John. He didn't want his proposal to cause problems for Esther, but he was confident she could work around John in her own way.

"She doesn't need to be a lawyer in order to qualify, John," he said reasonably. "Strength and intelligence are more important in giving an impartial hearing."

"Oh, Mama can certainly do that," Robert said, unable to remain silent. "She has been settling family disputes for years."

"Exactly," Kingman said as they all laughed at the boy's candid remark.

"I'm also thinking of recommending Caroline Neil from Point of Rocks and our own Franny Gallagher for other openings, but I'm not as certain they will qualify or be able to post bonds."

Esther was leaning forward at the table, resting on her elbows. She remained silent, stirring the spoon around in her coffee cup. Robert watched his father's eyes bore holes through her head, but Esther did not look at him.

"Archie and I could help her as clerks and show her the procedures of the courtroom," Robert said earnestly. Esther smiled at her son and Kingman knew then that she would do it, if not for herself, then for her boys, especially for Robert, who would be proud of her. She enjoyed that role. Robert sat next to John, whose arm was draped over the back of his son's chair, looking very much like him. Robert had inherited John's dark eyes and coloring, though Robert was of a slighter build and his features were finer.

"Tell me, John," Esther said, her blue eyes twinkling at Kingman, "would my friends be required to address me as Madam Justice or Judge Morris?" Before Kingman could respond, John tossed his napkin onto the table and scraped back his chair.

"And what would my friends call me?" he barked, knowing the men at the Grecian Bend would have fun at his expense. "Perhaps you would like to do my jobs at the saloon or the mine," he added. Robert could tell his mother longed to make the hot retort that rose to her lips, but she suppressed it and forced herself to rise without hurry from her chair and gather dishes from the table.

"Not tonight, thank you, Mr. Morris. Robert and I must get Archie's paper ready." The others remained silent until John left and the door closed behind him. Esther continued with her busywork at the table.

"It would be another first for our territory, Esther," Kingman said, finally breaking the silence.

"Yes, and you would be famous, Mother," Robert said in a rush. "You'd be part of our history and I could help you. There has never been a woman justice of the peace, has there?" Robert looked from Esther to Kingman.

"I must think about this," Esther said, although Robert knew she had already made up her mind. "Why don't you boys finish the pie," she said, heading toward the kitchen. Kingman slid another piece of pie onto Robert's plate.

"What do you think, Robert? Will she do it?"

Robert was enthused, but his brothers were not true advocates of suffrage. "She will ask my brothers for their opinions," he said, "but she will convince them to agree with her."

Kingman was confident Esther would accept, but he was not unaware of the domestic conflict it would cause.

"Your enthusiasm reminds me of my own son, Johnny, who is the same age. How he would love the excitement of building a new territory." Kingman recalled his recent trip to New Hampshire, where his wife Mary and their five children lived in his in-laws' comfortable fourteen-room house, furnished with the treasures of a lifetime. Mary would not join him in the West until their children were properly educated and the new territory had acquired some of the amenities to which she was accustomed. Kingman sympathized, even agreed with her. But in his heart he wished that Mary could toss it all aside and join him for an adventure.

As Kingman surveyed the sparse furnishings in the Morris home, he noted the incongruous mixture of an overstuffed mahogany settee and handmade pine chairs. But somehow, the room did not lack warmth and a feeling of comfort. The makeshift arrangement also held a vitality, a promise almost, of better things to come.

Finishing his pie, Kingman called into the kitchen. "Esther, if you are a true pioneer, you cannot refuse." When Esther came back to the table, trying to look serious, as if she were grappling with a difficult thought, Kingman rattled off a list of details involved in presenting a petition and posting a bond. Although she remained silent as her friend spoke on, Esther's imagination had already begun to enjoy her new role.

"I don't see that it will be any problem," Kingman said, smiling slyly, "that is, unless you have something to hide." They all laughed and, sensing Esther's decision, Robert clapped his hands. "Wait until I tell Franky about this!"

"We won't have to worry about getting the news out," Kingman quipped.

"Many, many years ago, I scoffed at the idea of doing a man's job when some of the citizens of Owego voted for me to be mayor of the town," she told Kingman. "Now I have learned more and have some wisdom. I can see that this is a first step I must take, the beginning of something, perhaps not just for me, but for all women."

Esther knew she could not refuse. Aside from her own enjoyment, she understood her obligation to all women. She would show that it could be done. But she also knew that although John would not oppose it openly, his displeasure would be apparent in his badgering and ridicule. His drinking was now a sickness like his rheumatism, and it had changed him. His humor was gone. He had always been stubborn but fair-minded. Lately he seemed to enjoy simply being disagreeable. It had never been easy for him to talk about his feelings, and she also knew that he was in pain a great deal of the time and tried not to show it. She was sure it had an effect on his mood.

Kingman broke into Esther's thoughts. "You aren't afraid, are you?"

Arching an eyebrow, Esther looked at Kingman haughtily and said, "I am in an elevated region, dear sir, where it's but a short step to heaven if the end should come." Kingman did not miss the hint of sadness in her sarcasm.

"There may be some rough cases," he said, "especially with some of our less-than-ethical attorneys acting as counsel. But a large part of the job is issuing bonds, deeds, and subpoenas. There's some money in it, too, I might add."

"Just as long as it doesn't interfere with my spring planting," she said, walking Kingman to the door. "And John," she said as he stepped onto the porch, "I will serve only until the end of Stillman's vacated term. I cannot make a career of this."

"That's all you need to do." Kingman smiled and touched his hat. Esther put an arm around her son's shoulder. "Well, Robert, let's see if we can make head or tail of Archie's paper."

Later that night, they heard John stumble on the porch. Robert lay stiffly under the thick feather quilt, waiting to hear if John would go sleep in his own room, or come in here to sleep in Ed's bed. Who would have to put up with his drunken snoring? When Robert saw John's shadow in the doorway and watched him try not to lurch into Ed's bunk, he imagined his mother's sigh of relief. Now she could stretch out peacefully under her big feather quilt, while Robert turned to the wall and drew myself into a compact ball, hoping to seal himself off from the night.

——

It was a blustery day in February, and as Esther sat on the edge of her bed, buttoning her gaiter boots, she seemed almost girlish, worrying a bit about doing the job properly. She put on the new black empress cloth dress she had made with the sewing machine the boys had given her, enjoying the heady scent of the new material. Her normally steady fingers fumbled with the garnet brooch she was trying to pin to the green velvet ribbon tied around her white lace collar.

She had tied on her small black bonnet before realizing she had forgotten her earrings. Impatient with her ineptness, she yanked the ribbons under her chin and tossed the hat aside while she put in her earrings. Finally deciding she was presentable, she took a deep breath and marched out to the porch. Archie and Ed were entertaining John and Robert with stories of their recent hunting trip. They would have venison and rabbit in the smokehouse.

"You look decidedly stylish, Ma," Archie said, offering his arm. John adjusted his waistcoat and sucked in his stomach. "And how do I look?" he asked. "Like a proper husband for a judge, I hope?" Esther detected a hint of jealousy, and she felt embarrassed for John because he could not find a place for himself somehow.

"You have always been a stylish man, Mr. Morris," replied Esther, always the politician. Despite the extra chairs, there were people standing in the low-ceilinged courtroom in the back of Major Baldwin's store when the family arrived. The Morrises all sat with John Kingman in the front row. Many friends and neighbors were there, anxious to show their support. Jim Stillman and some of his friends sat noisily across the aisle, the smell of whiskey apparent. John did not look at these men with whom he usually shared drinks at the Grecian Bend. Stillman, an educated man, had at one time been the editor of the *San Francisco Call*. His brother was a well-known banker in New York City, and his son, also named James, was in the middle of a messy and highly publicized divorce from his wife, Fifi.

The three members of the Board of County Supervisors filed into the room and sat down behind the "bench," a long plank table. John Anthony and Nat Daniels were both miners and ex-army officers. John Swingle was the town undertaker and a building contractor who liked to say, "We build 'em or bury 'em."

Esther responded in a firm and self-assured voice to routine questions from John Anthony as the men examined her petition. When Chairman Anthony called for a vote of the board, Nat Daniels, without hesitation, voted in the affirmative. He had known the Morris family well. On hearing this, John Swingle hopped up from his chair as if bitten by a rattlesnake. He had assumed they would all reject Esther's application. He felt it was merely an act of harassment from John Kingman and the Republican territorial administration.

Before the clerk had time to call his name, Swingle shook his head and shouted, "No, no, no!" His fleshy face vibrated like a pudding. Suddenly, Jim Stillman was on his feet.

"Now, Colonel Anthony, before you say your yea or nay, let me remind you that this board, in all seriousness to duty, cannot replace me with a woman. I—and you," he said, stabbing the air with his finger, "would be the laughingstock of the territory. Letting the ladies vote is one thing—they will vote as their husbands say—but they cannot decide a man's fate." The chairman leaned back in his chair and smiled at the crowd.

"I think they do that anyway, in the natural course of events, don't you agree, Jim?" The laughter in the room seemed to infuriate Stillman. Anthony stood up.

"Now, Jim," he said calmly but forcefully, "you gave up this job for other interests, and you have no say about who will get the job next."

"I will not be replaced by a woman," Stillman screamed, "and I will not release my records. I'll burn them before handing them over to a woman."

"And I'll help him," Swingle yelled from the bench.

"Sit down, both of you," Anthony said, raising his voice, "and keep quiet." Esther avoided looking at Stillman, but Robert knew she felt pity for the man, for making a fool of himself. She had told him that few people took him seriously anymore because of his drinking. Alcohol had been the ruin of many men Esther knew, even in her own family. Their faces suddenly flashed through her mind, her husband's face the most vivid in this sad parade—father, brothers, uncles, and Lotte's husband, Fred.

When he was sure he would be heard, the chairman put his hands on the table and leaned forward. "This puts me to my trumps," he said in a slow, deliberate voice. "But the lady is in every way qualified as to education and integrity. There is a vacancy to fill, she has filed the proper bonds—from Archie and Alphabet Dixon—and our democratic legislature has given the ladies equal rights as to the franchise and holding office with men. The question is proper, and I must in all conscience cast my vote for Mrs. Morris."

Esther's eyes filled as cheers broke out and Archie and Ed and Robert leaped to their feet, stomping and applauding. Ed clapped his brother on the back and grinned at Esther, who smiled and blinked rapidly a few times. Even John could not suppress a grin, although it was difficult to notice beneath his thick, gray, walrus-like mustache. He, too, finally stood and clapped. Swingle glared at Daniels and Anthony, who were leaning over the bench congratulating the Morris family. Stillman, his face red with rage, shouted above the noise.

"I will not be replaced by a woman!" He started for the bench and two men grabbed his arms when it appeared Stillman might take a swing at the chairman. More onlookers, attracted by the commotion, crowded into the doorways and peered through the windows. Stillman went back to his seat and picked up a large green clothbound book. He waved it at Anthony. "I will never turn this over to a woman," he shouted after glaring once more at Esther and the commissioners.

"We will have to issue a warrant for the return of the docket," Kingman called after him.

"Go ahead," Stillman shouted. He spit on the floor at Esther's feet and headed for the door. John stepped forward and slid his foot over the spot as if erasing it. The gesture surprised Esther, packed as it was with loyalty for her. As Stillman walked through the door, Kingman turned to Esther.

"Well, Judge Morris, it looks like you've got your first case." Chairman Anthony pounded on the table and when the room quieted, he looked at the clerk.

"Mr. O'Donnell, telegraph the world that Wyoming, the youngest and one of the richest territories in the United States, gave equal rights to women in actions as well as words today." The news of Esther's appointment reached Chicago and Boston even before it reached Edward Lee's desk in Cheyenne, where, as acting governor in Campbell's absence, he would make the appointment official.

⌒

The eastern press had been lukewarm to the passage of woman suffrage in Wyoming, preferring to publish "Wild West" stories of Indian raids and vigilantes. But the story of a female frontier judge appealed to their imaginations. As the story of Esther's appointment gathered momentum, it lost all semblance of truth. The family sat around reading the descriptions to each other, rolling over in mirth. Archie reprinted some of the better ones in his own paper. Adding as much as one hundred pounds and ten inches to Esther, some reports depicted a woman of gargantuan proportions. Western women, in the eyes of the eastern press, wore long bulky overcoats and high boots, with heavy pistols strapped around their waists.

"Is it true that Judge Morris just gave birth to a twelve-pound baby?" one correspondent wanted to know. Quick to defend the grace and propriety of western women, the Wyoming press exaggerated in the other extreme. One of these reports was picked up on the front page of the *New York Times* and described Esther as wearing a calico dress and green hair ribbons at her swearing-in. Esther's relatives in the East immediately dashed off letters begging her to deny that she had appeared publicly in such an unfashionable getup. It had been Archie's job as territorial clerk to administer the oath of office to his mother, and he decided it would also be his job to put to rest all the wild rumors. In his enthusiastic but heavy-handed editorial style, he composed a story for the *South Pass News*.

"As it is always interesting to note the exceptional circumstances, or rather to trace the causes which have led anyone to depart from the usual routine of life, and for the benefit of our eastern contemporaries who seem greatly exercised over the appointment of a woman to the office of justice of the peace, we give the following sketch," he began. After outlining the events of Esther's life, Archie added, "In her labors she has been the equal of man, and has felt the injustice of her position and the unequal opportunities of women; and while she advocates the elevation of woman, she does not wish the downfall of man. She says we must be as free and intelligent as man in order to be their companions."

Esther, meanwhile, was too busy to pay much attention to her new notoriety. When she went to hear her first case, the courtroom was crowded and noisy. She entered the room with a sense of anticipation and a bit of stage fright, hoping she would not disappoint her sex. Before she reached the bench, one man struck another and a general melee ensued. Esther's reaction was automatic.

"Boys, can't you behave yourselves?!" She said this with an air of authority, as she would have when her sons were young and battling with each other. Whether or not she could settle a legal case, she would at least reform the courtroom, with a slight feeling of contempt at such childish behavior. Esther had not raised her voice, but it was effective. Despite some snickering and scuffling, the courtroom quieted down. Esther sat down, too. The work of the court would begin. Robert stood at the end of the bench in his best black wool suit and a newly boiled shirt.

"The Territory of Wyoming versus James W. Stillman," he called out, his voice cracking only a little. Stillman sat in the front row, looking at the floor. His attorney, who had instructed him to keep his mouth shut, approached the bench and asked for a dismissal.

"On what grounds?" Esther asked.

"On the grounds that the court has no jurisdiction in this case, and also on the grounds of an incomplete warrant, uh, Your Honor." Stillman and his attorney had earlier denied any knowledge of the whereabouts of the docket. The constable had been unable to find it when he had searched Stillman's home and placed him under arrest. Esther assumed Stillman had kept his word and burned the docket.

Esther looked at Stillman, who sat in front of her looking wretched, his hands trembling. "He needs a drink," she thought. Esther knew there was no question about the court's jurisdiction. She could put Stillman in jail for this offense, or fine him heavily. She knew, too, that the people in the room were waiting for more theatrics, like those performed by Stillman at the hearing for her petition.

"I think the court must show mercy in considering this case," Esther said, finally. She looked directly at the defendant, who still avoided looking at her. "Mr. Stillman has a wife who depends on him. If he goes to jail, who will care for her? It is true, he has absconded with the court records, and that is a criminal offense. But we do not need the old record to administer future justice in this court.

"We have another docket for this court," Esther said, holding up the new docket book her son Robert had given her. "The charges against Mr. Stillman will be dismissed."

At supper that evening, John chided Esther for letting Stillman off so easily. "Weren't you sure about your authority? People will think you are afraid to take a stand."

"My dear," Esther said, straining her patience, "had you been on the bench, you would have rendered your own decision." She steered the conversation to Ed's job at the sawmill, refusing to allow her own supper table to become a court of judgment, and herself a defendant. "As usual," she thought, "men think first of posturing, making sure their own position is protected, whereas women can look past that at the wisdom of the ultimate decision."

While hearings and trials took place in the courthouse, the Morris home became Esther's office. It was here people came for subpoenas, deeds, and warrants, at all times of the day. Esther had converted her sewing table to a desk, arranging it closer to the front door, with chairs nearby for the comfort of her "clients."

All of them, and even John occasionally, assisted her with her work, but except for Robert they were not so inclined with the housework. It never bothered Robert, however, to sweep the floors or wash the dishes. He said he sometimes enjoyed it, seeing it as an avenue of order.

John's interest in his wife's job was almost obsessive. He had served as alderman, trustee, and coroner in Peru, and had authority in those roles. He wanted to know every detail and then proceeded to argue her decisions. He refused to give her credit for making a sound decision but, at the same time, complained that she was not paid enough for what she did. He became less active in his own affairs, griping about the saloon, the mining, and the government. Esther was dismayed at the increasing amount of time he spent sitting around the house, creating a tension she could relieve only with physical activity. Esther had always loved walking, but now she found herself walking faster, farther, and more often. John's rheumatism flared up more frequently, and he talked about taking the water cure at the hot springs in the Wind River Valley. Esther encouraged him. They all encouraged him. Archie said he would drive him there in the wagon.

Despite the frustrations of her own marriage, one of the duties Esther found most enjoyable in her job was marrying people, but when she legally joined a couple who had been living together for a year, some of her friends accused her of condoning sin.

"They have been kind to each other," she said, "and live no differently than any married couple. I felt they were sincere in their desire to do the right thing."

It soon became evident that Esther's cases were not being contested or appealed and that justice could indeed be dispensed by a woman, especially such a "courageous and intelligent woman," with such a "commanding appearance," as she was now described by the press. One correspondent said her profile "closely resembled the portraits of Queen Elizabeth."

The Wyoming press proudly asserted, "We hear nothing but golden opinions of Mrs. Morris's administration. Her decisions both on points of law and fact are of the soundest character and the tribunal over which she so gracefully presides is characterized by a degree of dignity and propriety rarely equaled in courts of inferior jurisdiction." After this article appeared, her sons began calling her "Golden Girl." Ed, always the practical joker, hung a board on the front of Esther's desk with the hand-lettered words "The Only Real Gold in the Territory."

Robert, who had recently read *Eminent Women of the Age*, wrote to cousin Libby Brown in New York.

"If your aunt is not yet one of the eminent women of the age, she is the first woman who has ever exercised the judicial power, at least on the American continent. I am glad to say my mother is perfectly at ease in her new position, and all our best citizens and the press are her open and declared advocates."

After a refreshing eight-mile walk one slow business day, Esther summed up her own feelings in a letter to Franky.

"My health was never better. My work pays well and I have more to spend on myself than ever before. I have been able to buy some velvet for a cloak (at $25 a yard) and all sorts of trimmings and laces for some new hats.

"Although I am confident in my work, I wish I was better qualified for it. Like all pioneers, I labor more in faith and hope. I really do have too much to do to do things well, but I guess I will be reinforced after awhile by volunteers.

"I shall take things as they come, even if I should be made President of the United States!"

CHAPTER NINETEEN

Casting Her First Ballot

On Tuesday September 6, 1870, Esther was up before dawn. In fact, she had hardly slept, such was her anticipation of going to the polls that morning. For the first time in the history of the United States and its territories, a woman would cast a ballot.

It was the beginning of something important, she believed. It was much like gardening. You plant a seed, it takes root, and something new grows from it—a beautiful flower, an asparagus stalk, or a tree filled with fruit. In her lifetime Esther had seen the beginning of so many things, from photographs to a machine to sew with and a machine to write with. She now rode in carriages drawn by a steam engine rather than horses. All of these advances began with an idea from someone who knew they would add to the common good. And she herself had shown that a woman could be as good a judge as a man and perhaps lead the way for the rest of the world. She felt sure that once all women could vote, it would be the beginning of making life better for everyone—women *and* men.

After making a breakfast of pancakes and fried eggs for the family and cleaning up the kitchen, Esther put on her best black alpaca silk dress, the one with the lace collar. She took pains in braiding her long hair that was now more gray than blond, winding it around the back of her head and fastening it with a tortoise shell hairpin. She tied her bonnet ribbons under her chin and declared herself ready to vote. Robert and Archie had already left for the polls set up in the back of Major Baldwin's store. As chief clerk of the territorial court, Archie was responsible for recording the proceedings, with the help of his brother, the assistant clerk.

"Are you coming with me to cast your ballot, Mr. Morris?" Lingering over his coffee at the table, John shrugged his shoulders.

"I'm not sure," he said. "With all those women at the polls, it may be harmful to my health." John never missed a vote, feeling it not a responsibility at all, but a privilege, given his gratitude to the country that made him welcome all those years ago.

"It's just as well," his wife teased, "for we would only argue about who is the best person to vote for."

"I'll go with Ma," Ed said, grinning at his father, who reluctantly got up and cuffed the side of his son's head good naturedly and put on his jacket. Despite his past indifference to suffrage as a political issue, John was more inclined to think it a good idea since his own Democrats had brought it about. Outside, the three Morrises joined their neighbors, Julia and Bill Bright and the Gallaghers, for the short walk.

"Good morning, Judge Morris," Archie said, greeting his mother with a grin as Marshal Church Howe tipped his hat. Five other towns-women were all greeted at the polls with the utmost courtesy. The atmosphere was quite low key compared with last year, when violence threatened as the first black men were escorted to the polls to cast their ballots.

That year, Election Day erupted like a Fourth of July celebration. As rowdiness gained momentum during the course of the day, stray bullets found their mark in wood and glass, but fortunately not in human flesh or bone. Saloons opened at sunrise and candidates began early buying votes with whiskey. Campaign posters were tacked to every fence and hitching post. Tension in the air was like an electric current. There were threats of violence by some of the men who had said they would "not let any niggers cast their ballots." Noisy crowds spilled out of the saloons. The promise of a more exciting confrontation hung in the air.

When a man suddenly stuck his head in the door of the store's back room and shouted, "Here they come!" the courtroom cleared out. Marshal Howe led fifteen newly enfranchised black men, including the Morrises' friend Jefferson Woffard, to the courthouse door. His hands were poised over the Colt pistols on his hips. Two deputies guarded the rear of the line, Winchesters ready. Some of the men on the porch locked arms to block the door. When the marshal, a staunch abolitionist from Massachusetts, ordered them to stand aside, no one moved. The wide brim of the marshal's hat dropped a curtain of shadow over his face, but his fiercely determined expression was plain.

"Stand aside," he said once more. In the few seconds of silence that followed, only the clicking of the rifle cocks could be heard. Robert said later it was the loudest noise he ever heard and it made his heart jump.

"Aw, let 'em go," a man on the porch finally said. "It's only fifteen votes." He freed his arms from the human chain and backed away. The others slowly followed. The marshal escorted the black men inside, where they predictably voted Republican before returning to their jobs on the ranches outside of town.

This year, however, with women casting ballots, there was no such tension, although the marshal was taking no chances and had called in some soldiers from the military post. Not every woman in South Pass City voted that day. Several who chose not to vote abstained either because they did not care about politics, or because they believed (as many women still did) that it was not a woman's place—or their husbands would not allow them to go. However, all thirteen women residing in Atlantic City, just eight miles away, had voted. As news came over the telegraph throughout the day, Esther and her friends learned that in Laramie, Amelia Post was hosting a party for all the politicians and friends of suffrage at the home she shared with her husband, Morton. Across the nation many eyes were on the new territory, and congratulatory telegrams came from Susan B. Anthony, Elizabeth Cady Stanton, Anna Shaw, Anna Dickinson, Isabelle Beecher Hooker, and other leaders of the National Woman Suffrage Association, who planned to visit as soon as possible to congratulate the women of Wyoming as well as the territory's forward-thinking legislators.

Mrs. Post and Esther were both invited to be Wyoming delegates at the National Woman Suffrage Association Convention in Washington early the following year. Amelia would attend, but Esther, knowing she would not be able to afford such a trip, sent her regrets with a letter to Isabelle Hooker, which would be read at the convention. She also asked Hooker to send some more association tracts to distribute.

At home the Morris family was helping Archie get ready for his wedding in Springfield, Illinois. Now twenty-eight, Archie was heavier than when he last wore his full Union army dress uniform. He donned the frock coat with its double rows of brass buttons and gold shoulder epaulettes, over sky blue trousers with a dark blue welt running down the side of each leg. A crimson sash was tied around his waist and over that, the sword belt. Esther teased her son while doing alterations that if she could make the suit fit, he was not to eat anything until after the wedding, when he could remove the belt and sash.

None of the family was able to go to the wedding, for in addition to the extraordinary expense, they all had to pitch in to cover Archie's jobs. John operated the sawmill with Ed, while Robert did his own as well as Archie's job in the clerk's office and at the newspaper with the help of his mother. But they thought of Archie and Sally every day and anxiously awaited the September 22, 1870, Chicago newspapers so they could read all about the wedding.

"The executive mansion at Springfield in this state was the scene of a wedding in high life on the past Thursday afternoon," Robert read aloud from the *Chicago Times* story entitled "An Interesting Society Event at Governor Palmer's Residence." "The principals in this matrimonial venture were Miss Sarah (Sally) Neely, sister of Mrs. Palmer, and the Honorable Edward Archibald Slack of Wyoming Territory. The bride was given away by His Excellency, Governor Palmer. The dresses were of the most elegant patterns, the bride especially being handsomely arrayed in a rich white satin. The bridal presents were numerous and of a costly kind."

"Oh, I wonder how they will get all those costly things home," Ed mused as they all peered over Robert's shoulder at the photograph of the bride and groom. "That is the best picture Archie ever had," Ed said.

"Yes, he is handsome in his dress uniform," Esther said, "and I am sure he was happier when he took it off." They all laughed with her, recalling the struggle she had to alter it so it would fit him.

"We should have been at the wedding," John said morosely. In the past, when the family had the means, they traveled often to visit relatives and friends, or simply to take a holiday. Esther, who would have given almost anything to watch her son being married, sighed.

"John, you know we could not raise enough money for such a trip. We must accept what is."

Robert continued reading aloud, raising his voice a bit to discourage an argument between his parents. "The groom is tolerable well known in this city, having attended the Chicago University for a term of three years. He served as a private in H Company of the 19th Illinois Infantry and was later appointed to the rank of colonel. Two years ago he was appointed clerk of the US District Court for Wyoming. He resides in South Pass City with his mother, who is a justice of the peace for that territory, she being the first and only lady ever elected to that position in this century."

"And what about us?" Robert complained. "No mention of his father and brothers. Hopefully our friend Seth Paine will give a better story to the *Chicago Tribune*."

The story added that the wedding was followed by an excellent collation prepared by the governor's private cook. Archie and Sally went to St. Louis and then to Chicago before coming to South Pass City.

———

As the family waited for the stage carrying the newlyweds, all were concerned at the new bride's reaction to such crude circumstances after living so well in Governor Palmer's home. They suspected that Archie had made the place sound more civilized than it really was, and they went to some pains to create order and comfort in his cabin. John and the boys moved his press to a corner, while Esther made a makeshift curtain to close the area off from the living quarters. Esther cleared the clutter of papers from the dining table and placed some dried flowers there.

"You should have seen her face when she saw Archie's home," Robert later wrote to Franky, describing the way his new sister's eyes widened and her inability to utter a sound as she looked around. Sally was almost as tall as Esther, but with a smaller frame, weighing just over one hundred pounds, with a lithesome build like Libby Brown. She had black hair and eyes. Robert thought Sally was a bit like Franky in her thoughtful demeanor, but not as intellectual as his cousin.

Sarah Frances Neely was born the same year as Archie to a poor pioneer family from Kentucky. Her mother died of cholera when Sally was eleven, and her older sister Malinda became a mother to her, the way Esther had cared for Lotte after their mother and father died. When Malinda married a young lawyer, John McCauley Palmer, when she was only fourteen, her husband took the siblings into his home, along with his own sister and brother and two other wards.

Esther gave a sociable to present her new daughter-in-law to the community and introduced Sally to the shopkeepers and local farmers who raised chickens and vegetables. Sally did her best to adapt, and Archie was tender in his actions with her. Late one afternoon, before Archie had returned from the sawmill, Esther heard screams from next door. Sally had been getting supper ready, and when she turned to set the table, she saw three faces with noses flattened up against the window glass, watching her. The Indians at the time were mostly friendly, but perhaps too much so, Esther thought, as she came out onto the common porch to ask the young braves to move along.

Sally would not have to endure South Pass City for too much longer, however. By the end of the year, the population was down by half as miners were attracted by new discoveries of gold and minerals in Salt Lake City and elsewhere. Stores, saloons, and gambling halls began closing. In the short term this was profitable for the Morris family, as they picked up business from those who left theirs. Robert had a job in the dry goods store in addition to being deputy county clerk, registrar of deeds, and deputy to the new justice of the peace. Ed, too, was balancing many jobs, helping Archie and his father.

Esther's term of office ended in November and the officers of the court gave her a celebratory dinner. The townspeople begged her to run for the office again so they could vote for her. Although she had rather enjoyed the job, Esther kept to her word to serve only for the remainder of Mr. Stillman's term. However, she did not have time to relax, having been asked to take over the departing Alphabet Dixon's job running the post office.

Archie sold the sawmill to the government, which planned to give it to the local Indians to help them develop a business. John's rheumatism was quite painful, and he went for six weeks to the Wind River Valley, thirty miles away, to bathe in the hot sulfur springs. Such bathing had always been popular in Europe and was becoming more and more popular in America. Perhaps John had been paying attention to Eliza Jane Hall's advice about the curative properties of mineral waters. After a few weeks John wrote to Robert, saying he was feeling better.

Over the following months, however, South Pass City became a ghost town. The Brights and many of their friends had moved on, and lack of company and the frigid winter were hard on Esther. She was unable to conceal her depression.

"We borrow books from the few remaining families and lawyers," she wrote Lotte, "for we read or play whist every evening; in fact, we play cards three or four nights. For the past two weeks it has been ten to twenty degrees below zero." Trying to cheer herself up, she added, "The air is so dry it does not seem so bad."

—◆—

Less than two years after arriving, all the family except John, who insisted on remaining with his mining investment, left South Pass City.

"Why can you not start a mercantile business in Laramie or Cheyenne, where there is a growing and stable population? You would have the same success you had in Peru," Esther assured him.

"I have everything invested in the mine, in gold and minerals, and I will see to it that I get the investment back with a profit," he declared.

"Even if it kills you," Esther added, understanding completely her husband's stubbornness. John had also taken over ownership of the Grecian Bend, the only saloon to serve the few remaining miners and the men of the nearby army fort. He also received an appointment as coroner for Sweetwater County, which would bring a small regular income. Most of the coroner's duties there, however, would be investigating the cause of death of men who were killed either in drunken brawls or from falling down a mine shaft.

There was nothing Esther could do for John, whether she stayed with him or not. She was not equipped to endure another winter with twelve-foot snowdrifts and nobody to talk to other than a brooding husband. Esther left most of the furnishings with her husband, but in addition to books and clothing, she took some of her dishes and her mother's Revere candlesticks. As she looked around, she thought of all the moves and all the things she always had to leave behind. While the garden here was nothing compared to what she had created in Peru, she nevertheless dug up the remaining root vegetables and put most inside for John, taking only a few cuttings to begin a new garden elsewhere.

With the boys now striking out on their own, Esther felt there was little reason to stay with her husband, but still, she was deeply saddened by the fact that her family was no longer together. The boys already had other work lined up. Robert was hired by Governor Campbell as a secretary. He and Ed, who was managing a lumberyard in Cheyenne, would board together. Archie took ownership of a larger newspaper in Laramie from a publisher who left the territory. Esther went to Laramie with Archie and Sally, who was now pregnant. She had a room in Archie's small brick house and was looking forward to her first grandchild.

When she got to Laramie, Esther learned from Amelia Post and Justice Howe that Governor Campbell had been offered a $2,000 bribe to repeal the woman suffrage bill. Happily, he refused.

CHAPTER TWENTY

A Trip to California

"THIS IS INDEED THE GARDEN OF EDEN," ESTHER SAID TO ELIZA JANE as they sat with legs outstretched on a hill overlooking the Pacific Ocean. "If the Yankees had landed here instead of Plymouth Rock, they would have gone no farther." Esther laughed and added, "If I had seen this before leaving Peru, I would not have stopped in Wyoming but come straight across to the Pacific Ocean."

The two old friends had walked along the Los Angeles coast for miles and were enjoying their first visit in nearly ten years. The soft scent of eucalyptus blended with the salty ocean air. It gave Esther such pleasure she thought she might swoon. Eliza Jane had traded in her favored turban for a wide-brimmed straw hat to cover her wild curly hair that was now gray. She wore pale gray canvas overalls over a white ruffled and embroidered blouse in the Spanish style. At sixty Eliza Jane was still thin and moved with her usual quick energy.

"Maybe Archie will want a paper here," Esther quipped. "I cannot wait to tell my boys all about this place." Eliza Jane's house—a small, low, adobe L-shaped building with a red tiled roof—was perfectly suited for the landscape. Esther had never before seen palm trees like those growing in the sandy loam around the house. She had also been introduced to her first taste of avocado.

"It is abundant in Mexico and part of the diet there," said Eliza Jane as they each scooped the velvety pale green fruit from a pitted avocado half. "Seasonal workers from Mexico come to help me harvest the citrus and they brought this to me. They are careful with how they handle fruit." Esther had already tasted the oranges growing on her friend's farm and declared them first class.

"Agriculture thrives all up and down the state," Eliza Jane said. "Sacramento has endless miles of good crops of vegetables. There is fish from the sea, and great timber from the north. And many Italians have come over here to begin vineyards on this fertile landscape. This is a place with a future," she added. "It is not like a gold mining town that offers nothing else, once the minerals are depleted." Esther had told her friend about the quick decline of South Pass City.

Eliza Jane had been thrilled to travel to San Francisco to hear her old friend and sister-in-law give a speech at the National Woman Suffrage Association Convention. Much as Esther enjoyed stating her mind when in conversation with others, the thought of addressing a large auditorium full of strangers filled her with dread. Nevertheless, she was humbled to see so many women eagerly awaiting her words. They wanted to know what it was like on the frontier. How had she convinced all those men to vote for suffrage?

"It was Bill Bright who got the bill passed. I only encouraged him," she said with a mischievous smile. "All the men were liberals from the East," she continued. "Many are Republicans, but both parties support suffrage." Esther also answered their questions about her job as justice of the peace and told them about the first all-female jury in Laramie. "Wyoming was pleased to go into the record books with the first all-female jury, but for some reason, it never happened again."

"Listen to what the *San Francisco Call* said about you," Eliza Jane said while they were riding the train to Los Angeles. "She is a courtly, self-possessed woman, full of natural dignity and ease, while her conversation clearly shows that she is possessed of more than an ordinary share of shrewdness and correct appreciation of human nature. Her manner of speaking is off hand, ready, and at times brilliant . . ."

"And here is more, my brilliant friend," Eliza Jane crowed, pushing the newspaper up to Esther's face. "In answering questions about woman suffrage she gave both sides of the question, wanting both perspectives to be fairly stated."

"Oh, Esther, you have always been a woman of ideas who can express herself well and forcibly," Eliza Jane said.

"Yes, and as Mr. Morris always said, 'a little too forcibly.'"

"Ah, but you are free from Mr. Morris now," Eliza Jane said, urging her friend to travel with the suffrage leaders and work for the cause. "We need you." Since the suffrage victory in Wyoming, Esther had enjoyed the company of many of the suffrage leaders, some of whom she had already met in New York or Chicago. But now suffragists came through Wyoming. Susan B. Anthony came to visit Governor Campbell and stopped in Laramie for a dinner with Amelia Post and Esther. Esther enjoyed the visits from the well-known suffragists, and she felt a responsibility to further the cause, but in her own way. She wanted equal rights for women, but felt it best to find a way to make it work in her favor rather than rebel outwardly, as her friend had done. She had accepted what she knew she could not yet change, although admittedly with less patience now.

"It will take men a long time, even after we all get the vote, to apply the idea of equality," Esther said to Eliza Jane. "As intellectually modern as Archie is, he is not so modern about his own wife. He expects her to fill the role, doesn't even worry about it. Although he treats her kindly, he is interested in his own growth. He left her in South Pass when the baby was only two weeks old to start his new paper in Laramie. I later took her and the baby on the train, so they could join him, but Sally has a sadness in her big dark eyes all the time.

"Robert, on the other hand, has great success in work he learned from women while at *The Revolution*," Esther said. "He can do shorthand and typewriting and works in politics," just as Libby Brown had predicted. Libby was still working with Anthony for the cause, although *The Revolution* had ceased publication the year before.

"Perhaps my girls are following your path, Esther," Eliza Jane said. "Look how Franky has maintained a good relationship with her father and married well. She is a homemaker, is she not? But she goes to college and she organizes the suffrage movement in Michigan.

"Libby, too, is for the cause, but she was very lonely here for lack of society," Eliza Jane added. "I think she may have married in haste to

Captain Moore, who is considerably older but can provide a comfortable life. Isn't that the reason so many women marry—to leave their family if they are not satisfied there?

"My children don't enjoy the farm," Eliza Jane lamented. "Charley does not want to work here. He wants to make money selling land and is already quite shrewd," she said of her son Charles Victor Hall, now twenty years old. "He has been devising schemes to rent out parcels of the farm to those who would work it and share the profits. These tenant farmers, he told me, would help increase our income."

"And what does Charley know about his father?" Esther asked, once again trying to challenge her friend on this subject. She felt Eliza Jane was wrong in denying her son a father, or at least knowledge of his father. Charley was born nine years after Franky, while Eliza Jane was still living in New York but traveling widely with her water therapy practice. She had never revealed the boy's paternity. When Esther pushed her about this, Eliza Jane said that she was a free woman and did not have to reveal anything she considered private information.

"Oh, Esther, you know I will never reveal this to anyone else, but you will be pleased to know I have talked with Charley and he does know who his father is."

"Well, we are grandmothers now," Esther said, understanding that her friend was not going to say more about Charley. "We have another generation to care for." She had proudly showed her friend a photo of Charles Henry Slack, "such a sweet baby."

"I see so little of Hobart," Eliza Jane said, "although Franky sends photographs and she is due to have another baby soon. Libby and I paid a visit last year to see him and his father, whom we had not yet met, for we could not go to the wedding." Esther, who had met Hobart before her trip to Wyoming, remembered him well.

"He has the same deep blue telescopic eyes as his mother," Esther said. "They widen in wonder while he listens to whatever you have to say to him. And those eyes are his grandmother's as well," Esther said, smiling at Eliza Jane. "Now we can see ourselves in a new generation."

"Yes, that is a good thing, so long as we don't see the bad as well," Eliza Jane said. "Oh, Esther, why don't you come here to live? I would love your company," she said wistfully. "You love gardening, and farming is not much different," she laughed, "only with much longer hours of labor."

"It is something to think about," Esther said, gazing again into the sea as if she feared it would not be there the next time she looked.

"The citrus market is growing now that the railroad goes across the country," Eliza Jane said, "so I am making better money." Esther knew her friend had suffered considerable hardship since investing the $3,000 from her settlement with Edmund. It was not enough to put the farm on a sure footing, and she had carried on her water therapy practice.

Esther envied her friend for what she had and at the same time was worried for her. While Esther would always promote suffrage and women's rights, she was a realist and not a dreamer. Marrying John Morris had been a decision based on compromise, and Esther was determined to make it work—and it did for much of her life. Thus, while she enjoyed her own intellectual power and her friends, she believed her first responsibility was to her children. Or perhaps she was simply afraid to go too far out on a limb. Eliza Jane, on the other hand, rebelled, set out on her own, and as a result created hardship for herself and her children. But then, she had this beautiful place to call her own.

As Esther traveled back to Wyoming on the train, she entertained the idea of living in such a comfortable and gentle environment as Los Angeles. What wonderful gardens she could grow there, and it was not very difficult anymore to make a visit to her family in Wyoming now that the trains ran everywhere. Didn't her brother Daniel tell her all those years ago that women could only live alone if they were old?

When Esther arrived in Laramie in August, however, any thought of moving to Los Angeles was immediately set aside. Her grandson, only ten months old, was gravely ill with diphtheria and died within a few days. The remembrance of the death of her own little Johnny, who would now be twenty-two years old, came over Esther like a dark cloud, and her heart broke for Sally and Archie. Sally was already pregnant with their second child, and she needed a mother right now to help her through the fear and stress. Esther remained by her side. When a daughter they named Esther lived only five weeks, Sally had an emotional breakdown. Esther grieved with her for the lost child, for her namesake, and wondered when it would ever be safe for women to have children. Libby Brown's sister Julia had married and gone to Nebraska, had lost all three of her infants, and was so broken that she divorced her husband and went back to Owego, vowing never again to become pregnant.

Sally, however, was at risk of dying herself if she could not be induced to eat and get some fresh air and exercise. She sat in a trance for most of the day, responding only in faint whispers to queries about her health. Archie was unable to console her, and also had his work at his growing daily newspaper to worry about. Esther humored and cajoled her daughter-in-law into accompanying her on long walks in the countryside.

"Come with me, Sally, so I am not walking alone." When Esther tried to interest Sally in the small garden she had started in back of their house, Sally said, "No, the plants would only die like my babies." There was a new school in Laramie, and Esther talked with Archie about getting Sally interested in a teaching job. The family doctor thought such work might help get Sally's mind off her own losses, but Archie thought being with other children would only make his wife more depressed about the loss of her own. Esther remained in Laramie with Archie and Sally until she was sure Sally would pull out of her depression, but Esther was restless and longed for her own space and more comfortable winters.

Esther's estranged husband was not well either. In addition to more acute outbreaks of rheumatism, John had developed dropsy, a condition that caused swelling and pain in his legs and feet and often left him breathless. He went to Cheyenne to see a doctor who gave him medicines to encourage his own body to release the fluid, but this did not always work. All of the family, including Esther, made periodic trips to visit John, and when he was feeling well enough, he came to Laramie or Cheyenne to visit them. But as his health continued to deteriorate, Ed decided to give up his job at the lumberyard and move to South Pass City to help his father with the work.

More change came for the family when Governor Campbell's term of office was over and Robert had to find a new job. Through family connections in New York and on the recommendation of Governor Campbell, Robert was offered a job as secretary to John Bigelow, the Erie Canal commissioner in Albany, New York. Esther decided to go with him.

CHAPTER TWENTY-ONE

A Sojourn Back East

ESTHER HELPED ROBERT SET UP HOUSEKEEPING IN A SMALL APARTment in Albany, but spent most of her time boarding with her niece Mary Jane Davie in Auburn, not far from Ithaca and Owego. The Davies had an estate farm, and Esther's widowed brother Daniel now lived there. Mary Jane was his only surviving child, and Daniel enjoyed the company of his grandchildren. Living there gave Esther the opportunity to help her family, especially her sister Lotte, who was not well, but she also enjoyed easy access to New York City by train, where she could visit Libby Chatfield and maintain her involvement in the suffrage cause.

In February of 1876, Esther, now sixty-three, was named vice president of the National Woman Suffrage Association celebration at Masonic Hall in New York. One of the speakers was Edward Lee, who had been the territorial secretary of Wyoming when the suffrage bill was passed. Lee, who had since returned to the Connecticut government, was invited to the Chatfields' for dinner after the day's speeches. He and Esther both had a chance to renew their acquaintance with Libby's friend Anna Dickinson, who was staying with the Chatfields while she finished writing her new play. General Chatfield was disappointed that he could not join them, but he had been called away to deal with an emergency at his and Libby's country home in Elizabeth, New Jersey.

In the elegant dining room of the Chatfields' brownstone, with its emerald green velvet drapes and long mahogany table, Libby and her guests dined on oysters and roast duck. Late into the night Esther,

Dickinson, and Lee regaled Libby with tales of their adventures in Wyoming.

Dickinson, now thirty-five, remembered Lee well, for he had been the one to rescue her from the wild men who mobbed her train when she tried to stop in Cheyenne to give a talk because the newspapers had been clamoring for the famous "Angel of the Civil War." A Quaker from Philadelphia and a college graduate, Dickinson was an ardent abolitionist and the first woman to speak before the United States Congress, where her impassioned speech drew a standing ovation.

"I no sooner stepped on the platform," Dickinson recalled, "than I was surrounded by a crowd of gaping men and had to get back on the train for refuge. But they continued to stare at me, flattening their faces against the car windows. I refused to stay in Cheyenne, but Mr. Lee came aboard and begged me to stop in September on my way back east."

"You certainly had the gift for gab," Esther said to Lee, laughing. "You could convince any woman of anything. You just keep talking until they say anything to make you stop."

"But it was you, Mrs. Morris, who convinced Miss Dickinson to return to Wyoming," Lee said.

"I told her the people there were hungry for enlightenment and they had the money with which to pay for it," Esther replied. "She could probably get a large fee for her lectures."

"You did it for Robert, too," Libby added, "for he was quite smitten with Anna."

"Yes, he had been so excited that Miss Dickenson would stop and he would see her again. He insisted he would be the one to drive the wagon to meet her train and deliver her to the speaker's hall." When Robert was working at *The Revolution*, he had become infatuated with this small, dynamic woman nine years his senior.

"Miss Dickinson is very good looking," Robert had mentioned to his mother more than once. Esther did not mention it now, but she knew that Robert had become disenchanted with Miss Dickinson since she had ceased her suffrage activities in favor of writing and acting in her own plays.

"Her true talent," he told his mother, "was to deliver a message to further this important cause." Robert had attended one of her plays, but he felt it was not very good and he was embarrassed for her. "She is not being true to her own self," he said.

Seated at the desk in his Albany apartment, Robert opened the letter from his brother Ed as his mother sat on the sofa reading the new *Atlantic Monthly* magazine. She had come over from Auburn for a weekend visit, and to congratulate Robert on his new job. Mr. Bigelow had been appointed New York's new secretary of state, and he brought Robert along from the canal commission as his secretary. Robert, now twenty-five, had grown a bit stout according to his mother and wore new spectacles because of continuing problems with his eyes. He had been staring at the same page of his letter for so long that Esther looked over.

"Has the news from your brother stunned you into silence?" Esther asked. "Or perhaps your new spectacles are not working." Esther knew the letter was from Eddie because she was there when the post arrived. "You have a letter from your dear brother," she had told him.

"He asks if I think you will come for a visit soon." It was February, and Ed knew that his mother would hardly venture into a Wyoming winter for the pleasure of it.

"Perhaps your father is not well," she said. John and Esther had lived apart for five years, but she visited whenever she returned to Wyoming in the summers, for he was still her husband.

"He doesn't say when," Robert said softly and looked over at his mother again. She had now put down her magazine and asked to see the letter. She would intuit the true meaning.

"He is trying to sound cheerful," Esther said, "as if he misses his mama." Ed rarely wrote letters, so Esther knew there was more here than he was saying.

"It could be that," Robert said. They had discussed this before, because they knew John's health would probably diminish if he persisted in a lifestyle that did not suit him. And they knew from the doctors and from others who suffered from dropsy that his heart would eventually give out. Robert occasionally got letters from his father, but they were mostly just news about South Pass City and about Ed. He only mentioned his health when he was feeling fairly good.

———

Esther left for Wyoming the next day, telling Robert she would wire him if he should come home, too. However, before she could reach Wyoming and South Pass City, John, now sixty-three, suffered a sudden fatal heart attack in the middle of a conversation with Ed. He died instantly.

"We were too late," she wrote to her family about John's death, and how she had to console her sons, especially Ed, who had witnessed his death. She tried to imagine his panic and distress at not being able to revive his father. There was no longer a doctor in South Pass City, but an army surgeon from the nearby fort was summoned to officially pronounce the cause of death as a heart attack. Ed had wired Archie, who went immediately to help his brother cope with the arrangements. They buried John in Lakeview Cemetery in Cheyenne next to Archie's two children. Archie, who now published the *Cheyenne Daily Sun* in that city, wrote an obituary about his father, a man who had accomplished a great deal since coming to America, had served his community, and had raised a fine family.

Along with her sons, Esther mourned her husband deeply. John had a gentleness that he tried to hide with gruffness, and he had loved the boys with all his heart, and made Archie his own. She had loved him for all those reasons. And while she never felt the kind of passion for John that she had for Artemas, she had never regretted her marriage to John. Over the years, they had forged a deep and affectionate bond over the care of their sons and their mutual pleasure in being pioneers in their little town of Peru. If only he had not been so stubborn and come with them to Laramie or Cheyenne, he might have spent his last years in some comfort and close to his family. She was glad Ed had stayed with him, although there was not much of a life for her son in South Pass.

Before she left John, years ago, he told her, "I failed you, Esther. I tried, but I failed." He looked at her with such sadness. "The census showed I was worth only $300 and you were worth $1,000."

Esther just shook her head at such pathetic logic. "My dear, the census taker was here when I was receiving a salary as justice, and your mine had not yet paid out. How can you look at our union in such a way?"

John tried to smile at her, but there was so little life force remaining in him that he said only, "You deserved a better man than me."

"Think of the good things that we have. Are you not proud of our boys?" Esther asked, taking his hand. "They are handsome and smart and honorable and will succeed well beyond what we two have accomplished."

She wondered if they had remained in Peru and continued the life they had before the war, whether John would have gotten so sick. The anxiety that came after wore out his heart, she was convinced. He was a proud man who would not admit defeat. After the funeral Robert went back to Albany, but Esther stayed on through the summer to help console her sons.

The following year, when Robert's term in Albany was up, he accepted another government job, this time in Springfield, Illinois, where the family had connections with Governor Palmer, who was now running for the United States Senate. Esther set up housekeeping for her son in a small rented house and made periodic visits to Uncle Watson, who was still playing checkers on the porch of the Mansion House Hotel in Pittsfield, although Aunt Diadema had passed away. The Watsons had also lost their daughter Sarah Jane to typhus, and now only Ellen and their grandchildren remained. On trips into Chicago, which now took only four hours by train, Esther visited Martha Ann Wallace and her daughter Isabelle, who was writing a book about her heroic father, General W. H. L. Wallace, whom Esther always remembered as the thoughtful young man she had met on her first landing in Peru with Uncle Watson. She affectionately called Martha Ann "Mrs. Judge Wallace" or "Mrs. General Wallace." Esther saw Mary Livermore and other suffragists and visited the Woman's Home that Seth Paine had set up for poor and abused women. Although Seth himself had died in 1872, his wife was carrying on his work.

In January 1881, with the Palmer family, Esther attended the inauguration of Shelby Moore Cullom, the new Republican governor of Illinois.

Sally had come up for that occasion as well, for she liked the chance to get away from Wyoming and spend time with her relatives.

While Cheyenne or any town in Wyoming would never be as interesting to Esther as Chicago or Springfield or New York, at the age of seventy she decided to settle down once and for all. She had forged an identity in that territory and her family was there. Eddie was getting married to Bertha "Bertie" Chambers, a young woman he had been introduced to through cousins in St. Louis. After raising three boys Esther was happy to have more daughters, and she especially wanted to be closer to her two-year-old granddaughter, Harriet (Hattie) Slack. When a hospital had been established in Cheyenne, Sally and Archie had felt it was safe to try to have children again.

Robert also came back to Wyoming after a failed attempt at a business partnership in a Chicago haberdashery. He accepted an appointment as secretary to Joe Carey, who had been elected the territorial senator for Wyoming. Robert was surprised at how much he had missed Wyoming, and although much of the year he would be in Washington with the senator, he was now able to buy a small house on Warren Street where Esther had a flower garden. It reminded her of the little house she had rented in Owego long ago, when she had a millinery business and cared for Lotte. She also had a housekeeper, which left her with plenty of time to entertain her friends and read many books. Most recently she had enjoyed *Ben-Hur*, written by another Civil War general named Wallace, this one named Lew Wallace.

Another granddaughter, Dora Slack, was born in 1885 and Esther delighted in the little girls. Sally and the babies had no problems this time, perhaps because there were now more and better doctors and a modern hospital. Archie published the leading daily newspaper in the West, advocating for modern roads, electricity in public buildings and in homes, and higher pay for schoolteachers, among other advancements. He and Sally had an active civic and social life in Cheyenne. Archie was talking of organizing an annual Wild West roundup and rodeo to be called Frontier Days. The idea began when a train agent stopped to chat with him one day and suggested that a good way to get more settlers into the state was to have a big western-type event. Archie began spreading the idea in his editorials and soon got the interest of other city leaders, and in July 1897 the first annual Frontier Days festival was held.

As Esther had always predicted, Ed became the most successful businessman of the family. Using the $2,000 John left him from the mining stock and with some additional funds from his brothers, he invested in a mercantile business in Green River and built a fine stone building on the main street along the river.

"It is like Peru, Ma," her son said, "but with better scenery." Ed had always loved the landscape of the West, and Green River had twin buttes shaped like giant Stetson hats serving as a backdrop to the town.

In addition to creating a thriving business with the department store and later a bank, and serving as the Sweetwater County clerk, Ed became the first mayor of Green River and was reelected five times. He organized the school district for Sweetwater County and fought to get funding from the federal government. He was involved in a great deal of charitable work through the Knights Templar and the Masons, secret societies the boys would never talk about. Esther often teased him about this, wondering if as women got more involved in men's work and politics, this was the one area they could keep to themselves. Esther visited Ed and Bertie often by train, now only a two-hour ride from Cheyenne.

"I wish your pa had lived to see you so successful," Esther told her son one day as she walked into Morris Bank. "He would be so proud."

CHAPTER TWENTY-TWO

The Old Politician

IN CHEYENNE THE DAY BEGAN WITH A LARGE PARADE OF CARRIAGES, floats, and marching bands from the high school and the military post. Two horses pulled a float carrying many women that was draped with a banner that read "Wyoming Statehood, July 10, 1890, The Equality State," the official slogan that had been suggested by Robert. Esther was among those on the float, and after the parade she joined officials on the reviewing stand draped in red, white, and blue bunting. She was recognized that day as the Mother of Suffrage by many of the speakers. Now young Therese Jenkins was trying to be heard above the commotion.

"We tread enchanted ground today. We're glorious, proud, and great. Our Independence Day has come . . . Wyoming is a state." Jenkins put down the paper and looked into the cheering crowd. "And it's the first state where women can vote and hold office and own property and be paid the same as men." The crowd burst into cheers again as she raised her arm in the air. She turned to smile at Esther and her family.

"In the days of the past there came to this region a woman who had been reared among the hardy minds of the East. She brought with her family, her garden seeds, her doctrine of woman's equality before the law. Her sons live to do her honor, her garden seeds have been planted, and she has proven to the world that this desolate plain can be made to blossom as the rose, and today she sits with us at the age of seventy-seven a free citizen equal with her sons. Esther Morris, like Queen Esther of old, has dared to brave the anger of man rather than her own people should perish.

"And now, before my voice gives way," Jenkins said, "I want to introduce someone who needs no introduction, a woman we all know and
love, Esther Morris." Esther, dressed in black silk with a white lace collar,
smiled and rose from her seat on the platform. Walking with a cane,
but standing very straight, she carried a folded flag and approached the
podium. The other people on the platform rose to applaud her.

"I'm afraid my voice cannot carry as far as Mrs. Jenkins," Esther said
to the crowd, "but then she has been practicing for two weeks out on the
plains. She told me that as her husband rode farther and farther away
from her, he shouted, 'Louder, louder,' until he could hear her a mile away.
Now Mrs. Jenkins can be heard all the way to Washington." The crowd
laughed as Esther looked out into the sea of faces, many familiar faces
and a few she did not yet know in this fast-growing state.

"I don't think we need another speech, but I want to tell you that
the women of this proud state have bought and paid for—with their
own hard-earned money—the first United States flag to fly here." Esther
turned to the people on the platform behind her. "May I ask the first
governor of the forty-fourth state of the Union, Francis E. Warren, to
accept this flag?" Warren, a man Archie's age with blond hair and full
mustache, was from Massachusetts and had won the Medal of Honor
for his heroism in the Civil War thirty-five years ago. He got up and
approached Esther with a grin.

Handing over the flag, Esther added, "And just let me say, Francis, it's
a good thing our first governor is a Republican." The governor laughed
as he took the flag from Esther and kissed her cheek. Esther turned and
walked to her seat, her family rising again as she approached them—
Archie, Sally, Robert, Edward, and Bertie, whose faces radiated the pride
they felt in their mother's accomplishments.

"I picked these from your own garden, Grandma." Ten-year-old
Harriet Slack jumped up to present her grandmother with a bouquet of
pink hollyhocks, while her five-year-old sister, Dora, clapped her hands
enthusiastically.

"These flowers are as beautiful and true as you are, dear Hattie."
Esther hugged her granddaughter as she accepted the flowers. Had it

really been six decades, she wondered, since she was Hattie's age and had first loved the hollyhocks in her mother's garden? "It was only yesterday," she thought.

—◦—

There was a large dinner celebration at Archie and Sally's stately home, where there was much jocular talk about how they finally became a state. When the Wyoming statehood committee, which included Edward Morris as well as other political leaders, first met to draft their petition for statehood, Republicans and Democrats argued on many issues but not on women's suffrage. All agreed that it must be part of their petition. But in Washington the battle raged for weeks, with the heaviest opposition coming from Southern Democrats who feared that black women would be able to vote.

Joseph Washington of Tennessee said, "Female suffrage is a reform against nature. It is unsexing and degrading to the womanhood of America." More thunderous opposition came from William Oates of Alabama, who said, "I like a woman who appreciates the sphere to which God and the Bible have assigned her."

The Wyoming delegation stood fast: Wyoming territorial senator Joseph M. Carey, thirty-five, known as "Little Joe," stubbornly refused to budge on the women's vote issue. Men stood and shouted from the balcony in the Senate building, crowding the rows of women sitting near the railing, leaning forward. As Senator Carey's secretary, Robert witnessed all of this and told this story many times to his family. Carey kept trying to be heard above the commotion. The Speaker of the House, Thomas Brackett Reed, a Republican of Maine, banged the gavel.

"Order, order; quiet down here. The gentleman from Wyoming Territory has the floor."

"Mr. Speaker," shouted a man with a stout frizzy beard, "the gentleman from Wyoming is out of order!" The gavel banging continued.

"Mr. Speaker, if I may continue my petition for statehood," Carey said, keeping at it until his voice nearly gave out. The men around him hissed and booed and stamped their feet. The speaker rapped the gavel again.

Another man, waving his fist at Carey, said, "Drop women's suffrage from your petition and we will let you continue." Carey had heard this before and he had the answer, indeed the answer all of the statehood committee members had unanimously agreed upon.

"We may wait a hundred years to come into the Union," Carey said, "but we will come in with our women." He had shouted the message many times that day, and it was obvious there was no compromise on this point. The speaker was still banging the gavel. "Gentlemen, can we call the roll. Do we accept Wyoming's petition as it is?"

A tall, thin man who looked eerily like Mr. Lincoln jumped up from his seat so high, he looked like a jack-in-the-box. "That's ridiculous, Mr. Speaker. The remaining western territories will want suffrage, too. And nigger women will vote!"

The speaker, truly exhausted from this battle, banged his gavel yet again.

"Call the roll!" He was yelling now, as if at a house full of naughty children. It took two more months to get the bill through the Senate, but Congress finally relented, and on July 8, 1890, President Harrison signed the bill making Wyoming the forty-fourth state and the first state in the Union where women could vote.

Esther remembered well the day Wyoming got the news. "We were all outside the telegraph office, waiting," Esther had written Franky. The operator was bent over his machine while a crowd of men and women tried to squeeze into the tiny office with him. All were watching the keys of the machine clicking as the crowd outside pressed against the windows."

"Okay, here it is," he said when the keys stopped. "The Senate vote is . . . 39 opposed and 47 in favor . . ." The people in the office jumped up and down, yelled and screamed, and hugged each other. The telegraph operator, grinning broadly, leaned out the window. "We're in! Wyoming is the forty-fourth state of the United States of America."

Pandemonium erupted and the crowd went berserk. Men on horseback rode in circles, shooting pistols into the air. Fireworks exploded. People danced in the street.

"What a party we had that day," Esther later wrote to Franky.

Five years after statehood, Esther, now affectionately known as "the Old Politician," was nominated as Wyoming's representative to the Convention of the Republican League in Cleveland. Her sons were worried that at eighty-three she should not take such a trip by herself, but she was anxious to go so that she could also meet with her old friends in Illinois.

"It could be the beginning of something new," she insisted, imagining future conventions and more female delegates. In 1892 her friend Therese Jenkins had become the first woman delegate to any Republican National Convention. Esther's sons insisted she have a chaperone, so when her neighbors Mr. and Mrs. Burke offered to accompany her to Cleveland and from there to Chicago, where Esther would stay at the Great Northern Hotel, the boys relented.

Although Esther claimed no personal political ambition, she had made her mark in every place she lived, including South Pass City. She enjoyed a notoriety that was nurtured by Archie, now the most influential newspaper editor in the West. Her garden was a stopping place for the city's residents, with whom she often shared seeds and cuttings. For the rest of her life she remained influential in women's rights, politics, and civic affairs—and in her sons' lives. Her only worry was for Ed, who, like his father, suffered from rheumatism. When he developed diabetes and began losing weight, Esther's worry increased, but he promised to obey his doctors and eat according to his diet. When Ed began gaining weight, Esther was convinced he would be healthy again.

"My children are my greatest treasures," she said, "and if they are not perfect, then as good as I could expect, considering who their mother is!" Esther died peacefully when she was nearly ninety, but not before she experienced the beginning of a new century.

"When my mother died," Robert later wrote his cousin Franky, "it was like a generator going off. We could all feel our energy shrinking."

AFTERWORD

ARCHIE, WHO HAD DEVELOPED BRIGHT'S DISEASE, DIED FIVE YEARS after his mother, at the age of sixty-five. Cheyenne's annual Frontier Days, the world's largest outdoor rodeo and western celebration, continues to this day. In 1997, on the one hundredth anniversary of the event, a life-size bronze statue of Archie created by a Cheyenne artist was commissioned by the *Tribune Eagle*, the successor to Archie's *Cheyenne Daily Sun*. A. E. Slack, as he was known, leaning against a lamppost and reading a newspaper, stands at the site of the Frontier Days arena. Small versions of the statue are used each year as community spirit awards.

All of Esther's descendants came through Archie's daughter Dora, who married William DuBois and had five children, fourteen grandchildren, and twenty-eight great-grandchildren. Today there are eighteen great-great-grandchildren. Esther's great-great-grandson, William R. DuBois III, taught American and frontier history for thirty-seven years in Cheyenne high school. Bill served on the State Historic Preservation Board and is past president of the Wyoming State Historical Society. Active in the music world, he was inducted into the Frontier Days Hall of Fame, "largely because I sang the national anthem 240 times to open the rodeo for forty years." He was also the founding director, in 1978, of the Cheyenne Frontier Days Old West Museum.

Edward's health declined after his mother's death, and he died five months later of complications from diabetes, a condition that had little effective treatment before the discovery of insulin. He was fifty-one years old, and given the largest commemorative funeral and service in Green River history with his Knights Templar and Masonic friends as pallbearers and speakers. He had no children, and his widow, Bertie, remarried a year later and moved to Denver, Colorado.

After his mother's death, Robert moved to Green River to care for his brother and take over the operation of Morris Mercantile and Morris Bank. Robert donated "the great trunks of the family books that followed us wherever we moved" to the new Carnegie Library in Cheyenne, built by a young architect named William DuBois, who became the husband of Dora Slack. Robert Morris died at age seventy, a year after woman suffrage was finally ratified nationwide.

In July 1927, Florence Moore Kreider, Eliza Jane Hall's granddaughter, wrote to her Aunt Franky in Flint, Michigan: "I sat next to Carrie Chapman Catt at dinner. She said Aunt Esther was now considered one of the outstanding American women and that a history was being written of her."

Esther's legend again surfaced in 1950 when Wyoming wanted a statue to symbolize the spirit of the state. After a long debate Esther finally won out over a horse, and her statue was erected in front of the capitol in Cheyenne in 1960. A copy is in the Hall of Statues in Washington, DC. Today the entire town of South Pass City, including Esther's house, has been restored as a historic site. Her home on Front Street in Cheyenne is also a historic building.

In the 1970s Wyoming was one of the first states to ratify the Equal Rights Amendment. When "some fool" attempted to repeal it several years later, the motion was quickly put down. Equality has been Wyoming's pride since 1869.

Acknowledgments

Many people have been helpful to me over the years of gathering material for this book.

Grateful thanks and affection to William (Bill) DuBois III, great-great-grandson of Esther Morris, who gave me access to his files and introduced me to the Wyoming Historical Society archives. Bill has always been involved in Wyoming's history, both as a high school history teacher for thirty-seven years, and as an officer of the State Historic Preservation Board and the Wyoming State Historical Society and the American Heritage Board with the University of Wyoming. He, too, is pleased that his great-great-grandmother's story is finally coming to light.

The late Rosalind Day of California, a great-granddaughter of Esther's niece Frances "Franky" McQuigg Stewart, whom I met through Bill DuBois, provided a trove of correspondence between Esther and her sons and Franky. Roz's spirit is here in these pages.

And all those years ago, a young woman named Anne Grant (now Anne Grant West) first made me aware of Esther Morris through her research in women's history. She produced with New York City Now *Our North American Foremothers*, which became a Bicentennial ABC documentary-drama, *The American Woman: Portraits of Courage*, in 1976, for which Anne won an Emmy.

Much love and gratitude goes to my daughter, Karen Leifsen, for patiently reading several versions of this manuscript.

And many, many thanks to my agent Rita Rosenkranz, and my editors Erin Turner and Lynn Zelem at Globe Pequot for believing in this story and making the book possible.

About the Author

Marian Betancourt has written scores of articles for the Associated Press and for *American Heritage, Irish America, Promenade*, and many other magazines. She is the author of several books on women's issues and health. With Globe Pequot she has published two history-related cookbooks as well as *Heroes of New York Harbor: Tales from the City's Port* (2016). Her published fiction includes a short story, "In the Ferry's Wake," in *Iris*, a journal of the University of Virginia.